ALSO BY PATRICK ANDERSON

Nonfiction

The Presidents' Men (1968)
High in America (1981)
Electing Jimmy Carter (1994)

Novels

The Approach to Kings (1970)
Actions and Passions (1974)
The President's Mistress (1976)
First Family (1979)
Lords of the Earth (1984)
Sinister Forces (1986)
The Pleasure Business (1989)
Busybodies (1989)
Rich as Sin (1991)

The Triumph of the Thriller

THE TRIUMPH

OF THE THRILLER

How Cops, Crooks, and Cannibals
Captured Popular Fiction

Patrick Anderson

 RANDOM HOUSE | NEW YORK

Published in the United States by Random House,
an imprint of The Random House Publishing Group,
a division of Random House, Inc., New York.

RANDOM HOUSE and colophon are registered
trademarks of Random House, Inc.

Grateful acknowledgment is made to Henry Holt
and Company, LLC, for permission to reprint
excerpts from *E Is for Evidence* and *M Is for Malice*
by Sue Grafton, copyright © 1988, 1996
by Sue Grafton. Reprinted by permission
of Henry Holt and Company, LLC.

ISBN 978-0-345-48123-8

Printed in the United States of America
on acid-free paper

www.atrandom.com

9 8 7 6 5 4 3 2 1

FIRST EDITION

Book design by Dana Leigh Blanchette

For
Ann Michael Hendell
and
Merry Louise Hendell

Contents

I. CRIME PRESENT AND CRIME PAST

1. A New Beat *3*

2. Crime Past: *Poe, Doyle, Christie* *12*

3. American Style: *Hammett, Cain, Chandler* *27*

4. Tough Guys: *Spillane, MacDonald, McBain, Macdonald, Willeford* *47*

II. CHANGING CRIMES

5. The Birth of the Thriller *69*

6. Tom Clancy's Literary Offenses *82*

7. Dangerous Women: *Grafton, Paretsky, Highsmith* *93*

8. Lawyers at Large: *Turow, Grisham, Lescroart* *108*

9. Spy Masters: *McCarry, Littell, Silva, Furst* *122*

10. Literary Thrillers, Killer Clowns,
     Barroom Poets, Drunken Detectives,
     Time Travel, and Related
     Curiosities *139*

III. FOUR MODERN MASTERS

11. Thomas Harris: *Learning to Love
     the Doctor* *151*

12. George Pelecanos: *Bulletins from the
     Front* *165*

13. Michael Connelly: *Death Is My Beat* *176*

14. Dennis Lehane: *No Turning Back* *190*

IV. TALENT, TALENT EVERYWHERE

15. Favorites *205*

16. More Favorites: *Brits* *223*

17. Three Young Writers: *Karin Slaughter,
     Peter Craig, Charlie Huston* *233*

18. No More Mr. Nice Guy *244*

19. The Question of the Series *258*

20. Parting Shots *263*

Personal Favorites *271*

I.

CRIME PRESENT AND CRIME PAST

Wherein a middlebrow ventures onto the thriller

beat, Edgar Allan Poe inflicts bloody murder

on the Rue Morgue, Arthur Conan Doyle sends

forth the original dynamic duo, Agatha Christie

takes on Shakespeare and the Bible, hard-drinking

Americans invent the hard-boiled detective novel,

and postwar Americans graduate from the pulps

to semirespectability.

1.

A New Beat

In 2000, Marie Arana, the editor of *The Washington Post Book World,* put me on the thriller beat. I had for years reviewed both fiction and nonfiction for *Book World,* but now Marie wanted me to focus on the crime-related novels that have come to dominate the bestseller lists. Soon I began reviewing a new book each Monday in the *Post*'s freewheeling Style section.

Over the years, reading purely for pleasure, I'd become a fan of such writers as John D. MacDonald, Lawrence Sanders, Elmore Leonard, Ross Thomas, Ed McBain, James Lee Burke, Thomas Harris, and Michael Connelly. Now, reading thrillers on a regular basis, I learned how much more talent was out there. I discovered people like Dennis Lehane, Ian Rankin, Donna Leon, Robert Littell, George Pelecanos, John Lescroart, Philip Kerr, and Alan Furst. I reviewed best sellers by John Grisham, Tom Clancy, Sue Grafton, John Sandford, James Patterson, and Patricia Cornwell; some I admired, some I deplored, but their success says something about our popular culture. I've had the pleasure of telling our readers about new talent like Karin Slaughter, David Corbett, Robert Reuland, and Charlie Huston.

The more I read, the more I was struck by the transformation in America's reading habits. I grew up with the blockbuster novels of the 1950s and 1960s, written by people like James Michener, Harold Robbins, John O'Hara, Jacqueline Susann, Herman Wouk, and Irving

Stone. They explored sex, money, movie stars, war, religion, and exotic foreign lands but rarely concerned themselves with crime. In those days, crime novels were trapped in the genre ghetto, often published as paperback originals, and rarely won a mass audience.

Today, those blockbuster novelists have been replaced on the best-seller lists by the crime-related fiction we loosely call thrillers, which includes hard-core noir, in the Hammett-Chandler private-eye tradition, as well as a bigger, broader universe of books that includes spy thrillers, legal thrillers, political thrillers, military thrillers, medical thrillers, and even literary thrillers. I have a copy of the December 25, 1966, *Book World*—incredibly enough, I had a review in it. Starting at the top, the ten authors on the fiction best-seller list are Robert Crichton, Allen Drury, Jacqueline Susann, Rebecca West, Mary Renault, Edwin O'Connor, James Clavell, Bernard Malamud, Harold Robbins, and Harry Mark Petrakis. Two political novelists, two or three literary writers, two grand masters of sex and schlock—but no crime fiction.

Compare that with a *Book World* list in February of 2006. By my count, nine of the ten books listed were thrillers, including Dan Brown's *The Da Vinci Code,* Sue Grafton's *S Is for Silence,* and John Lescroart's *The Hunt Club.* Another Sunday that month, *The New York Times Book Review* had fifteen thrillers among its sixteen hard-back best sellers, including those on the *Post*'s list plus Greg Iles's *Turning Angel,* and various lesser works. The transformation between the lists in 1966 and 2006 could not be more dramatic. To oversimplify a bit, John Grisham is the new James Michener and *The Da Vinci Code* is our *Gone with the Wind.*

In this book, I'll look back to the origins of modern crime fiction— to writers like Edgar Allan Poe, Arthur Conan Doyle, and Agatha Christie—to examine how the modern thriller has evolved. The triumph of the thriller, I call this transformation. We will grapple with questions of definition. Just what is a thriller? How is it different from a mystery or a crime novel? The terminology is far from precise, but let me suggest a few guidelines.

Agatha Christie and her imitators wrote mysteries that stressed intellectual solutions to crimes. Her tradition continues in so-called cozies, which appeal to readers who want no violence, and in more ingenious novels by writers like the American Martha Grimes.

In this country, around 1930, Dashiell Hammett invented the

American crime novel, also known as the detective or private-eye novel, and Raymond Chandler built on Hammett's work. Their hard-boiled tradition prevailed for several decades, but by the 1970s the crime novel began to mutate into something that was bigger, darker, more imaginative, and more violent: the modern thriller. Certain novels have been milestones in expanding the boundaries of the thriller—among them Lawrence Sanders's *The First Deadly Sin,* Frederick Forsyth's *The Day of the Jackal,* Scott Turow's *Presumed Innocent,* Tom Clancy's *The Hunt for Red October,* John Grisham's *The Firm,* Thomas Harris's *The Silence of the Lambs,* and Dennis Lehane's *Mystic River.*

John Updike said this while reviewing Robert Littell's surreal spy novel *Legends* in *The New Yorker* in 2005: "The slippery difference between a thriller and a non-thriller would hardly be worth groping for did not the thriller-writers themselves seem to be restive—chafing to escape, yearning for a less restrictive contract with the reader. They write longer than they used to, with more flourishes." Updike notes that Agatha Christie's ambitions never extended past the lean, efficient mysteries she wrote, but "Littell and le Carré and the estimable P. D. James give signs of wanting to be 'real' novelists, free to follow character where it takes them and to display their knowledge of the world without the obligation to provide a thrill in every chapter."

The estimable Updike might have gone further and added a number of other thriller writers to his list of restive souls, many of whom have gone beyond *wanting* to be real writers to *doing* it. Novels like *Bangkok 8, Hard Revolution, Tropic of Night, Done for a Dime, Red Dragon, Lost Light,* and *The Way the Crow Flies* are simply some of the best fiction being written today.

I had misgivings when Marie put me on the thriller beat. I was an English major in the uptight 1950s, when the high modernists—T. S. Eliot, James Joyce, William Faulkner—were force-fed to undergraduates, and for years I felt a tremor of guilt when I stooped to popular fiction and certainly to thrillers. A lot of people of my generation felt that way. When my political thriller *The President's Mistress* was published in 1976, *The Washington Post*'s reviewer declared that she locked herself in her office until she finished it. It was, she said, "a Mt. Everest among cliff-hangers." I was feeling pretty good until she sandbagged me at the end: "Of course, I always did like Chinese food."

In other words, I'd given her a few hours of guilty pleasure, but I wasn't a serious writer providing solid sustenance. I was guilty as charged, of course, but consoled by a $250,000 paperback sale and a movie deal. A few years later I saw another review in which that same writer confessed that, after much soul-searching, she had decided it was *all right* to enjoy popular fiction. I was happy for her.

A lot of people have a hard time making the leap from officially approved "literary" fiction to novels that are fun, and they aren't all refugees from the fifties. I received an e-mail recently from a college student in Houston, an English major, asking what thrillers he should read—or whether he should read them at all. "I am racked with guilt if I read any of this stuff. Life is short. I haven't finished all of Dickens or Shakespeare. Do I have time for detective novels?" I could only advise him that life is a lot longer than he at present understands and there is time for, say, Elmore Leonard and Dennis Lehane along with Dickens and Shakespeare.

The more I read, the more I saw that Marie, in putting me on the thriller beat, had given me the new mainstream of American popular fiction to splash about in. I want to examine this new mainstream and how it came about. I want to show who the good writers are and why—and, to a lesser degree, who some bad ones are and why. It seems to me beyond dispute that the level of talent at work today in thrillers and crime fiction is superior to anything that has previously existed in America or Great Britain. I say this having recently reread a number of acclaimed crime novels that I first read several decades ago. Alas, the books we loved in our youth, like the sweet young things we dallied with, have not always aged well. Our memories play tricks on us and often we have been misled by movies that vastly improved the original material. Nostalgia is the sweetest of drugs, but it will cloud our minds, distort our memories, and lead us into error if we let it.

We must ask why thrillers have become increasingly popular. Of course, stories of danger and suspense have always had visceral appeal. Lee Child, author of the Jack Reacher series, once summed this up nicely:

In human evolution we developed language, we developed storytelling, and that must have been for a serious purpose. I think right from the caveman days, we had stories that involved danger and peril, and eventually safety and resolution. To me that is the story. And that's what we're still telling today, 100,000 years later. That's what a page-turner is.

But there are contemporary reasons for the triumph of the thriller as well. One is the transformation of the book business. Once hailed as a "gentleman's profession," publishing today is more like a barroom brawl as corporate takeovers have intensified bottom-line pressures on editors. And the bottom line is that thrillers sell, which means there is a continuing scramble to find the writers who can produce books that translate into corporate profits. There are other social and cultural factors, of course. Decades of war, recession, and political and corporate corruption have made Americans more cynical—or realistic—and thus more open to novels that examine the dark side of our society. And yet most thrillers manage some sort of happy ending. They have it both ways, reminding us how ugly and dangerous our society can be and yet offering hope in the end. Thrillers provide the illusion of order and justice in a world that often seems to have none.

Of course, we read for fun too. We love the excitement of suspense. We want to know whodunit. Indeed, these days, we love suspense more than sex, at least in books. In the fifties and sixties, sex was a huge element in popular fiction, from *I, the Jury* to *Peyton Place* to *Portnoy's Complaint* and countless others. Today, we're up to our ears in sex. Who wants to *read* about it? The books I'm discussing contain relatively little sex and dirty talk, nothing like what we endure on HBO. In the modern thriller, suspense has replaced sex as the engine that drives popular fiction.

As thrillers have become more popular and their potential rewards greater, more of the most talented young writers, those who a generation ago would have produced anguished novels about their unhappy childhoods, are instead trying to become the next Grisham or Grafton. The level of their work has risen until the best of today's thrillers are the white-hot center of American fiction. We hear talk about this or that "golden age" of yesteryear. Forget it. Right here, right now, is the golden age of thrillers, some of which transcend genre. *The Silence of the Lambs* and *Mystic River* are excellent examples. Both novels—and the Oscar-winning movies made from them—are vastly more sophisticated and powerful than their counterparts from earlier eras.

This book is not about me—often a vital point for a writer to grasp—but it is indisputably *by* me, so I think it reasonable to say a little about my background, preferences, and prejudices. The central fact is that, as reader and reviewer, I fall into three related categories: bookworm, middlebrow, and writer.

The turning point in my life came when I was four and spent a year living with my maternal grandparents. My grandmother was a fussy little woman who decided it was high time I learned to read. I remember sitting on the floor as she stood at a blackboard and taught me my ABCs. Soon I was reading the Sunday comics and then books. I still have the copy of *Huckleberry Finn* she gave me the Christmas I was six. I was never much of a student—I was bored in the early grades and rebellious in high school—but I read a lot and could always write an essay or book report; in a pinch I would make up the book. Most of what I learned in my early years resulted from taking the bus to the Fort Worth Public Library each Saturday morning, checking out the maximum five books, reading them, and going back the next Saturday for five more. The Hardy Boys were my first crime series, if you don't count the Dick Tracy comic strip.

My mother kept best sellers around the house. The first grown-up novel I remember reading, at twelve or so, was *The Robe,* which featured one hell of an exciting sword fight. I loved George Orwell's *Animal Farm* without having a clue about its political message. I devoured the short stories of Mark Twain, who did a great deal to corrupt my young mind. When I was a teenager, you could feel awfully isolated in Texas if you weren't part of its dominant culture, which worshipped football, oil, Cadillacs, and country clubs. You were always listening for faint signals from afar, evidence that others out there shared your discontent. By high school I was deep into Somerset Maugham, whose views were decidedly un-Texan, and Sinclair Lewis, who encouraged me to scorn the George Babbitts and Elmer Gantrys I saw around me.

I spent two years at North Texas State, in nearby Denton, where my fellow students included Pat Boone, who joined my fraternity before he dashed off to stardom, and Bill Moyers, whom I would meet again a decade later in the White House. Larry McMurtry arrived on campus just after I left; we both took a writing course from Dr. James Brown.

Life was good at North Texas—except that, like many an impression-able lad of that era, I had come under the spell of F. Scott Fitzgerald. I dreamed of Princeton's ivory towers. Alas, I lacked the money—not to mention the grades—to enter that distant paradise. But I had a friend at the University of the South, in Sewanee, Tennessee, and I managed to scrape together the wherewithal to enroll there.

Until then I had read at random. At Sewanee, people were actually teaching me. I took a good course on Shakespeare and a great one on the Renaissance poets, taught by an incomparable Alabaman, Dr. Charles Trawick Harrison. It was the most important course in my col-lege career. Once you begin to appreciate the majesty of Andrew Mar-vell's "But at my back I always hear / Time's wingèd chariot hurrying near" and the music of Robert Herrick's "Gather ye rosebuds while ye may, / Old Time is still a-flying," you start to grasp the potential of our language. I also took a course on Romantic poets that bored me and one on literary criticism that baffled me. I was starting to realize that there were highbrows in the world and there were middlebrows, and I was among the latter. I sat in Lit Crit with young men who would go on to be distinguished professors at leading universities—John Fleming at Princeton, John Evans at Washington and Lee, Bernie Dunlap at the University of South Carolina, Henry Arnold at Sewanee—and it was clear that they had intellectual concerns that I didn't share.

In my contemporary lit class, I delighted in Hemingway and Fitzgerald but never ventured far into Faulkner. Today, I would say that my favorite novels are *The Great Gatsby, Huckleberry Finn, Lone-some Dove,* and *Riddley Walker,* and I've taken pleasure from many other writers, including Graham Greene, Philip Roth, John Updike, John O'Hara, Flannery O'Connor, Ann Beattie, and J. D. Salinger, as well as many of those I'll discuss in these pages.

Upon graduation, when my more scholarly classmates went off to graduate school, I got myself hired as a $65-a-week reporter for the *Nashville Tennessean.* It was there I did my first professional book re-viewing—I guess you'd call it professional; they didn't pay me, but I got to keep the book. Later I made my way to Washington to work in the Kennedy Administration and then to pursue a writing career.

Which brings me to my third category: writer. I've published nine novels, at least two of which weren't bad (*Lords of the Earth* and *The President's Mistress,* if you must know), and several books of nonfiction. I review novels as one who has written them. I know all the problems and most of the tricks, and I usually know when the writer is at the top of his game and when he's faking or just doesn't have the moves.

I have vast sympathy for writers. It's not so hard to write a publishable novel, given certain basic skills, but it's damned near impossible to write a really good novel, and I respect those who do. Writing is a tough, lonely business. You see illiterate hacks getting rich while you can't pay your rent. No matter how good you are, there are people who are better, legions of them. When you're young and your book is published, you race out each Sunday morning and seize *The New York Times Book Review,* searching for the acclaim that will bring you fame and fortune, and it takes many months to grasp that they aren't going to review you.

The *Times* once published a brief, harsh review of a first novel. A few Sundays later they ran the author's one-sentence letter to the editor: "You have broken my heart." Writing can indeed be heartbreaking, but sometimes, if you have talent, perseverance, and luck, you can survive, even prosper. As McMurtry notes somewhere, after a lifetime of toil, you might advance from "promising" to "minor."

It annoys me to see fine writers dismissed as genre writers—crime novelists, spy novelists, and the like—by those who salivate over the latest incomprehensible postmodern gimmickry. A book is a book is a book. Labels are necessary to organize bookstores, but serious readers should pay them no mind. In these pages, I will follow one paramount rule: to judge writers not by their reputations but by the words they put on paper. Reputations are what other people think; this book is what I think.

I don't expect everyone to agree with my views. We all have different tastes, often amazingly so. Not long ago I mentioned my admiration for George Pelecanos and Michael Connelly to a crime writer I respect. He replied that "for reasons I can't fully comprehend I can't force myself through Pelecanos" and that he finds police procedurals "to be tediously dull—so there goes Connelly." I thought this quite perverse—but probably no more so than readers will find some of my opinions.

I should issue two warnings. First, there are scores of fine writers at work today, and I can't include them all. I wish I could. Second, in discussing books, I will from time to time reveal their endings. So if you don't want to know who killed Roger Ackroyd, or who plotted the Kennedy assassination in *The Tears of Autumn,* or what surprise brought joy to Harry Bosch's tormented life, proceed with care, because in these pages the truth will sometimes out.

While I was writing this book, more than a hundred writers formed International Thriller Writers, Inc. The group's Web site, thrillerwriters .org, contains a list of all-time top thrillers. Their definition of a thriller, like my own, is inclusive, and reaches back to such classics as Wilkie Collins's *The Woman in White,* Robert Louis Stevenson's *The Strange Case of Dr. Jekyll and Mr. Hyde,* Oscar Wilde's *The Picture of Dorian Gray,* and Bram Stoker's *Dracula* before advancing to Graham Greene's *The Third Man,* Patricia Highsmith's *Strangers on a Train,* Richard Condon's *The Manchurian Candidate,* Thomas Harris's *Red Dragon,* and John Grisham's *The Firm,* among many others. Neither Hammett nor Chandler is listed, because they are viewed as having written private-eye or detective novels, not thrillers. (However, to further complicate matters, most of today's private-eye novels are considered thrillers, simply because of their level of violence.)

Lists are fun, but all contemporary judgments are suspect. The only real test of literature is what one of my professors called "universal acceptance." That doesn't mean that Tom Clancy is a great writer because he's sold millions of books. It means that Mark Twain and Charles Dickens are great writers because educated opinion has for more than a century continued to regard them as such—and because we common folk have continued to read them. The future will have the last word. But that doesn't mean we shouldn't duke it out in our own time.

Jonathan Yardley, the *Post*'s Pulitzer Prize–winning book critic, once wrote that Edmund Wilson "saw it as his mission to introduce worthy writers to intelligent lay readers." Clearly I'm not Wilson and the authors I'm championing are not the celebrated modernists he admired, but I like to think I share that admirable goal—to introduce worthy writers to intelligent readers. There are a lot of both out there, and I hope this book helps bring them together.

2

Crime Past:

Poe, Doyle, Christie

A case can be made that the first great thrillers were classics like *Oedipus Rex* (king/investigator finds killer: himself) and *Hamlet* (prince/investigator dithers), but it is generally agreed that the detective story was invented by Edgar Allan Poe in "The Murders in the Rue Morgue," published in April 1841 in *Graham's Magazine* in Philadelphia. In concocting that story, Poe moved beyond another, related genre he had already perfected: the tale of horror. I remember at age twelve or so discovering Poe's horror stories—"The Pit and the Pendulum," "The Cask of Amontillado," "The Tell-Tale Heart"—and being dumbfounded. Nothing in *Black Beauty* or *Lassie Come Home* had prepared me for Poe's dark vision. He was a troubled man with a wildly inventive mind who was far ahead of his time.

"The Murders in the Rue Morgue" is plenty horrific but, unlike Poe's horror stories, it held out the possibility that human reason—in the person of a private detective, a man of superior intellect—could triumph over madness. It is also an extremely odd story. In the edition I have, it's forty-five pages long and the first four and a half pages—a tenth of the story—are devoted to tedious remarks on "the analytical power." A modern editor would have cut this digression, in part because Poe's detective makes the same points again in the body of the story.

Finally the real story starts:

Residing in Paris during the spring and part of the summer of 18—, I there became acquainted with a Monsieur C. Auguste Dupin. This young gentleman was of an excellent—indeed of an illustrious family, but, by a variety of untoward events, had been reduced to such poverty that the energy of his character succumbed beneath it, and he ceased to bestir himself in the world, or to care for the retrieval of his fortunes.

The unhappy Dupin and the unnamed narrator decide to share a house. The narrator soon concludes that Dupin is the most fascinating fellow he's ever met. He is particularly taken by Dupin's "peculiar analytic ability" and gives us a dramatic example. The two of them are out walking and have been silent for fifteen minutes. Abruptly, Dupin refers to an actor they both know. The narrator had indeed been thinking about that very actor, and says, "Dupin, this is beyond my comprehension. I do not hesitate to say that I am amazed, and can scarcely credit my senses. How was it possible you should know I was thinking of ——?" Dupin explains that fifteen minutes earlier a man carrying a basket of apples had nearly knocked the narrator down, and goes on to explain the train of thought that led him from the apples to the actor.

This demonstration of Dupin's mental powers is followed by their reading in the newspaper about the murder of a mother and daughter at their home in the aptly named Rue Morgue. The murders were unspeakably violent and clearly committed by someone of great strength. Neighbors heard the women screaming. Before they were able to force their way into the women's fourth-floor apartment they heard a shrill voice that spoke in a language no one recognized. The doors and windows to the apartment were locked from the inside. There seemed to be no way anyone could have entered or left the apartment.

Dupin receives permission for himself and the narrator to examine the crime scene. He studies it and the victims' bodies and soon deduces the identity of the killer, which he explains as the narrator listens "in mute astonishment." When examining the windows that appeared impossible to open, Dupin found concealed springs that make them open easily. Having discovered how the killer could have come and gone, he noticed a lightning rod that he could have used to climb up to the windows. He further discovers a "little tuft" of hair in the "rigidly clutched fingers" of one of the victims. He notes that the bruises on the throat of one victim are too small to have been made by a human hand. He has also found a piece of ribbon the police missed, the sort that sailors use to tie up their hair.

Putting all this together, and noting that the killer seems stronger, more agile, and more brutal than a human, Dupin concludes that the killer was a "large fulvous orangutan of the East Indian Islands."

He puts an advertisement in *Le Monde* in which he claims to have found a lost orangutan and invites its owner to come claim the creature. Before the sailor arrives, Dupin and the narrator arm themselves lest he proves violent. As it turns out, the sailor admits that his orangutan escaped from him and carried out the killings. He agrees to tell the police what happened. The Prefect of Police, rather than thank Dupin, says he should mind his own business, but Dupin tells the narrator, "I am satisfied to have defeated him in his own castle."

Thus ends the world's first detective story. It works because Poe, like Arthur Conan Doyle after him, exploits our willingness to identify with the brilliant detective and to scorn the clueless cops. The solution of the mystery—death by killer ape—is colorful but not really satisfactory by today's standards. In real life one could go decades, perhaps centuries, without seeing two women murdered by an escaped orangutan armed with a razor. Poe's genius was in inventing the genre, not in creating a murderous monkey. In one burst of inspiration, he gave us the private detective who scorns the inept police, the locked-room mystery, and the detective's sidekick/narrator who became the model for countless other second bananas of criminal detection, most notably Dr. Watson.

Nothing is more striking about the story than our awareness of how much Doyle would soon borrow from it. The eccentric and moody Holmes has much in common with Dupin. The narrator of the Dupin stories, like Dr. Watson, not only moves in with his hero but tells us endlessly how brilliant he is. Dupin's seeming ability to read the narrator's mind is reflected in the many times Holmes dazzles Watson by announcing that some passerby is a left-handed Lithuanian who loves polkas and hates his mother. Dupin's putting an ad in the newspaper to summon the criminal, and the two men arming themselves, are devices often seen in the Holmes stories.

Poe wrote two more Dupin stories, "The Mystery of Marie Roget" and "The Purloined Letter." The former is sixty-seven pages long and all but unreadable. Poe tells the story of Marie Roget's death—her body is found in the Seine—by having Dupin and the narrator read newspaper accounts of the crime and discuss what they prove or don't prove. Once again, many of the clues are absurdly simple—a cloth is tied around the victim's body with a "sailor's knot," which leads Dupin to suspect a young naval officer. The point of the story is that Dupin solves the crime without even visiting the scene. It is enough for him to apply his intellect to the facts. Other armchair detectives would follow, starting with Sherlock Holmes's smarter brother, Mycroft.

The other story, "The Purloined Letter," concerns a missing letter that could somehow inspire a royal scandal. The police search the apartment of the suspected thief, a government minister, without success; only Dupin, by putting himself inside the mind of the villain, realizes he would not conceal the letter but would leave it out in the open—hide it in plain sight.

Writers have offered complex interpretations of the Dupin stories. David Lehman, in his book *The Perfect Murder,* suggests that Poe's invention of the detective story is connected to the death of Romanticism "with its worship of the noble savage." Surely it is no accident, he says, that in the world's first detective story, "the culprit turns out to be a ghoulishly transmogrified version of the noble savage." He says that the orangutan's dark deeds were those of "the id on a monstrous rampage, primitive energy uncontrolled, Romanticism gone haywire."

Perhaps so, but for our purposes let's just call a spade a spade and an orangutan a bloody ape and keep in mind that poor doomed Eddie Poe paved the way for Sherlock Holmes.

TWO CLASSICS

Wilkie Collins (1824–89) was a close friend of Charles Dickens and, like Dickens, he wrote big complex novels packed with characters and events, notably *The Woman in White* (1860) and *The Moonstone* (1868). Collins was the first writer to see that mystery novels could be as rich and ambitious as those of his friend Dickens. *The Woman in White* is a strange, mysterious tale of love, deceit, mistaken identity, a forced marriage, a loyal sister, and retribution; there had been nothing like it before. *The Moonstone,* even more exotic, concerns a priceless diamond, stolen from India and brought to England with a curse on it that leaves death and destruction in its wake. T. S. Eliot called it the first and best of English detective novels. In it, departing from Poe's incompetent cops, Collins introduced the admirable Sergeant Cuff of Scotland Yard. Collins was overshadowed by Dickens as a novelist and by Doyle as a crime writer, but these two novels hold up admirably today, certainly better than Doyle's. His tale of the cursed Indian moonstone is echoed in Doyle stories like "The Sign of Four," and the gothic scope of his novels influenced twentieth-century writers like Lawrence Sanders and Thomas Harris. *The Moonstone* and *The Woman in White* are the first great crime thrillers, essential reading for anyone with a serious interest in the literature of suspense.

ELEMENTARY, MY DEAR WATSON

There are people who study the Holmes stories with Talmudic zeal. King Lear and his fool have never been examined with more intensity than have Holmes and Watson by these Sherlockians, as they call themselves. The more extreme Sherlockians reject Arthur Conan Doyle and treat Holmes as a historical figure whose adventures were written by his friend, Dr. Watson. Doyle is dismissed as Watson's literary agent.

I am no Sherlockian, but in rereading some of the stories I enjoyed them. How could anyone who admires vivid, imaginative, fast-moving, suspenseful prose not? Yet I think the greatness of the stories is widely misunderstood. Holmes is famous as the ultimate genius of crime fighting, a mental superman whose brooding mind saw answers that were invisible to ordinary mortals. He endlessly lectures Watson—and us— on the powers of deduction, and generations of readers have bowed to his superior intellect.

All this is twaddle. Doyle's genius was his ability to play games with us. Time after time, Holmes's supposedly dazzling solutions turn out to be simple, even silly. The writer holds all the cards in this game. He has crafted his puzzle in advance and tosses out various clues, some relevant but most there to tantalize the reader. We don't reread the Holmes stories because of the puzzles but despite them, because we love the exciting, comforting, now-vanished world that Doyle summons up. With this in mind, let's look more closely at his work.

We start with the young Conan Doyle, who in the spring of 1886 was practicing medicine at Southsea but burned with a passion to write. He had been deeply impressed as a medical student by a professor who stressed the use of close examination and relentless logic in diagnosing patients. Doyle had read Poe and Collins and he had the idea for a detective, not unlike Dupin but English, who would solve crimes by his powers of observation and analysis.

Doyle's first published story, "A Study in Scarlet," is an odd, awkward tale. It opens with Watson's first-person account of meeting Holmes. We learn that Watson has been an army doctor in "the second Afghan war." He was wounded there and sent to London to recover. The first thing Holmes says to him is "You have been in Afghanistan, I perceive." "How on earth did you know that?" Watson replies—"in astonishment"—but Holmes only chuckles. The two men agree to share lodgings at 221B Baker Street. Holmes tells Watson more about "the science of deduction" and confesses, "I have a trade of my own. I suppose I am the only one in the world. I'm a consulting detective." Watson says agreeably, "You remind me of Edgar Allan Poe's Dupin." Holmes rejects the compliment, saying that he found Dupin "a very inferior fellow."

The loyal, plodding Watson is never as colorful or interesting as Holmes, but he is absolutely central to the stories' success. We see Holmes through his eyes, with his mixture of affection and awe. Watson never tires of telling us that Holmes is the most fascinating man on earth and most readers come to accept his judgment even when the evidence does not support it.

Scotland Yard asks Holmes's help. An American has been found dead in a deserted house. The clues include a woman's ring, the word *Rache* written on the wall in blood, and footprints and tire tracks that Holmes understands but the police do not. When one of the policemen announces that obviously a woman named Rachel is the key to the mystery, Holmes informs him that *Rache* is German for "revenge." Holmes calls upon "six dirty little scoundrels"—the Baker Street Irregulars—to assist his investigation, showing that Doyle appreciates the utility of children in fiction. After a second American is killed, Holmes calls for a cab and, when the driver arrives, snaps handcuffs on him and announces that he is the killer. This man, Jefferson Hope, confesses.

We have been reading for thirty-five pages, we have the killer, and we have no idea who Jefferson Hope is or why he killed the two Americans. Doyle then launches part two of the story. Watson's narrative stops and we begin a third-person account that is set in "an arid and repulsive desert" in "the central portion of the great North American Continent." It is some years earlier, 1847, and a man and a little girl, the only survivors of a wagon train, are rescued by a group of Mormons headed for their Promised Land in Utah. The Mormons demand that the man join their religion along with the child, whom he has adopted. He does, although he never adopts their polygamy.

Some years later the brutish Mormons demand that he give up his adopted daughter to a man who already has seven wives, but the father refuses. He is killed and the young woman is forced into marriage and dies. She is survived by the man she truly loved, Jefferson Hope, who vows revenge and obtains it years later when he follows the Mormon who stole his love and another man to London. This flashback takes twenty-five pages. Then Watson resumes his narrative and Hope confirms that he had become a cabdriver in London and thereby tracked down his victims. The problem of what to do with Hope, whose crimes seem justified, is solved when he dies of a heart condition.

For all Holmes's deductive skill, the turning point in the case came when he sent a telegram to Cleveland, where the first victim had been living, and inquired about the man's marital status. The Ohio police sent back word that the man "had already applied for the protection of the law against an old rival in love, named Jefferson Hope, and that this same Hope was at present in Europe." It was a simple matter for Holmes, aided by his "Arab detective corps," to find the cabdriver named Hope, who has helpfully continued to use his real name. Scotland Yard could as easily have asked the right question of the Cleveland police. The story ends with Watson vowing to tell the world of Holmes's amazing powers.

In fact, Holmes's amazing powers consisted of sending a telegram. Realizing that his crime story was thin, Doyle then took us halfway around the world to portray a lurid tale of rape and murder among the Mormons. Doyle surely hoped that such scandalous events would strengthen the chances of selling his story.

As it turned out, he had a hard time selling it. It was an awkward length, long for a story and short for a novel. Two publishers turned down "A Study in Scarlet" before Ward Lock & Co. offered to include it in *Beeton's Christmas Annual for 1887*. Then Doyle got lucky. An editor of *Lippincott's Magazine* liked the story and asked Doyle for a follow-up. Consider Doyle's plight at this point. It has taken him more than a year to get his first story published. Now he is given one more chance to get Holmes before the public. So what does he do? He does what any writer worth his salt would do: He writes his ass off.

Holmes's second adventure, "The Sign of Four," probably contains more thrills per page than any other story ever written. In its opening sentence, Holmes is injecting himself with cocaine (the famous seven-percent solution), much to Watson's displeasure. Soon a young woman arrives, a damsel in distress. Her soldier father, she explains, has vanished some years earlier, but she has been sent "a very large and lustrous pearl" every year since, and now she has been summoned to a mysterious meeting by an "unknown friend." Holmes agrees to accompany her. Watson, for his part, is already falling in love with Miss Mary Morstan. She produces a letter of her father's that refers to "The Sign of Four." That night, after a wild ride in a closed carriage, they are admitted to an isolated house "by a Hindu servant, clad in a yellow turban" and meet the master of the house, a bizarre little man named Thaddeus Sholto. He says that Mary will be given a vast fortune in jewels that her father brought back from India. However, Sholto's brother has the treasure chest, and when they reach his house the brother is dead, in an inaccessible locked room, apparently killed by a poisoned thorn. Holmes finds evidence of a "wooden-legged man" and footprints suggesting that the killer was only half the size of an adult man. "Holmes," Watson gasps, "a child has done this horrid thing." The treasure chest is missing.

Holmes employs a dog named Toby to help him track the killers (dogs, like children, are mainstays of adventure stories), and unleashes the Baker Street Irregulars to find the killer's boat, which leads to a wild chase down the Thames ("Our boilers were strained to their utmost"). Holmes captures the peg-legged killer and his tiny dark-skinned associate ("that little hell-hound Tonga," he of the poisoned darts), and we learn the story of how some Englishmen stole a fortune in jewels during the Indian Mutiny. The "Four" of the title were convicts who thought the treasure theirs. Holmes solves the locked-door murder—that little hell-hound Tonga, like the orangutan in "The Murders in the Rue Morgue," could scramble to places most mortals cannot. The jewels are lost at the bottom of the Thames, but Watson marries Mary, the true treasure. Whether she is his first or second wife is a subject of continuing debate among Sherlockians.

In short, Doyle's first two stories are less exercises in deduction than exotic action adventures, with innocent virgins dragged to harems in Utah and pint-size savages wielding blowguns on the streets of London. Holmes, hitching rides on the backs of carriages, racing down the Thames in a speedboat, and sending his scruffy little "Arabs" into the street, has less in common with C. Auguste Dupin than with Indiana Jones. Yet the stories are gloriously readable. In 1890 "The Sign of Four" was published in *Lippincott's* American and English editions and came out in book form. Doyle was sufficiently encouraged to close his medical practice and launch a series of stories in the *Strand Magazine* that made him famous. There is a saying among writers that you must trust your material. As his success grew, Doyle came to have more faith in Holmes and Watson and to feel less need for polygamy and blowguns.

Doyle's next story, "A Scandal in Bohemia," is simple compared to the first two. Holmes and Watson are visited by a huge masked man who proves to be the king of Bohemia. He explains that he is about to marry but fears that a former lover will use a photograph to embarrass him. This is, he declares, "a matter of such weight that it may have an influence on European history." It happens that the woman in question, Irene Adler, is the woman in the world Holmes most admires, but that is not central to the events that follow. The king, whose agents have already broken into Adler's house and searched without success for the photo, persuades Holmes to try to find it.

Holmes arranges for his confederates to fake a fight outside Adler's home during which an old clergyman is seemingly injured. She takes the poor fellow inside to recover. Watson, outside, shouts "Fire!" The woman hurries to the photograph's hiding place ("a recess behind a sliding panel") before she realizes there is no fire. The clergyman is Holmes in disguise, so now he knows where the photograph is hidden. Here is Holmes's superior intellect at work: "When a woman thinks that her house in on fire, her instinct is to at once rush to the thing which she values most." This is genius? The story, a jazzed-up variation on Poe's "Purloined Letter," is child's play as to criminal detection but pulls the reader in with fancy talk about changing the history of

Europe and dark hints of the scandalous ways that fine ladies and Bo-
hemian kings conduct their romances.

Must I continue? In story after story the solution is childlike in its
simplicity. Even run-of-the-mill crime writers today devise more ingenious plots than Doyle. And yet Doyle's stories have survived for a reason. He was a *writer*. His stories capture us not with their "scientific
deduction" but with their zest, their portrait of London, and the chem-
istry between his two great characters. They are an excuse for us to
enter a world that is ordered and dignified, a world where rationality
triumphs over evil, a world still innocent of the horrors that began in
1914. The Holmes stories made it clear for the first time that mysteries
could attract a vast audience. The excitement that surrounded the
Holmes collections, particularly when Doyle brought Holmes back
after his apparent death, wasn't equaled in England until the Harry
Potter books a hundred years later. Indeed, the secret of the Holmes
stories is that they are magnificent boys' adventures that continue to
work after the boys grow up. If, indeed, we ever grow up.

Others share this view. Christopher Morley, in his introduction to
the complete Sherlock Holmes, wrote, "Even in the less successful stories we remain untroubled by any naïveté of plot; it is the character of
the immortal pair that we relish." Somerset Maugham wrote in his
essay "The Decline and Fall of the Detective Story," "For an anthology
of short stories that I was preparing several years ago, I re-read the col-
lected stories of Conan Doyle. I was surprised to find how poor they
were. The introduction is effective, the scene well set, but the anecdote
is thin and you finish the tale with a sense of dissatisfaction. Great cry
and little wool." Yet Maugham goes on to say, "No detective stories
have had the popularity of Conan Doyle's, and because of the invention of Sherlock Holmes I think it may be admitted that none has so
well deserved it." The Holmes stories remind us that the tales we love
best are character-driven. With that in mind, let us turn to Doyle's most
successful imitator, Agatha Christie.

THERE IS NOTHING LIKE A DAME

My first encounter with Dame Agatha Christie (1890–1976) was a
happy one. I must have been in my early teens when I saw René Clair's

movie of Christie's *And Then There Were None*. I remember the moody black-and-white photography and the devilish plot in which ten strangers are summoned to a deserted island, where someone starts to kill them. Finally, the last survivors, two young lovers, confront each other, each believing the other is the killer. But, of course, Christie still has tricks up her sleeve.

I read a few of Christie's novels in my youth but I was essentially innocent of her work when I sat down one autumn day in Paris to read *Peril at End House,* a 1931 Hercule Poirot mystery that I'd picked at random at Shakespeare & Company. The novel opens with the Belgian Poirot and his friend Captain Arthur Hastings vacationing on the Cornish coast. They are obviously modeled on Holmes and Watson, the brilliant world-famous detective and his stolid biographer friend. Although Hastings later married, he and Poirot once shared lodgings, like Holmes and Watson, and they bicker like an old married couple.

The first thing Poirot says to Hastings is, "Your remark is not original." Hastings recalls a mystery "solved by Poirot with his usual unerring acumen." Poirot says he wishes Hastings had been with him during that case. "As a result of long habit," Hastings reflects, "I distrust his compliments." Sure enough, Poirot adds, "One needs a certain amount of light relief." Poirot claims to be retired from the detective business and Hastings urges him to reconsider. No, Poirot says. "They say of me, 'That is Hercule Poirot!—the great—the unique! There was never anyone like him, there never will be!' *Eh bien*—I am satisfied. I ask no more. I am modest." Poirot is "almost purring with self-satisfaction." Later—when Hastings insists that Poirot's career is not finished—"Poirot patted my knee. 'There speaks the good friend—the faithful dog. And you have reason, too. The grey cells, they still function. . . .' "

By then I was in shock. Christie had transformed Holmes and Watson from the sublime to the ridiculous. She had made them comic characters—the fussy, absurd little Belgian with his "egg-shaped head" and his dense oft-ridiculed sidekick. Holmes and Watson were classics of male bonding, up there with Mark Twain's Huck and Jim and Larry McMurtry's Gus McCrae and W. F. Call. Poirot and Hastings are closer to Abbott and Costello. And there is a cruel undercurrent to the exchanges. *Light relief! The faithful dog!* Holmes was a gentleman who treated the loyal Watson with respect. Poirot needs a punch in the nose.

I tried to imagine what Christie was up to, for she was a clever woman whose books have been outsold only by Shakespeare and the Bible. I can only surmise that, setting out to imitate the Holmes stories, she decided to alter the formula. If Holmes had any fault as a character it was that he was both rather grim and a bit of a smarty-pants. That did not impede his success, but it could perhaps be improved upon. So Christie made her master detective not only a foreigner (not French but close to it) but also a rather absurd one. We could laugh at Poirot and still reluctantly admire his alleged genius. He provided comedy and intellectual fireworks in the same package. It is true, too, that Christie began writing in the immediate aftermath of World War I, with its unspeakable loss of life, and she may have felt that people needed to laugh.

Peril at End House is a comedy of manners, built around mysterious events and the murder of one minor character. Poirot and Hastings meet Nick Buckley, an attractive young woman who owns End House. She is a modern woman who drinks martinis and has a "hint of recklessness" about her, and it appears that someone is trying to kill her. The plot expands to include a young pilot who is attempting to fly around the world (heady stuff in those days), the death of the richest man in England, a secret engagement, a poisoned box of candy, a drug fiend, a forged will, and finally a séance at which Poirot exposes the killer—who turns out to be the lovely Nick herself! It's harmless fun, but I never got over the shock of meeting the comedy team of Poirot and Hastings.

Wanting to be fair to Dame Agatha, I sought out one of her most admired novels, *The Murder of Roger Ackroyd,* which was published in 1926 and inspired Edmund Wilson's famous 1945 *New Yorker* essay, "Who Cares Who Killed Roger Ackroyd?" In the essay the great critic declared that detective fiction was a minor vice, somewhere between crossword puzzles and smoking, but confessed his weakness for the Holmes stories. *The Murder of Roger Ackroyd* is a far better novel than *Peril at End House;* take off Christie's name and you wouldn't think the same person could have written them both. Captain Hastings does not appear. Poirot has settled in an English village where he is a neighbor of Dr. Sheppard, who narrates the novel and who at the outset thinks Poirot a hairdresser.

The opening chapters, in which we meet the people of the village, are a model of deft exposition. The writing is both amusing—particularly the sketch of Dr. Sheppard's nosy sister—and perceptive about the place and its inhabitants. Abruptly, the village's leading citizen, Roger Ackroyd, dies in his home under mysterious circumstances. Poirot solves the murder, which involves the use of a Dictaphone (high technology for that day) to imitate the voice of the dead man, the faking of footprints, and the use of a stranger to make a crucial phone call. In the end, Poirot shows that the killer is none other than Dr. Sheppard, our helpful narrator. Poirot permits the duplicitous doctor to kill himself rather than face justice—this, like Jefferson Hope's heart attack in "A Study in Scarlet," removes the need for a messy trial. The ending of the novel aroused a noisy debate. Many readers felt that Dame Agatha had broken the rules by letting the narrator be the killer. Imagine, a mystery novelist deceiving her readers! But the lady was well aware that there are no rules in writing except what works. The writer, if she is good enough, makes the rules.

Christie wrote for some fifty years and produced more than sixty novels, as well as short stories, plays, and an autobiography. There were thirty-three Poirot books alone. Some of her most-admired novels, in addition to *Roger Ackroyd,* are *The ABC Murders, And Then There Were None,* and *Death on the Nile,* and the Miss Marple series has devoted fans. On the basis of the two novels just discussed, we must call her output uneven, but that is inevitable. (Her rivals Shakespeare and the Bible are also uneven.) Dame Agatha had a genius for clever plots and her success inspired other writers, many of them women. Some wrote mysteries that were more sophisticated, but none was more popular.

PUZZLES

Starting with Christie's *The Mysterious Affair at Styles* in 1920, the English mystery focused on a "closed circle" of suspects, often in an isolated country house. The suspects are part of an elite that plays bridge and dresses for dinner. A body turns up on page one but no one really mourns the victim. The mystery is what matters. The police are baffled and the case is solved either by a private investigator like Poirot or by a gifted amateur like Miss Marple or Dorothy Sayers's Lord Peter

Wimsey or G. K. Chesterton's Father Brown. Over time, as the genre evolved, the stories advanced from the ingenious to the preposterous. In *Peril at End House,* Nick Buckley murders her cousin so she can claim the fortune that the cousin's secret fiancé, a dashing young aviator who is conveniently lost at sea, inherits from his fabulously rich uncle. Say *what?*

In *The ABC Murders,* the victims are killed in alphabetical order, with A and B dispatched only to divert attention from the real target, C. On this side of the Atlantic, Ellery Queen wrote *The Chinese Orange Mystery,* in which a corpse is found in a locked room where everything is backward—furniture is upended, paintings are turned to the wall, the victim's clothes are reversed—all of which is intended to disguise the fact that the victim was a priest, a man who wore his collar backward. We have entered what Aristophanes called Cloud-Cuckoo-Land.

Up to a point, we accept an improbable plot if the story is fun, but there are limits. In time, such novels became too precious to be taken seriously. In 1928, S. S. Van Dine, author of the Philo Vance mysteries, wrote an article called "Twenty Rules for Writing Detective Stories." The detective story is "a kind of intellectual game," he said, and self-respecting writers must follow certain unwritten rules. The reader should have the same opportunity as the detective to solve the crime, no tricks can be played on the reader that aren't played on the detective, the detective should have no love interest, the villain must play a prominent role in the story, and the culprit must be an amateur, not a professional criminal. Van Dine also listed devices that were forbidden, such as a séance that frightens the culprit into a confession, using a dummy to create an alibi, having someone's twin commit the crime, and so on. The essay was amusing, but his point was serious. A genre that has become that ritualized cannot last.

The next year, 1929, two first novels were published that would point the way for the divergent paths that American crime fiction has followed ever since. The first of these was *The Roman Hat Mystery,* which was attributed to Ellery Queen and featured an aristocratic detective with that name. The authors were in truth two cousins, Frederic Dannay (originally Danny Nathan) and Manfred B. Lee, both born in 1905. During a childhood illness, Dannay devoured the Sherlock Holmes books. In their early twenties, as one cousin worked as a publicist and the other in advertising, they decided to collaborate on a crime series. Thus was born the brainy, rather effete Ellery Queen, who drove a Duesenberg and kept an apartment on Manhattan's Upper West Side. The Queen books, movies, and magazines were hugely popular for more than forty years. Inevitably, the quality of their work declined. The cousins, talented hustlers from the first, became a brand name, a book factory, and thus anticipated current writers like James Patterson and Tom Clancy.

But something else was happening as the twenties neared an end. Readers were increasingly disenchanted with "puzzle mysteries," particularly in America, where various factors—the Depression, the influence of Ernest Hemingway, the rise of pulp magazines—were moving us toward a new kind of crime fiction. The other writer whose first novel was published in 1929, and whose short, tormented career would be far more important than Ellery Queen's, was Dashiell Hammett, the father of hard-boiled American crime fiction.

3.

American Style:

Hammett, Cain, Chandler

odern American crime fiction starts with these opening lines
of Dashiell Hammett's 1930 novel *The Maltese Falcon:*

> Samuel Spade's jaw was long and bony, his chin a jutting v under
> the more flexible v of his mouth. His nostrils curved back to
> make another, smaller v. His yellow-grey eyes were horizontal.
> The v *motif* was picked up again by thickish brows rising out-
> ward from twin creases above a hooked nose, and his pale
> brown hair grew down—from high flat temples—in a point on
> his forehead. He looked rather pleasantly like a blond satan.

This is the work of a supremely confident writer. He's found his
voice, he's found his hero, and he knows you're going to be as hooked
as he is on this blond satan, this Sam Spade. Having introduced his
hero, in prose as sardonic as Spade himself, Hammett wastes no time.
In the next paragraph, Spade's adoring secretary, Effie Perine, announces that a Miss Wonderly wants to see him. Miss Wonderly enters—a knockout, as Effie promised—all aflutter, another damsel in
distress. Except she's not. Her real name is Brigid O'Shaughnessy and
she's a con artist, nonstop liar, and possible murderer. Spade suspects
the worst but is happy to take her money. He assigns his partner, Miles

Archer, to follow one Floyd Thursby, who Brigid says is leading her sister astray. There is of course no sister.

That night Archer is shot dead on the assignment. Soon Thursby too is dead. Thus begins the tale of the elusive bejeweled Maltese Falcon that, as novel and movie, is a classic of hard-boiled crime fiction and film noir. *The Maltese Falcon* wasn't Hammett's first novel but it was his best and, because of John Huston's 1941 movie, is by far his best known. It isn't the greatest noir film—that would be Billy Wilder's version of James M. Cain's *Double Indemnity*—but the combination of Humphrey Bogart's snarling Spade, Sydney Greenstreet's obsessive Falcon hunter Kasper Gutman, Peter Lorre's effete Joel Cairo, and Elisha Cook Jr. as Wilmer, the surly young gunsel, makes it irresistible.

I reread the novel, after several decades, to see how it held up and in particular to see if what I have long considered the major fault of the movie came from the book. That is the character of Brigid, as played by Mary Astor, an actress whose charms elude me. I can never believe that Bogart would give a damn about this woman, beyond the obligatory one-night stand. As a result, the dramatic ending of the movie, when he agonizes about his love for her, never worked for me. Even if she hadn't killed his partner, I couldn't believe that Bogart would fall for this creepy woman with the bizarre hairdo who lies endlessly. Contrast Astor's Brigid with Barbara Stanwyck's delicious Phyllis Dietrichson in *Double Indemnity* or the heartbreaking Gene Tierney in Otto Preminger's *Laura*—dames any guy might play the sap for!

The novel is written with economy, energy, and flair. The Hemingway-influenced dialogue is dazzling and the characterization of the cynical, calculating, violent, fiercely independent Spade is a marvel. (We will often see the influence of Hemingway in the decades ahead. Writers like Hammett and Cain knew they were influenced by him; today we have young writers who are influenced by him and don't even know it.) Hammett's talents, along with the romance and mystery of the centuries-old Falcon and Gutman's obsession with it, make *The Maltese Falcon* memorable. Yet I find many problems in the novel, faults we may overlook because we read it a long time ago or because we loved the movie or because we admire Hammett. Here, as elsewhere, nostalgia can cloud our minds.

It is basic to *The Maltese Falcon* that everyone is intimidated by Spade. The cops defer to him (one keeps saying, "Aw, be reasonable,

Sam") and even the local DA is speechless when Spade bawls him out. When Gutman and his gang are threatening him with death, he laughs and says he won't be influenced by the guns they're pointing at him, and he defies the gang to torture him. If men defer to Spade, women adore him—the long-suffering secretary, Effie; Miles Archer's widow, Iva, who fancies that Spade loves her; even the duplicitous Brigid. He awes all these people not with his intellect, like Dupin or Holmes or Poirot, but with his physical prowess, his fearlessness, his moral superiority. Hammett had been a Pinkerton detective and knew that private detectives do not often talk back to cops and keep their teeth. But he had also written for the pulp magazines and knew that a cop-baiting private eye made great copy.

Years later, Ed McBain had his detective, Frank Carella, observe that "the last time [he] had met a private detective investigating a murder was never." Hammett didn't care. Poe, Doyle, and Christie had perfected the brilliant private investigator who could run circles around the lamebrained cops. Hammett made the detective a man of action, and as such he became the central hero of modern crime fiction. When Hammett started writing, America's police were notoriously corrupt and brutal, and the incorruptible PI made a dramatic foil. Sam Spade ushered in a half century in which the private eye replaced the lone cowboy as the iconic American hero.

One problem with *The Maltese Falcon* is its homophobia, although Hammett's is not as blatant as Raymond Chandler's a decade later. Perhaps it's a holdover from writing for pulps, but it's clear that both writers are doing it to amuse readers who want to laugh at these repellent creatures—or watch them get roughed up or even killed. The main target in *The Maltese Falcon* is Joel Cairo. When Cairo first turns up in Spade's office, Effie brings in his perfumed card and announces, "This guy is queer." Then we are off to the races:

> Mr. Joel Cairo was a small-boned dark man of medium height. . . .
> His black coat, cut tight to narrow shoulders, flared a little over
> slightly plump hips. . . . He . . . came towards Spade with short,
> mincing, bobbing steps. The fragrance of *chypre* came with him.

Cairo's effeminacy is remarked on throughout the novel, and apparently he is the lover of Wilmer, whose "curling lashes" are fre-

quently cited. Today, the problem is not only that the gay-baiting is repugnant but that it's so dated. (What the hell is *chypre?*)

Gays aside, there are several scenes and plot twists in the novel that
don't make sense. For example, the scene in which Brigid and Cairo are
in Spade's apartment and the police come to the door. Spade won't let
them in, but then Brigid and Cairo get in a fight and he screams and the
cops rush in, whereupon Spade concocts a ridiculous story that it was
all a joke they put on to fool the police. If the scene has a point it is to
show again how easily Spade can manipulate the dumb cops. It's silly
in print and silly on film; there's nothing to be done with it.

Spade leads a charmed life. Wilmer and Cairo keep pointing guns at
him but he only laughs and takes their guns away. Spade's impassioned
argument that he and Gutman had to give the police a fall guy—
Wilmer—to blame for the murders is double-talk, since Wilmer would
eagerly turn on them. Equally improbable is the revelation that Brigid
killed Miles Archer. Her confession serves mainly to set up the high
drama when Spade agonizes about his love for the woman who murdered his partner.

Where is the evidence of this love? The first hint of romance between Brigid and Spade comes while he is trying to get the truth about
the Falcon out of her. "I have always been a liar," she confesses. Spade
laughs and says he'll make coffee, whereupon "She put her hands up to
Spade's cheeks, put her open mouth hard against his mouth, her body
flat against his body." As Spade embraces her, "his eyes burned yellowly." Thus ends Chapter 9. It's not terribly romantic (his eyes burned
yellowly?) but it serves to get them in bed, where we find them the next
morning. As Brigid sleeps on, Spade dresses, takes her room key from
her purse, and hurries to her hotel to search vainly for the Falcon. Then
he buys some eggs, goes home, lies about where he's been, ignores the
gun in her hand, and makes breakfast. When he tries to question her
again, she protests. "You can't ask me to talk about that this morning
of all mornings."

That's Brigid as a blushing bride, on her morning of mornings, and
it's about as romantic as it gets for these two. Nobody likes or trusts
Brigid except Effie, who keeps going on about what a swell kid she is.
There is a later scene with Spade, Brigid, Gutman, Cairo, and Wilmer
when someone has stolen a thousand-dollar bill from Spade. Ever the

gentleman, he takes Brigid into the bathroom and tells her to take her clothes off. She refuses. "All right," he says. "We'll go back to the other room and I'll have them taken off." She protests that he'll be killing something. "I don't know anything about that," Spade tells her. "Take them off." She does.

After the Falcon has proved a fake and Gutman and his friends have fled, Brigid admits that she killed Miles and Spade tells her, "I'm going to send you over." He taunts her by saying that she'll probably be out of prison in twenty years and he'll wait for her. He says he didn't give a damn about Archer but says that if your partner is killed, you're supposed to do something about it. Spade admits that "maybe you love me and maybe I love you" but when she keeps babbling about love, Spade tells her angrily, "I won't play the sap for you." The police come and take her away.

High drama, but I don't believe a word of it. Someone reading the book or seeing the movie for the first time, caught up in the story, might buy this moment of love and heartbreak or not be bothered by the holes in the plot, but if you look closely it is hard to deny that the novel, so tough, so readable, so influential, is noir with plenty of smoke and mirrors.

Much of the enduring popularity of *The Maltese Falcon* is because of John Huston's shrewd film adaptation. The dialogue in the movie is almost all from the novel, but Huston cut a great deal of weak or superfluous material. He shows a lot less of Ivy, Archer's widow. He cut Gutman's daughter, who turns up drugged in a pointless scene. He plays down the homophobia and drops the suggestion of a relationship between Cairo and Wilmer. Nor does he tell us at the end, as Hammett did, that Wilmer killed Gutman shortly before he was arrested. Huston understood that it was better to leave us thinking that Gutman might yet spend the rest of his life in a hopeless quest for the Falcon. It was Huston, too, who had Spade invoke Shakespeare to tell us that the Falcon was "the stuff that dreams are made of." How much better to remember the movie in those terms than to recall the novel's final lines, when Effie tells Spade that the creepy widow Iva has come to see him and he "shivered" and said, "Well, send her in."

Huston also made changes in the relationship between Spade and Brigid, all intended to make the climactic "maybe I love you" exchange more believable. After they first spend the night together, Huston cuts the scene when he searches her apartment and she pulls a gun on him. He also cuts Spade's telling Brigid to take off her clothes or he'll have them taken off—pulp-magazine sadism that has no place in his movie.

After a recent viewing of the film, I still think Brigid is a serious flaw, but I no longer blame Astor; the character is impossible. Still, Huston made a classic movie out of a fitfully brilliant novel, one that had been produced twice previously with dismal results. Hammett's reputation today rests in large part on the enduring popularity of Huston's film.

Hammett served in World War I, was a Pinkerton detective for eight years, and in the mid-1920s began writing for the pulp magazine *Black Mask*. The best of Hammett's novels are *The Maltese Falcon* and *The Glass Key*. The latter features Ned Beaumont, a gambler who becomes the close friend of a political boss. Beaumont is a tough and resourceful fellow, but he isn't larger than life like Spade, nor does his involvement in corrupt politics and murder capture our imagination the way Spade, Gutman, and the Falcon do. Hammett's last novel, *The Thin Man,* was his weakest, but its Nick and Nora Charles inspired a popular series of movies that starred William Powell and Myrna Loy as upscale crime solvers.

When World War II began, Hammett enlisted, at the age of forty-eight, and worked on an army newspaper in Alaska. He had for years been active in liberal causes, and after the war he was called before Congressional committees and questioned about his work with the Civil Rights Congress, which the FBI called a communist front. He refused to answer and served six months in a federal prison. After he was sentenced, the government moved to have his books removed from libraries that received federal funds and his publisher suspended publication of *The Maltese Falcon* to please the witch-hunters. After Hammett's death, he was buried, as a veteran of two world wars, in Arlington National Cemetery.

CAIN

James M. Cain didn't invent a genre, like Hammett, nor was he as skilled a writer as Raymond Chandler, but between Hammett's last novel and Chandler's first he published two best sellers, *The Postman Always Rings Twice* (1934) and *Double Indemnity* (1936), that were flawed classics and live on as notable movies. Cain was an insurance salesman after college and then a reporter in Baltimore; both pursuits contribute to his fiction. In 1924, in his early thirties, he joined the *New York World.* He wrote a play that closed quickly but gave him credentials for screenwriting, and he went to Los Angeles in 1931 to write for Paramount. He had little success as a screenwriter, both because he didn't like the movie business and because he drank too much, so he decided to write a novel.

Cain had been fascinated by the 1927 trial of Ruth Snyder, who, along with her salesman lover, Judd Gray, was convicted and executed for murdering her husband. Several details stuck in Cain's mind, including the fact that Snyder had taken out a double-indemnity policy on her husband and that she arranged for the postman to ring twice when he delivered payment coupons. Also, the murder was poorly planned (the dumbbell murder, it was called), and Snyder and Gray blamed each other in the end. As a novelist, Cain mined the case for two titles, a theme, and many details. He was further inspired when, driving outside Los Angeles, he met a sexy young woman who ran a gas station with her husband, and later he read that she had been charged with killing him.

The Postman Always Rings Twice and *Double Indemnity* are short novels, not much over a hundred pages, and both have the same basic story. A cocky, good-looking young man meets a married woman he can't resist. They become lovers and decide to murder the husband, disguise it as an accident, and collect his double-indemnity insurance policy. Although the murders are poorly planned, they get away with them but turn on each other and finally are punished.

Cain could repeat his plot because he put his two sets of lovers in different worlds. In *Postman,* Frank is a drifter and small-time hustler. In its famous opening line he tells us, "They threw me off the hay truck about noon." He stops at the Twin Oaks Tavern, a filling station and sandwich joint, and meets Nick, its Greek owner, who offers him a job. Frank gets a glimpse of Nick's wife, Cora, and accepts. Frank is dumb but thinks he's smart. Cora is so dumb she agrees. They become lovers, decide to kill Nick, and bungle the first attempt. Then Frank kills Nick with a wrench and they fake an auto accident. The police know what has happened but a slick lawyer named Katz gets them off. The lovers fear each other, consider murder, and then decide they're in love, whereupon fate intervenes. There is no postman in the novel, unless the title is taken to mean death, like the iceman in Eugene O'Neill's *The Iceman Cometh*. That postman does ring twice.

The novel was considered scandalous, although it is tame by today's standards. Cora likes it when he bites her. The novel's sexiest moment comes just after the lovers are freed from jail:

> I ripped all her clothes off. She twisted and turned, slow, so they would slip out from under her. Then she closed her eyes and lay back on the pillow. Her hair was falling over her shoulders in snaky curls. Her eye was all black, and her breasts weren't drawn up and pointing up at me, but soft and spread out in two big pink splotches. She looked like the great-grandmother of every whore in the world. The devil got his money's worth that night.

Hot stuff in 1934.

In *Double Indemnity,* the characters are middle class and more polished, if not much smarter. Walter is a thirty-four-year-old insurance salesman. He falls for Phyllis and they agree to kill her husband. They do this by faking an accident—a fall from the back of a slow-moving train—and Walter thinks he's committed the perfect crime. The only one to suspect murder is his boss, Keyes, a student of insurance fraud. Walter and Phyllis beat the rap but face another kind of justice.

Cain, like Hammett, was well served by the people who put *Double Indemnity* onto film: director Billy Wilder and Raymond Chandler, working on his first screenplay. Their movie version opens and closes with brilliant noir scenes, neither of which is in the novel. In the new opening, amid the shadows of LA at night, the dying Walter staggers from his car into his office to confess his crimes into a recorder. Probably to defer criticism, Wilder and Chandler thus make clear at the outset that crime doesn't pay. Then they return to the novel's opening, when Walter goes to a client's house and meets his wife, Phyllis, played by Barbara Stanwyck, who is as sexy as she is scary.

Wilder and Chandler cooked up suggestive dialogue that sneaked around the censorship of the era, but they couldn't get around the major flaw in the novel, which is Walter's perfect crime. As Keyes points out, men who fall off the back of slow-moving trains don't often die, as the husband supposedly did. But the brilliance of the directing, the dialogue, and the photography and the acting of Fred MacMurray, Barbara Stanwyck, and Edward G. Robinson sweep us past the weak spots. In Chandler and Wilder's ending, Walter goes to Phyllis's home. She wears white silk. They talk in the shadows. The dreamy ballad "Tangerine" plays in the distance. She shoots and wounds him. She admits she never loved him, that she's rotten, but she won't shoot him again. He takes the gun and shoots her. Then he goes back to his office to confess and die.

The Wilder-Chandler ending is inspired, particularly when compared with the truly dreadful ending of the novel. There, Walter and Phyllis are freed and put on a ship bound for Mexico. Both are so overcome by guilt that they agree to jump into the ocean, where a shark awaits them. Perhaps Cain, reacting to the controversy that greeted *Postman,* thought justice-by-shark was the price he had to pay for an amoral novel. Chandler and Wilder had the good sense to dispense with the shark and have Phyllis die at Walter's hand—and in his arms—in the most beautiful scene in all film noir.

PULP WRITER AND POET

I'm going to spend more time than I should on Raymond Chandler because he troubles me. He is everywhere hailed as the master of the crime novel. He was praised by the likes of T. S. Eliot and W. H. Auden—although I suspect that when Evelyn Waugh called Chandler "the best writer in America," he was having a bit of sport with fellows named Hemingway and Faulkner. Despite all the praise, and despite his obvious strengths and historical importance, Chandler strikes me as an uneven, overrated writer. I say this having reread his three most admired novels: *The Big Sleep, Farewell, My Lovely,* and *The Long Goodbye* and found it an often agonizing experience.

Raymond Chandler was intelligent, well read, and talented, but he was in many ways a bitter, insecure man. He was scornful of foreigners, blacks, homosexuals, rich people, and women, among others, and it is no accident that in these three novels the villain always turns out to be a rich woman. It is generally agreed that Chandler's plots are convoluted at best and incomprehensible at worst, but his admirers say his virtues compensate for the confusion. For me, the plots are only the start of the problem. Chandler was capable of colorful, inventive, lyrical prose, but he was also a woefully self-indulgent writer who junked up his books with cruel asides and inane similes. He was in urgent need of a good editor, but he couldn't tolerate criticism and once fired his agent because an assistant in his office, after reading the first draft of *The Long Goodbye*, told the author, not unreasonably, that his beloved Philip Marlowe was becoming "too Christlike."

Chandler was born in Chicago in 1888. After his father deserted the family, he and his mother wound up in London, living off the charity of rich relatives. His uncle staked him to a taste of college; then he was obliged to take a civil service job. Unhappy there, he tried freelance writing and then moved America. He settled in California, soon followed by his mother, and lived there until his wartime service in the Canadian army. He returned to California, where he became part of a rich artistic crowd, and in 1919 he fell in love with an attractive, sophisticated woman named Cissy Pascal. Their romance was complicated not only by her marriage but by the fact that he was thirty-one and she was a good bit older. Cissy divorced her husband, but marriage was not possible as long as his mother was alive.

In 1920, Chandler was hired by a small oil company and became a well-paid executive. He lived with his mother and supported both women until 1924 when, soon after his mother's death, the lovers married. They seem to have been happy at first, although she had deceived him about her age. When they married, he was thirty-five and she was fifty-three, not the forty-three she had claimed. By the late 1920s both were drinking heavily and he had at least one affair at his office. They periodically separated, with Chandler moving into hotels to drink alone.

In 1932, Chandler was fired because of his drinking. Fortunately, he had savings to draw on, and at age forty-four he made a bold decision: He would be a writer. Chandler admired Hammett's work and decided to try to write for *Black Mask*. He spent five months on "Blackmailers

Don't Shoot" and *Black Mask* bought the story, which his biographer Tom Hiney says "has an almost completely indecipherable plot." But Chandler wrote richer, more colorful prose than any other *Black Mask* contributor, and before the decade was over he published twenty-one stories there, earning $300 to $400 for most of them. He became the best pulp writer in America because the quality of his writing transcended the magazine's formula of sex, sadism, and violence. In 1938, an agent showed his stories to publisher Alfred Knopf, who asked for a novel. Chandler quickly wrote *The Big Sleep* (i.e., death) that summer. He wove in characters and scenes from several of his *Black Mask* stories, which helps account for its disjointed plot.

At the outset, as Philip Marlowe goes to meet a rich new client, he tells us proudly, "I was neat, clean, shaved, and sober, and I didn't care who knew it. I was everything the well-dressed private detective ought to be. I was calling on four million dollars."

Chandler, like Hammett before him, had found his voice and his man. The writing is precise in its descriptions and sardonic in its tone. Marlowe is modeled on Sam Spade but different too. He's better dressed. He speaks in the first person. And his clients are rich, unlike the gang of crooks Spade came up against.

In the novel's second paragraph, Chandler tells us that the front door of the Sternwood mansion "would have let in a troop of Indian elephants," which is typical of the overstatements he gloried in, and he also tells us about the "stained-glass panel showing a knight in dark armor rescuing a lady who was tied to a tree and didn't have any clothes on." He fantasizes about helping the knight save the damsel. That is the first hint that we are to regard Marlowe not simply as a private eye but as a knight in shining armor. The opening chapters also feature Marlowe's fiery independence. He is approached by Carmen Sternwood, who is twenty or so and has "little sharp predatory teeth." She giggles, sucks her thumb (she does that a lot), and falls into his arms, explaining, "You're cute."

He escapes from Carmen and goes to see her father, in the celebrated greenhouse scene. General Sternwood is a wonderful old man, who declares that neither of his daughters has any more moral sense than a cat. They get to business: An art dealer named Geiger, who is really a pornographer, is asking Sternwood to pay Carmen's gambling debts, in what sounds like blackmail. Marlowe boasts that he'll handle the matter so that Geiger will think a bridge fell on him. There is also talk of a Joe Brody, to whom the General has paid $5,000, and of the Irish bootlegger Rusty Regan, who is the third husband of Sternwood's older daughter, Vivian, and has been missing for several weeks. The General calls Vivian spoiled and ruthless. In the movie, which stars Bogart as Marlowe, Vivian is played by Lauren Bacall, and she is toned down to allow for Bogart-Bacall flirtation. The scene with Sternwood, like much of the novel, is as readable as it is confusing, particularly as to the roles of Geiger, Brody, and Regan—and Eddie Mars is soon added to the mix.

Marlowe is summoned to meet Vivian. They banter and she declares she doesn't like his manners, to which he replies that he's not crazy about hers either, but he likes her legs. Soon she says admiringly, "My God, you big dark handsome brute. I ought to throw a Buick at you." Despite Marlowe's arrogance, haughty rich girls throw themselves (and sometimes Buicks) at him and old millionaires love him like a son.

I won't try to summarize the plot of *The Big Sleep*. I'm not sure I could. There is a well-known story that when Howard Hawks was filming the novel, neither he nor his screenwriters could figure out who had killed the Sternwood chauffeur. Hawks cabled Chandler for an explanation and he cabled back: NO IDEA. In truth, it doesn't matter. The chauffeur existed only so we could learn that Vivian once had him arrested under the Mann Act for running off with Carmen, but dropped charges when she realized that thumb-sucking Carmen cooked up the trip.

Near the end of the novel, Marlowe drives to an isolated house where he thinks Eddie Mars's missing wife is being held. Two men overpower him and he winds up inside with his hands cuffed behind his back. His hostess is Eddie Mars's elusive wife, whom he calls Silver-Wig because she's wearing one. Although a gangster is coming to kill him, Marlowe continues to emit snappy dialogue. She asks how he feels. Great, he says. "Like someone built a filling station on my jaw."

Silver-Wig cuts loose the ropes that bind him and explains that Canino, the gangster who is coming, has the key to the handcuffs. Despite the handcuffs, they kiss and then he flees. Marlowe gets his gun out of his car and, after Canino arrives, survives a shootout with his hands handcuffed behind his back, a first in the extensive literature of gunfights. Marlowe escapes death because Silver-Wig has risked her life for him. Handcuffed, seemingly a goner, Marlowe survives because he is both Don Juan and Deadeye Dick.

The novel's final revelation is that it was poor sex-crazed Carmen who shot Regan, because he spurned her advances. Then, having pinned the crime on Carmen, Chandler waffles. He reveals that she suffers from epileptic fits, raising the possibility that illness, not sheer rich-bitch malice, caused her to plug her amiable Irish brother-in-law.

In case we fail to grasp this knight-errant's nobility, Chandler has Vivian offer Marlowe money to keep quiet, whereupon he responds with a long speech declaring that he's risked his life for $25 a day and now she's insulting his honor. The book would have been stronger without this self-serving pronouncement, but Chandler loved his hero too much to cut it.

Chandler's second novel, *Farewell, My Lovely,* opens with what I can only call a malicious minstrel show. Marlowe is at work in a black neighborhood when he notices a man who was "not more than six feet five inches tall and not wider than a beer truck." This giant, garishly dressed, enters a Negro bar and throws a young man out into the street: "It landed on its hands and knees and made a high keening noise like a cornered rat." Marlowe explains that "it" was "a thin, narrow-shouldered brown youth in a lilac-colored suit and a carnation. It had slick black hair. It kept its mouth open and whined for a moment." There's more about "it."

"A dinge," the big man explains. He introduces himself as Moose Malloy and insists that Marlowe accompany him while he looks for his ex-girlfriend, Velma. It becomes clear that Velma sang in this club when it was a white club but now it is a black club, and Malloy can't quite grasp that concept. The club has a bouncer who laughs at Malloy. The big man tosses him across the room. The bartender is a thin worried-looking Negro who moves as if his feet hurt. When Malloy questions him about Velma, "his Adam's apple flopped around like a headless chicken" and he starts "rolling the whites of his eyes." When

Malloy goes into the manager's office, the man tries to pull a gun, whereupon Malloy breaks his neck.

Malloy departs but Marlowe stays to explain things to the police. The detective sighs and says, "Another shine killing." He waxes nostalgic. "One time there was five smokes carved Harlem sunsets on each other down on East Eighty-four." *Harlem sunsets?* One doesn't know if that lovely phrase emerged from the streets or from Chandler's exquisite imagination.

All this, while eye-catching, is a throwaway. Malloy is not central to the story and soon disappears. The scene exists to give *Farewell, My Lovely* an opening that would be irresistible to readers who like to laugh at black people.

Chandler has equal scorn for one Lindsay Marriott, who asks the detective to come to his house to discuss a job. Marriott lives by the ocean, and as Marlowe nears his home we get this description:

> I got down to Montemar Vista as the light began to fade, but there was still a fine sparkle on the water and the surf was breaking far out in long smooth curves. A group of pelicans was flying bomber formation just under the creaming lip of the waves. A lonely yacht was tacking in toward the yacht harbor at Bay City. Beyond it the huge emptiness of the Pacific was purple-grey.

That's nice and harder than it looks. Much of Chandler's best writing involves nature. He likes the sky, sunsets, trees, rain, mountains, and the sea far more than he does people.

Few of Chandler's characters are less attractive than Lindsay Marriott. We are told that he is tall and blond and wearing a white flannel suit and a violet satin scarf around his "thick, soft brown neck, like the neck of a strong woman."

Marlowe enters the man's house and tells us he smelled perfume on his host and describes Marriott's artworks in scornful detail. He declares that it was the kind of room where people sit with their feet in their laps and sip absinthe through lumps of sugar "and talk with high affected voices and sometimes just squeak." When Marlowe glances at an odd-looking artwork, Marriott says it is Asta Dial's *Spirit of Dawn*. Marlowe replies, "I thought it was Klopstein's *Two Warts on a Fanny*."

Marlowe has it both ways: he insults Marriott but still persuades him he needs his help. They proceed to the job, which is to drive to a nearby beach where Marriott is to give money to some men in return for stolen jewels. The mission is a failure: When they arrive at the beach, someone sneaks up on the detective and knocks him out. When he wakes, a young woman is pointing a gun at him. Marlowe laughs at her gun but is impressed by her toughness, particularly when she tells him his client's fate: "He's dead all right. With his brains on his face."

Chandler has gone to great lengths to ridicule a gay man, only to kill him off and tell us, with apparent delight, that he has his brains on his face. He likes that line so much he uses it again. What is the matter with this man? Is he simply homophobic? Does he think nastiness will sell books? Did he pick up bad habits writing for the pulps and find himself unable to break them? His books abound with references to pansies and fags and niggers and shines. Elsewhere, in *Farewell, My Lovely* we get a "dirty wop," someone "sneering . . . the way Jap gardeners do" and a chapter that begins "The Indian smelled."

I don't know how people can read Chandler today without his misogyny lessening their pleasure in his work. It isn't enough to say that Chandler reflected the prejudices of his day. You can find scenes in Hemingway, Fitzgerald, and Faulkner that reflect those prejudices, but they didn't savage blacks and gays, didn't batter them, wipe the floor with them, and then laugh at them, as Chandler so gleefully does. The point isn't political correctness, just basic decency. Chandler ridicules people who have done nothing to him and can't fight back. He could write gorgeous prose, but he could also write like a sick, sadistic son of a bitch.

Chandler's portrayal of Marlowe and sex is monumentally weird. Women cannot resist this handsome brute and yet Marlowe is forever rejecting them. At the start of *The Big Sleep*, Carmen literally throws herself at him, and the thrice-wed Vivian is just as adoring. Later, after Marlowe has rescued Vivian from a gunman outside a gambling club, they are alone in his car. "Hold me close, you beast," she commands. They kiss and she tells him to take her to his place. Whereupon he announces that her father didn't hire him to sleep with her. (Has this man never heard of fringe benefits?) She curses him and eventually takes out her handkerchief and slowly tears it to pieces with her teeth.

Marlowe gets rid of her and goes home, only to find that sly little Carmen has talked her way past his landlord and is waiting in his bed. She giggles and sucks her thumb and throws back the covers to reveal herself "naked and glistening as a pearl." He tells her that he's rejecting the offer because he's working for her father, and notes smugly that it's hard for women to realize that their bodies are not irresistible. And yet, after he gets rid of Carmen and sees the imprint of her "small, corrupt body" on his sheets, he "tore the bed to pieces savagely." It's been a bad night for handkerchiefs, sheets, and heterosexuality in general.

In *The Long Goodbye,* a rich, beautiful woman summons Marlowe to her bed. She "thrashed around and moaned" and Marlowe admits, "I was as erotic as a stallion. I was losing control." Then, Candy, the Hispanic houseboy, appears at the door and "saves" him. Marlowe rushes after the man. When he returns, the woman is still moaning for him. Marlowe hurries downstairs and starts swigging from a bottle of Scotch "until the flames reached my brain."

What is going on here? Chandler seems determined to deny sex to Marlowe in these tortured, bed-destroying, Scotch-swigging scenes. Most fellows, if they're as erotic as a stallion and an eager filly is at hand, tend not to go off and suck on a bottle of Scotch. In my experience, if a novelist is having an enjoyable sex life, he's forever looking for ways to translate it into print—and forever finding original sex scenes damnably hard to write. Chandler, far from celebrating sex, keeps having Marlowe scorn it. Candy saved him? Saved him from what? A romp with a woman who is rich, beautiful, and eager? It would seem that Chandler had serious frustrations. He was in his fifties when he started publishing novels and in his mid-sixties when he wrote *The Long Goodbye.* Alcoholism may have diminished his capacity for sex, and his wife was eighteen years older and in poor health. He cared for her lovingly in her old age, but there is every reason to think he was a frustrated man. After she died, he lived in London for a time and was notorious for making drunken passes at women who were trying to befriend him at a time when he was widely thought to be suicidal.

Most good writers have a personal mythology that underlies their work. Chandler's seems based on his hatred of the rich relatives whose charity he was obliged to accept as a child and of domineering women who threaten his manhood. This mythology is reflected, in the three novels discussed here, in that the killer, when finally revealed, is always a rich, decadent woman. I mentioned minstrel shows. In a minstrel show, fake black people act ridiculous for the amusement of white people. In Chandler's novels, rich women are presented as murderous drugged-out whores who debase themselves for our amusement. It's entertainment, but of a most odd and perverse kind.

Chandler's first two novels, *The Big Sleep* and *Farewell, My Lovely,* sold poorly. He didn't achieve much attention until two things happened. After his and Billy Wilder's film of *Double Indemnity* was a hit, Chandler suddenly had his pick of top-dollar film jobs, although he never had another success equal to the first one. His other break came when Knopf finally published his novels in mass market editions, and they were highly successful.

Chandler produced weak novels for the better part of a decade and then scored a comeback with *The Long Goodbye* in 1953. I was stunned when I started reading this last of his major novels. It isn't just that there are no minstrel shows or gay-bashings or sex-crazed women in the opening chapters—the writing is gorgeous, glittering. It suggests a tougher, more cynical Scott Fitzgerald. The plot in this longest of Chandler's novels becomes mind-bogglingly complex and there are predatory women and loathsome gays ahead, but it is here that Chandler most fully realizes his potential.

When Chandler is at his best, as he is here, the writing is what matters. He once told Charles Morton, editor of *The Atlantic Monthly,* "The only fiction of any moment in any age is that which does magic with words." At his best, this is what Chandler did. The plots and the bigotry are maddening, but if you are going to like him it is because he can write sublimely. Of course, just what is his best writing is open to question. He gloried in one-liners like these:

"He looked a lot more like a dead man than most dead men look."
"The green stone in his stickpin was not quite as large as an apple."
"A blonde to make a bishop kick a hole in a stained-glass window."
"I was as hollow and empty as the spaces between the stars."

Such lines, and there are hundreds of them, are central to Chandler's style. At best they are poetry ("The sunlight was so bright that it danced"); at worst they are shtick ("The sunshine was as empty as a headwaiter's smile"). I wish he'd used fewer because the weak ones detract from the best. There is some wonderful writing near the end of *The Long Goodbye,* when Marlowe catches a ride on a speedboat out to a gambling ship. I particularly liked the line "A faint music came over the water, and music over the water can never be anything but lovely." But lines like that didn't make him famous; lines like "I felt like an amputated leg" did.

Having praised the writing in *The Long Goodbye,* I won't try to deal with its plot. It is enough to say that Chandler's novels raise the question of how much plot matters in heavily atmospheric crime novels. Biographer Hiney says that when Chandler started writing for the pulps, he decided that "the best way to stop the reader guessing the end of a story . . . was not to know how it ended yourself." Whether this was a strategy or a rationalization is debatable. Hiney also quotes director Howard Hawks as saying, after the filming of *The Big Sleep,* "I never figured out what was going on, but I thought that the basic thing had great scenes and was good entertainment. After that I said, 'I'm never going to worry about being logical again.' " Hawks and his screenwriters (William Faulkner, Jules Furthman, and Leigh Brackett), may have given up on logic, but the *New York Times* reviewer Bosley Crowther, cursed with a literal mind, called the film "a web of utter bafflement."

Among other things, *The Long Goodbye* is a hymn to drinking. There are gorgeous scenes in elegant bars with somber discussions of the virtues of this cocktail versus that one. But the hymn grows dark. Chandler had a serious problem. Marlowe drinks more or less constantly but rarely suffers more than a manly hangover. In this novel, however, two other characters reflect the realities of alcoholism. In the novel's first sentence Marlowe sees Terry Lennox drunk in a Rolls-Royce Silver Wraith outside a club called the Dancers. He takes Lennox home to sober up and the two become drinking friends. Lennox flees the country after his rich wife is beaten to death. Marlowe is then hired to find an alcoholic writer named Roger Wade. Wade eventually dies, a possible suicide, and leaves a long, anguished note behind. A typical line says, "The worms in my solar plexus crawl and crawl and crawl." There's more, even more scary. After Wade is dead, Marlowe says of him, "He was a bit of a bastard and maybe a bit of a genius too. . . . He was an egotistical drunk and he hated his own guts." It's not a pretty portrait, particularly if we take it as a self-portrait.

Chandler's best writing often recalls Fitzgerald's, never more so than in *The Long Goodbye*. Even its plot echoes *The Great Gatsby*, with a doomed wartime romance that ends with the woman married to another man. Chandler was surely aware of his debt to Fitzgerald, and it is a shock to come across a barbed reference to him in the novel. Marlowe has been seeking Eileen Wade's missing husband and she shows him a note the writer left behind: "I do not care to be in love with myself and there is no longer anyone else for me to be in love with. Signed: Roger (F. Scott Fitzgerald) Wade. P.S. This is why I never finished *The Last Tycoon*."

Marlowe asks the woman what the note means. She replies that her husband was a fan of Fitzgerald, whom he considered "the best drunken writer since Coleridge, who took dope." This passage can only be read as a gratuitous insult to a writer who is (1) far more talented than Chandler and (2) dead. It is yet another example of the mean-spiritedness that afflicts even Chandler's best work. *The Long Goodbye* does have a nice scene near the end when Marlowe surrenders to Eros. Her name is Linda and she is rich and beautiful and has a black chauffeur named Amos who admires T. S. Eliot. Linda comes to Marlowe's apartment and pours champagne and says she wants to go to bed. He asks how much money she has, she says eight million dollars, and he quips that he's decided to accept her offer. The sex must have been as good as the banter because an hour later she suggests marriage. Marlowe says it wouldn't last six months. She calls him a fool and cries. The next morning, Marlowe muses, "To say goodbye is to die a little." We get the impression he wouldn't mind another romp with Linda. This is progress.

As promised, I have gone on too long about Chandler, but it is hard to think of another writer whose mingled gifts and weaknesses are so extreme. He was a strange hybrid of poet and pulp writer, and his novels were both brilliant and maddeningly flawed. Chandler had a right to be Chandler, but we have a right to wish he'd had discipline equal to his talent. Of course, if he had, he might never have written anything, for his extremes, good and bad, were reflections of the reckless way he lived his life.

4.

Tough Guys:

Spillane, MacDonald, McBain, Macdonald, Willeford

I f the first great era of American crime fiction burst spontaneously
from the primordial soup of Hemingway, Hammett, political and
police corruption, tabloids, pulps, and the Depression, the next era was
profoundly influenced by World War II. By the time the war was over,
Hammett had fallen silent, Cain's best work was behind him, and
Chandler was preoccupied with film projects. The vacuum was soon
filled by a new generation. Most were veterans, and it showed in the violence and nihilism of their work. They had seen slaughter on a scale
unimagined by writers who had only glimpsed it as reporters or Pinkerton detectives.

If many veterans came home and never wanted to speak of what
they had seen, others wanted to bear witness. Writers like Norman
Mailer, James Jones, and Irwin Shaw wrote powerful novels of war,
and crime writers too drew upon their hard-won knowledge of man's
inhumanity. Some made violence explicit, and others kept it implicit,
smoldering beneath the surface of middle-class life, but the war and its
lessons were always there.

Film noir emerged in the postwar years, and it both inspired and fed
off hard-boiled American crime fiction. The growing popularity of paperback novels, selling for a quarter in every drugstore and bus station,
often featuring lurid covers that promised sexual revelations within,
helped writers reach ever-larger audiences. Publishers were still wary of

explicit sex or profanity, but writers pushed the limits and readers were ready for more candor. The emerging writers exhibited a dazzling variety of concerns, from fun in Florida to generational mysteries in California to angst on the streets of New York. The first of them to gain fame wrote with the subtlety of a pair of brass knuckles—he named his hero Hammer—and his overnight success announced a new day, both in terms of violence and sales.

ME 'N MICK

Frank Morrison (Mickey) Spillane was born in Brooklyn in 1918, an Irish bartender's son. In high school he played football and wrote his first fiction. After a brief fling at college in Kansas he returned to New York and started writing for comic books and pulp magazines. He was a pilot during the war and, after it ended, he wrote *I, the Jury* in nine days. The novel was rejected by four publishers as too violent and then appeared in 1947, introducing Spillane's savage alter ego, Mike Hammer. Hammer is a descendant of Sam Spade and Philip Marlowe but tougher than either. The war had happened and Spillane was in it and his man didn't mess around with pretty words or knight-errant poses; he'd as soon kill you as look at you. Still, Spillane wasn't a bad writer, sentence by sentence. Consider the opening lines of *I, the Jury,* when Hammer arrives at the scene of his best friend's murder:

> I shook the rain from my hat and walked into the room. Nobody said a word. They stepped back politely and I could feel their eyes on me. Pat Chambers was standing by the door to the bedroom trying to steady Myrna. The girl's body was racking with dry sobs. I walked over and put my arms around her.

A moment later, Hammer gazes on the body of the army buddy who had "stopped a bastard of a Jap from slitting me in two." He gazes on his friend's body and makes a solemn vow:

> I'm going to get the louse that killed you. He won't sit in the chair. He won't hang. He will die exactly as you died, with a .45 slug in the gut, just a little below the belly button.

Noir doesn't get much better than that. Spillane was writing for men like himself who believed in the problem-solving value of violence and had zero interest in literary flourishes. His words grabbed you like a meat hook. Hammer eventually identifies his friend's killer as a Park Avenue psychiatrist. When he confronts her, she starts to undress, trying to stop him from killing her. Instead, he shoots her in the gut—as he had promised—inspiring the famous final exchange:

> "How c-could you?" she gasped.
> I only had a moment before talking to a corpse, but I got it in.
> "It was easy," I said.

The Signet edition of *I, the Jury,* with a cover portrait of Hammer holding his gun on the woman as she unbuttons her blouse, won a huge paperback audience. Next, in a remarkable burst of creativity, Spillane published five more Hammer thrillers in 1950–52—*My Gun Is Quick, Vengeance Is Mine, One Lonely Night, The Big Kill,* and *Kiss Me, Deadly*—great titles all. Other books followed and many movie and TV portrayals of Hammer, but Spillane's importance rests on those early novels, which shocked America with sex, sadism, and raw violence, and made him one of the world's best-selling writers. Spillane was a great primitive; his stories exploded off the page. He was denounced for corrupting America's youth but he was, in fact, a revolutionary. Like Hugh Hefner, Elvis Presley, Alfred Kinsey, and Lenny Bruce, in their different ways, he challenged the pieties of the fifties and helped create the anything-goes society that followed.

I read Spillane's novels in my early teens, and if they corrupted me I was a willing victim. At a time when most boys that age were profoundly ignorant about sex, Spillane's books, along with Erskine Caldwell's *God's Little Acre* and *Tobacco Road,* were treasured as a source of titillation and possible enlightenment. Actually, the novels were suggestive rather than explicit ("Her head nestled against my shoulder and she moved my hand up her body until I knew there was no marvel of engineering connected to the bra because there was no bra"), but they were all we had. That the novels abounded in sexism and McCarthy-style politics was lost on me; those ladies with no bras were my concern. The good parts, as they were known to a generation of young Americans.

I remember my shock at the end of *Vengeance Is Mine,* which featured a statuesque woman named Juno. Hammer was drawn to Juno's beauty but there was something troubling about her that he couldn't quite put his finger on. In the climactic scene, Hammer forced Juno to remove her clothes, which produced a mind-boggling revelation: "Juno was a man." *What?* How could Juno be a *man?* Juno was a *woman!* Juno's secret was more than my innocent mind could comprehend, and I was left more confused than ever by the mysteries of sex. Happily, a girl named Patti, sweet sixteen and wise beyond her years, came along to elucidate those mysteries, and Spillane's books were only a brief detour in my progress from the Hardy Boys to Hemingway. Still, Mick was there when I needed him and I've had a soft spot in my heart for him ever since, even though a woman I admire insists on calling him a trenchcoat fascist. I was thus saddened to read a novel he'd written in his eighties that was close to a parody of his early work. But no matter—the real Mick had made his mark a half century before, and there's never been anyone else quite like him.

GAWAIN IN GATOR COUNTRY

John D. MacDonald was born in 1916, earned a BA from Syracuse University and an MBA from Harvard, and served as an intelligence officer during World War II. After the war he moved to Florida and became a prolific writer for the pulps and then of paperback novels. In the early 1960s he decided to build a series about one character. Thus was born the immortal Travis McGee, who first appeared in *The Deep Blue Good-by* in 1964 and returned in twenty more novels, until the series ended with 1985's *The Lonely Silver Rain.* MacDonald died the next year. He wrote some forty non-McGee novels as well.

Jonathan Yardley discovered MacDonald's work in 1976 when he was book editor of *The Miami Herald.* MacDonald's non-McGee *Condominium* was a Book-of-the-Month Club selection, and Yardley went to interview him. But first he immersed himself in MacDonald's work. "I was bowled over. This man whom I'd snobbishly dismissed as a paperback writer turned out to be a novelist of the highest professionalism and a social critic armed with vigorous opinions stingingly expressed." Yardley added, "For my money, John D. MacDonald's

Travis McGee is one of the great characters in contemporary American fiction—not crime fiction, fiction period."

I agree. Travis McGee is a great hero of popular fiction, a wonderful fantasy figure. We might admire the toughness of Sam Spade, Philip Marlowe, and Mike Hammer, but not many of us would actually want to *be* those guys, who are variously broke, drunken, semiliterate, and bedeviled by sexual hang-ups. But what red-blooded American male wouldn't like to be McGee—big, bronzed, and rugged, living on a houseboat in Florida, adored by endless bikini-clad lovelies, working when he feels like it, and invariably winning his confrontations with evil men?

McGee lives on the *Busted Flush*, his 52-foot houseboat. His address, Slip F-18, Bahia Mar, Lauderdale, is as well known in some circles as Holmes's address on Baker Street. He is a veteran of World War II, six-foot-five and tough as an old boot, but with the fair sex he is the most tender of lovers, even if he rarely lingers past breakfast. In a famous passage in the first McGee novel, he makes clear his scorn for the tentacles that doom most of us to mundane lives: "credit cards, payroll deductions, insurance programs, retirement benefits, savings accounts, Green Stamps, time clocks, newspapers, mortgages, sermons, miracle fabrics, deodorants, check lists, time payments, political parties." Who would not second this manifesto?

MacDonald gave McGee a good friend at Bahia Mar, the "semi-retired economist" Meyer. Meyer is McGee's Dr. Watson, although he doesn't narrate the novels, McGee does. He is no a clown, no Captain Hastings, but McGee's more reflective older brother, a purveyor of advice and wisdom. McGee deals in what he calls salvage work, which means if you've lost something he'll find it and take half. But salvage work can be defined to include missing persons. Such is the case in *A Tan and Sandy Silence,* first published in 1971. (All the McGee books have a color in the title, and several of the titles, including this one, refer to death, following the tradition Chandler started with *The Big Sleep.*) I read most of the McGee books for fun in the 1970s and 1980s, and recently picked up *Tan* at random for a closer look.

The novel begins with McGee kneeling in eight inches of oily water in Meyer's cabin cruiser, the *John Maynard Keynes,* repairing the automatic bilge pump. We get the details; MacDonald often shows us how things work—condos, smuggling operations, boats—to ground his novels in reality. McGee goes back to the *Busted Flush* and is met by an obnoxious businessman named Harry Broll. Broll's wife, Mary, has left him and he's convinced she's with McGee. He pulls a gun and starts shooting. McGee escapes with a minor wound, disarms Broll, and sends him on his way. Meyer arrives and warns McGee that he's getting careless. The two men proceed to a party given on the yacht of Gillian (Jilly) Brent-Archer, a rich widow of uncertain years. She is beautiful and sexy, and in bed she and McGee have exchanges like:

"Are you going back to sleep, you wretch?"

"Not with you doing what you're doing."

"This? Oh, it's just a sort of reflex thing." She adds, "A nice rain always makes me very randy."

The problem is that Jilly wants more than recreational sex. She wants McGee to come live with her but he resists. He digresses on the kind of kept man he despises, although no one can really imagine McGee being such a fellow. When Jilly begs him for just one week of his time, he tells her he has to go look for a friend. That's Mary, the missing wife, and the rest of the novel is his search for her.

McGee continues to agonize about rich Jilly and delivers a mock-Hemingway hymn to her charms:

I like the textures and juices, spices and rhythms of her, all her tastes and tastings. We truly climb one hell of a hill, Papa, and when we fall off the far side together, it is truly one hell of a long fall, Papa. . . .

This goes on for three pages, and it's not MacDonald at his best. McGee concludes that he's gotten soft and must test himself:

Get out there on the range and go down to the pits and stand up for a moment and see if they can pot you between the eyes. If they miss, maybe you'll get your nerve back, you tinhorn Gawain.

Tinhorn Gawain? McGee is too modest. Gawain was King Arthur's nephew, a good and brave knight, but overshadowed by Sir Lancelot. McGee is a Florida knight-errant, at least as brave and formidable as those in Los Angeles, and much more deft with damsels than Sir Philip of Marlowe or even Sir Sam of Spade. McGee is no tinhorn but a Gulf Coast Gawain in dazzling armor.

McGee's advice to himself was to get back onto the field of battle, and he does. He and Meyer are taken captive by a psychopath named Paul who has already killed Mary and others. Paul forces McGee to wire Meyer's wrists and ankles and then his own. The situation is dire but fortunately, as crazed killers do in books, instead of killing his prisoners the villain raves on about why and how he's going to kill them. Meanwhile, McGee is working on the wire that binds his wrists and finally it breaks. ("By happenchance, he'd made a bad choice of wire.") Thus it is the psychopath who dies a horrid death, not our heroes.

The novel came out when America was in turmoil over the war in Vietnam but it is of no concern to McGee. One night he watches the news and it's all bad—inflation, murders, drugs, body counts—but McGee is not interested:

> News has always been bad. The tiger that lives in the forest just ate your wife and kids, Joe. There are no fat grub worms under the rotten logs this year, Al. Those sickies in the village on the other side of the mountain are training hairy mammoths to stomp us flat, Pete. They nailed up two thieves and one crackpot, Mary.

In short, the world is mad and a wise man retires to Florida and cultivates his houseboat.

Let us note that Paul was one of the first serial killers we've encountered. In the drawing-room mysteries of the 1920s, one murder was proper, two could be tolerated, and more than that was bad form. Today people are shot and strangled, gutted and broiled, sliced and diced by the scores. Probably it was Ted Bundy, whose murders began in 1974, who did most to popularize serial killers. These days, it often seems that half the novels published are about them. The thought of all those writers in their musty little rooms, conjuring up new methods of mass murder, boggles the mind. In real life, most serial killers are cretins, but in novels they are increasingly geniuses: this fantasy achieved its zenith in Dr. Hannibal Lecter. MacDonald was one of the first novelists to feature psychos like Paul, and he was good at them. Often they are thuggish rednecks with names like Junior and Joe Bob, the sort of narrow-eyed no-neck Neanderthals too often encountered in dark corners of the sunny South.

So what is the verdict on John D. MacDonald? My view is that, in terms of sheer male-fantasy entertainment, McGee is the grandest character since Sherlock Holmes. If MacDonald were a rock band, he'd be the Beach Boys, blasting out fun, fun, fun, till Daddy takes the T-bird away. Still, there is a certain sameness to the McGee novels: sexy ladies, curbstone philosophy, and last-chapter heroics. It is pointless to criticize the McGee books for not being "serious"—that wasn't MacDonald's intent, except in his heartfelt scorn for our increasingly regulated society. Certainly I have enjoyed the McGee books; reading one is like downing a few rum-and-cokes with an old friend.

MacDonald was immensely popular and deservedly so. He fathered a school of Florida writers that has included Charles Willeford, Carl Hiaasen, Edna Buchanan, Randy Wayne White, and James W. Hall, and McGee was the model for John Sandford's equally popular Lucas Davenport. The McGee novels are marvelous entertainment, but in terms of realism they do not approach the series created by MacDonald's equally prolific contemporary Evan Hunter, aka Ed McBain.

THE URBAN JUNGLE

In 1954 a young writer who called himself Evan Hunter seized national attention with his first novel, *The Blackboard Jungle,* a story of a teacher's battle against teenage louts in the classroom. In 1956, writing as Ed McBain, he published his first 87th Precinct novel, *Cop Hater.* McBain died in July 2005, at seventy-eight, with another 87th Precinct novel, the fifty-fifth, *Fiddlers,* set for publication. Writing as McBain, Hunter also published thirteen books about lawyer Matthew Hope, plus eight stand-alone novels. As Evan Hunter he has published another twenty or so novels, plus two collections of short stories, children's books, and assorted screenplays and teleplays. Call it a hundred books in fifty years and you're not far off.

The amazing thing, beyond the Herculean volume of McBain's work, is its quality. He won every major prize available to a crime writer. The 87th Precinct novels, upon which his reputation will rest, are as impressive a body of work as exists in his chosen genre, the police procedural. That term, incidentally, was coined by Anthony Boucher, the esteemed reviewer of crime fiction for *The New York Times* in 1951–68, and McBain didn't like it. He thought he just wrote novels about cops.

Insofar as McBain has been overshadowed by Hammett, Chandler, and MacDonald, there may be two reasons. First, it is easy to take someone so prolific for granted—and the output of anyone who averages two novels a year will be uneven. Second, the 87th Precinct's Everycop, Detective Steve Carella, is not a larger-than-life warrior/lover/philosopher like Spade, Marlowe, or McGee. Nor is he angst-ridden like Michael Connelly's Harry Bosch or Ian Rankin's John Rebus. Carella is a relatively sane fellow who loves his wife and kids, pays his bills, and is more bureaucrat than action hero. His normalcy may be a weakness in terms of commercial fiction, but in terms of what police work is really like, McBain is probably closer to the truth than any other American writer, at least until Michael Connelly came along.

We learn that, in college, Carella liked to quote lines from T. S. Eliot's "The Waste Land" to impressionable coeds. As a detective, Carella is a melancholy poet of urban crime, trying to bring order to the wasteland of Isola, his fictionalized New York City. *Isola,* Italian for "island," suggests isolation, which abounds in McBain's urban jungle. One of McBain's late novels moved Marilyn Stasio, the reliable crime reviewer of *The New York Times Book Review,* to write, "Years ago, I thought Ed McBain's books were sexy love songs to a cold, violent city. Now, I think they are sad, slow dances in a city where everyone dances alone."

McBain was born Salvatore Lombino in 1926 in East Harlem, the only child of Charles and Marie Lombino. His father worked for the post office and played the drums in a band. While serving in the navy in 1944–46, young Lombino read Hammett, Hemingway, and Cain and started writing short stories and sending them to magazines. All were rejected. After the war, he entered Hunter College on the GI Bill and took all the writing courses he could, as well as writing for the school newspaper and starting a drama club. He wanted to go to Paris and write, like Hemingway, but when his wife became pregnant he took a job teaching at a vocational school in the Bronx. The students, he once said, "didn't give a rat's ass" about literature; he immortalized their surliness in *The Blackboard Jungle.*

In 1950 he quit teaching and was selling lobsters when he answered an ad in the *Times* and was hired as a reader/editor by the Scott Meredith Literary Agency, which handled, among others, Mickey Spillane. For forty dollars a week he read short stories and decided which might be sold. Soon he was writing his own stories for the pulps. After earning $2,500 for writing a science-fiction novel, he quit his job and wrote *The Blackboard Jungle*. He used the name Evan Hunter, which he later made his legal name, because an ethnic name like Lombino was thought to be a handicap. Following the novel's success, an editor at Pocket Books, hoping that McBain could duplicate the success of Erle Stanley Gardner's Perry Mason books, urged him to attempt a series of paperback originals about the police. Thus was born the 87th Precinct series, under the name Ed McBain.

For McBain to undertake a series of novels about big-city detectives was by no means the obvious move after the success of *The Blackboard Jungle*. If he wanted to write crime fiction, private-eye novels were the tradition. Or he might have undertaken mainstream novels, as in fact he did, as Evan Hunter, along with his police series. Not long before his death, I asked McBain about his choice and got this reply:

> I thought I could do both. I've always been blessed (or cursed) with being a fast writer. (A damn good one, too, he added modestly.) So I knew I could handle the additional work load of a mystery series. In 1956, for example, I published the first three McBain mysteries, plus an Evan Hunter novel titled *Second Ending*. (After the success of *The Blackboard Jungle,* it sold perhaps twelve copies, six to my mother.) In 1957, there were just another two McBains, no Hunter at all. But in 1958, I published an Evan Hunter novel titled *Strangers When We Meet*—a *New York Times* best seller—plus three new McBains. And so on through the years. In 1961, for example, I published another Evan Hunter best seller, *Mothers and Daughters,* plus one McBain. It wasn't until later that I realized the "qual lit" community was dismissing me as a "serious" writer because I also wrote mysteries, and the mystery community didn't fully accept me into *that* clan because they thought I felt I was slumming by writing mysteries. In 2001 I published *Candyland,* by Evan

Hunter and Ed McBain, to show the difference between the two writers' styles and subject matter. The critic for the daily *New York Times* thought it was a stunt. If so, my entire writing career has been a stunt.

I recently read two 87th Precinct novels at random, *Ten Plus One* from 1963 and *Long Time No See* from 1977. *Ten Plus One* begins with a businessman walking out of his office one spring evening and being shot dead by someone on a nearby roof. Carella arrives a few minutes later and reflects that it's too early in the season for flies but there they are, "feeding at the open hole between the man's eyes."

Carella returns to his office and makes a recurring point: that police work is a team effort and the detective is an organization man. Yet, a page later, McBain reminds us of the human side of the job. The detective, he says, seeing endless human violence, sometimes becomes an observer,

> a visitor from somewhere far in space studying a curious race of insect people, who rip each other apart, who tear each other limb from limb and drink each other's blood; he stands appalled, a civilized human who momentarily renounces his citizenship, unable to believe such cruelty can exist in men who have almost reached the stars.

A few days later, when a second man is shot on the sidewalk, Carella and his colleagues fear the possibility of a sniper. Snipers terrify them because they are often skilled marksmen, with army training, who strike at random. The third sniper victim is a prostitute who once attended a local college. They visit the college, where the woman was active in the school drama club, and learn that the first victim also attended that college. The fourth victim is an Italian fruit peddler with no apparent connections to the others.

The next victim is an assistant district attorney and all hell breaks loose. This inspires a truly ugly scene. Although his novels mostly admire the police, McBain knows the underside of police work. When the prosecutor's slaying brings intense pressure to find the sniper, two tough cops—bulls, they are called—interview a young ex-convict who might know something. The young man has a job and is trying to go straight, but that does not impress the bulls, who beat him to a pulp and then accuse him of attacking them. He is sent back to prison.

Finally Carella figures out that the first six victims were all in the eleven-member cast of a college production of Eugene O'Neill's *The Long Voyage Home*. From there it is simply good police work to find the five others, figure out who had a motive for murdering them, and catch him before he kills again. Along the way, McBain tosses in a nice digression. Carella and his partner Meyer go see a gag writer named Cohen. He starts telling them about the gag-writing business, and soon Meyer and Carella forget about the murder case and are simply two professionals who are fascinated by the details of another man's work. McBain was, of course, himself the consummate professional, able to appreciate both Carella's craftsmanship and that of the gag writer.

On the surface, *Long Time No See* resembles *Ten Plus One*. Someone is killing blind people and Carella has to find out why. But *Long Time No See* (an unpleasant title, in context), written fourteen years later, is a more complex, sophisticated work. It opens with this: "He thought of the city as a galaxy. A cluster of planets revolving around a brilliant sun. Asteroids and comets streaming through the blackness of space."

These are the thoughts of Jimmy Harris, age thirty, a black man who was blinded by a grenade in Vietnam and makes his living begging on the streets of Isola. We spend five pages getting to know Jimmy and then someone slits his throat. Carella interviews Harris's wife, who is also blind, and arranges to pick her up the next morning to identify the body. Before he does, someone cuts her throat too.

There is a third murder of a blind person and an attempt on a fourth. We see Carella's methodical investigation. We meet cops who aren't very bright and cops who are bigots. Sex is central to the novel. Harris's wife was having an affair with her boss. When Carella meets another woman while examining Harris's army records, she suggests they have drinks and stresses that her husband is out of town. He declines. Carella interviews a young woman who works in a massage parlor because she wants a Mercedes-Benz. ("I give really good blow jobs.") He stretches this scene to fifteen pages, perhaps to give us relief from the grim story of blind people being murdered. Later, Carella studies a brochure that describes in detail various sex toys, including a life-sized doll complete with breasts and "vaginal pocket" and an "autosuck vagina" that operates from a car's cigarette lighter. As he puts down the brochure, "Carella suddenly had the feeling that he could hack his way through the dense undergrowth of this city forever and still not reach a clearing where there was sunlight."

McBain has a healthy ego and he makes clear his disdain for his competition. He writes scornfully of television shows in which every crime is logical—missing "the purely accidental nature" of much violence. Cops know that Sherlock Holmes and his brilliant deductions are bullshit, McBain declares. Most pointedly, he tells us that Carella didn't agree with the theory that all homicides are rooted in the distant past:

> He would leave such speculation to California mystery writers who seemed to believe that murder was something brewed in a pot for half a century, coming to a boil only when a private detective needed a job.

The California writers McBain had in mind were clearly Raymond Chandler and Ross Macdonald, whose stories were often rooted far in the past. The irony is that to solve the murders of the blind people Carella must go back ten years to Jimmy Harris's military service.

These are not cheerful novels. McBain could be hilarious, but most often the crimes in his novels are terrible. A decade ago, I reviewed *Privileged Conversation,* an Evan Hunter stand-alone that was one of his darkest novels. It concerns a psychiatrist who has an affair with a younger woman while his wife is at the beach. Problems arise: The woman is crazy and someone is stalking her. I wrote:

> The other striking fact about *Privileged Conversation* is its exceedingly dark view of the human condition. A casual affair between two attractive people swiftly spirals into a panorama of deceit, rape, incest, murder, and madness. Chapman, a decent enough fellow, is quick to betray his wife. Kate's family background proves to have been a chamber of horrors. One of Chapman's colleagues is having an affair with a nineteen-year-old

patient. The stalker is evil, mad and lethal. Even Chapman's wife proves not to be the saint she at first appears. . . . Virtually everyone in the book is weak at best and monstrous at worst, and no one escapes unscathed.

In 2000, McBain published *The Last Dance,* the fiftieth novel in the 87th Precinct series. Reflecting his lifelong interest in the theater, it told of the murder of a man over the rights to a Broadway musical. Then came *The Frumious Bandersnatch,* to remind us how easily McBain could move between comedy and tragedy. *Bandersnatch* concerns Tamar, a twenty-year-old who has a hit song by that name, words by Lewis Carroll set to a hip-hop beat. Her record company gives a launch party on a yacht and McBain has a lot of fun with the music-world culture—how could he not? Tamar is so young she doesn't know who Mick Jagger is, and the music moguls have never heard of Lewis Carroll but love the song "Bandersnatch" because it sounds dirty. Then three intruders, armed and masked, arrive by speedboat and abduct Tamar.

Carella is on the case. So is Detective Oliver Wendell "Fat Ollie" Weeks, a capable detective but otherwise a buffoon and bigot who earlier had his own novel, *Fat Ollie's Book.* Fat Ollie is a great comic character, McBain's Falstaff. He's an aspiring novelist and would-be ladies' man who at one point tells a woman he's trying to impress:

"Take a truly great master of literature like James Patterson, are you familiar with his uv?"

"His what?"

"His uv. That's French for 'body of work,' an *uv,* they call it."

That's McBain again having fun with other writers—this time, one who wasn't fit to empty his wastebasket—and also reminding us that his own *uv* (or, dare we say, *oeuvre*?) is among the finest in American crime fiction.

Bandersnatch is mostly McBain in an antic mood, but it suddenly turns dark. Tamar's captors are two men and a woman. One of the men wants to rape the girl but the woman, Kellie, has protected her. Then things go sour, the kidnappers fear capture, and Kellie is left to guard the frightened singer:

> "You can describe me."
> "Lots of girls look like . . ."
> "Lots of girls didn't kidnap you," Kellie said, and raised the AK-47 onto her hip. The three shots blew off the back of her skull and splashed gristle and blood all over the radiator behind her.
> Wow, Kellie thought.

Thus McBain, near the end, still casting a cold eye, not giving an inch. He was a master, and his tales of the city are timeless.

DARKNESS IN CALIFORNIA

Ross Macdonald, the pen name of Kenneth Millar, wrote eighteen novels between 1949 and 1976 that moved some critics to call him the finest American crime writer. His novels often dealt with tormented families with secrets buried deep in the past, and his admirers find echoes of Freud and Oedipus in his work. I read one of Macdonald's novels years ago, didn't like it, and didn't return to him until a recent reading of two of his most highly regarded, *The Chill,* from 1964, and *The Far Side of the Dollar,* from 1965. I found him awfully grim and convoluted.

David Lehman, in his book *The Perfect Murder,* praises Macdonald for endowing the private-eye novel with "a degree of high-mindedness it had never known before." He says Macdonald's novels are "gothic psychodramas," have a tone of "weary resignation" and an atmosphere "heavy with guilt." I agree. The question is whether Macdonald is too high-minded, too weary, too heavy. Reading him, I yearned for Fat Ollie Weeks to swagger in for comic relief.

Macdonald (1915–83) came by his angst honestly. He survived a difficult childhood, took refuge in books, and became a Phi Beta Kappa graduate of the University of Michigan and a student of literature. After service with the navy during the war, he married another writer, endured a difficult marriage, and saw his only child succumb to drug addiction. Lehman declares that "Macdonald's stroke of genius was to transform the hard-boiled romance into a species of what Freud called the family romance." In other words, Macdonald took crime out of the world of petty criminals and put it into the middle-class world, where every crime is wrapped in long-hidden secrets.

That is certainly true of *The Chill*. Its plot is far too complicated to explain, but I will suggest a few highlights. A young man approaches Macdonald's private detective, Lew Archer, in Pacific Point, a fictional city south of Los Angeles. The young man is honeymooning, but his bride has run off after a man with a beard visited her in their hotel. Archer discovers that the man was the bride's father, recently released from prison after serving ten years for killing her mother.

Archer visits the local college the girl attended and meets Helen, a member of the faculty, who tells him that someone has threatened to kill her. That night someone does kill her and the missing ex-convict is suspected, as is his daughter, the runaway bride. Archer learns that twenty years earlier, Helen's father, a policeman in the Midwest, covered up the murder of a rich man named Luke Deloney. Archer is soon convinced, without much evidence, that all three murders—that of Helen, in the present, of the bride's mother, ten years earlier, and of Luke, twenty years back—may be the work of one killer.

Women play a central role in all this. Two have been murdered, a third is suspected of at least one of the crimes, and another five or six, wandering about, are the mothers, widows, sisters, and ex-lovers of various characters and are all but impossible to keep straight. In the end, the plot turns on the fact that a middle-aged man's supposed mother, with whom he lives, is in fact his wife. This may have been suggested by Chandler's marriage to a woman eighteen years his senior.

For me, *The Chill* (another title that means death) raises questions about just how much complexity I am willing to put up with. At some point the reader has a right to say, "What the hell is going on here?" A lot depends on the context. We tolerate Chandler's plots for the sake of his characters and his prose. My problem with *The Chill* starts with the fact that it is extremely hard to follow, and when you do decipher it you have to accept that the same woman would kill three people over a twenty-year period. Moreover, this baffling series of events is embedded in an extremely dry account of some exceedingly unattractive people.

The Far Side of the Dollar is more straightforward. A young man is missing, perhaps kidnapped, and Archer is trying to find him. The plot takes us into the past—one couple gave the boy up for adoption, another couple raised him—but most of the action is in the present and it moves along crisply, with some nice descriptions and writing. My problem with the novel is Archer himself. Macdonald's main device for advancing his plot is for Archer to talk to people who invariably blurt out everything they know. He can't buy a pack of gum without the clerk giving him some vital clue. He's an insufferable busybody. People say, "I shouldn't be telling you this," or "I ought to order you out of my house," but they keep on spilling their guts. Wives and husbands have violent arguments, revealing horrid secrets, as he stands by contentedly, all ears. Most crime novels feature a cop or PI who asks a lot of questions and worms the truth out of people, but Macdonald milks this device to the point of absurdity.

Archer is not only a busybody, he's a moralist, forever telling people how they should live their lives. Everyone else is weak, crooked, and hypocritical; only Archer is wise and good. He tells the rich man he's working for, "You don't know how sick it makes me to sit here and listen to you while you dabble around in your dirty little warmed-over affairs." (He then adds that he was "astonished" that he'd said such a thing. I wasn't.) For all his Calvinism, Archer can be weird about sex. Macdonald introduces a sweet virginal girl of sixteen and three times has Archer comment on her breasts: "the bud-sharp outlines of her breasts . . . her little breasts. . . . Her small breasts brushed my shoulder like a gift of trust."

In the Chandler tradition, the cold-blooded killer proves to be a rich woman. When her guilt is clear, she tries to buy Archer off with money but of course he can't be bought. In the final scene, when the woman proposes to kill herself, Archer plays God, telling her she must face justice. Then, having established Archer's nobility, Macdonald has it both ways by letting the woman kill herself in a wildly melodramatic fashion before our eyes.

Macdonald's writing is cool, crisp, and unrelieved by humor. One could praise its purity or damn it as mind-numbing. He seems to be exorcising his own demons with the psychodramas he inflicts on his characters. I respect Macdonald's narrative skill, his seriousness, and his willingness to probe the dark secrets that torment even the best families, but he's too grim, pious, and demanding to be one of my favorites. Not to put too fine a point on it, Lew Archer is a colossal pain in the ass.

KISS YOUR ASS GOODBYE

During his lifetime, Ross Macdonald was the most critically acclaimed of these fifties writers. Probably this was because he was the most serious. High-minded critics who were loath to enjoy John D. MacDonald or Ed McBain could find it respectable to admire the austere Macdonald, who adorned his novels with references to Shakespeare, Eliot, Tennessee Williams, Gerard Manley Hopkins, and many more literary figures. He was the thinking man's crime novelist. Charles Willeford (1919–88) was more or less the opposite. His hardscrabble career brought him little financial or critical success until shortly before his death, but his reputation has grown steadily since then, while Macdonald's has declined.

Willeford was born in Arkansas and orphaned at eight. He lived with his grandmother in Los Angeles for a few years, but the Depression had begun and she had no money, so at twelve he struck out on his own. He rode the rails, held odd jobs, and at sixteen lied about his age to join the army. During the war, he was decorated for his service as a tank commander in Europe, and he retired as a master sergeant after twenty years. While still in the military he began publishing poetry and writing novels.

His first novel, *High Priest of California,* was published in 1953. It concerned an ill-starred three-way romance between a car salesman, a dance-hall girl, and her ex-boxer husband. Willeford thus began twenty years in the jungle of paperback originals, where the pay was low and publishers changed the names of his books and sometimes misspelled his name on the cover. His second novel, *Pick-up,* was published in 1955 and concerned a doomed love affair involving a failed artist who's working as a short-order cook. In 1960 he wrote *The Woman Chaser* in a month to earn money for graduate school.

Cockfighter, from 1962, examines the world of cockfights. Roger Corman's 1974 film version, starring Warren Oates, became a cult classic. Willeford wrote the screenplay and played an aging referee. By the

1970s, Willeford was living in Florida and being published in hardback. His popular success began when St. Martin's published *Miami Blues* in 1984. (He wanted to call it *Kiss Your Ass Goodbye*.) A psychopath named Freddy Frenger is released from San Quentin and told to get out of California. He mugs some people in San Francisco for airfare and flies to Miami. Arriving in the airport he breaks the finger of a Hare Krishna. The fellow goes into shock and dies, whereupon homicide inspector Hoke Moseley gets on the case. Frenger has by then begun a one-man crime wave. At one point, he steals Moseley's gun, badge, and false teeth. Here and elsewhere, Willeford mixes broad humor with serious violence.

After the success of *Miami Blues,* which was made into a nice little movie, the publisher asked for another Hoke Moseley novel, and a series was born: *New Hope for the Dead, Sideswipe,* and *The Way We Die Now* followed. The last earned Willeford his first six-figure advance and was published in March 1988. Willeford had just received advance copies of the novel, and signed a few for friends, when he died on Palm Sunday.

Early in the new century, Willeford's 1955 *Pick-up* was included in the Library of America's collection *Crime Novels: American Noir of the 1950s,* which called it a "nihilistic early novel" that "follows the pilgrimage of two lost and self-destructive lovers through the depths of San Francisco." Others in the collection include Jim Thompson's *The Killer Inside Me,* a searing study of a psychopathic deputy sheriff; Patricia Highsmith's *The Talented Mr. Ripley,* about a charming American psycho adrift in Europe; and Chester Himes's *The Real Cool Killers,* which features Harlem detectives Coffin Ed Johnson and Grave Digger Jones. The recognition of these novels by the Library of America, some fifty years after they were first published, mostly as two-bit paperback originals, is a nice reminder that today's cheap thrills can be tomorrow's classics.

II.

CHANGING CRIMES

<hr>

After assassinations, war, and rebellion, new voices

are heard and the private-eye novel begins to

evolve into something bigger, darker, more violent,

and more ambitious—the modern thriller—as

trailblazers like Lawrence Sanders, Elmore Leonard,

Tom Clancy, Sue Grafton, Thomas Harris, and Scott

Turow take aim at the best-seller lists.

5.

The Birth of the Thriller

The triumph of the thriller built slowly but reached a tipping point in 1981, when an unprecedented four crime novels were among the year's fifteen best-selling books.

Looking back, we can see the transformation begin with the 1963 assassination of John F. Kennedy, on a November day that was the end of innocence for a generation. The madness continued with Lyndon Johnson's escalation of the war in Vietnam and the resurrection of Richard Nixon. By the time the war fizzled out and Nixon slouched into exile after Watergate, the old America was gone. The fifties world of Doris Day movies, the Hit Parade, sock hops, slumber parties, virgin brides, and cockeyed optimists had become a darker place. Bob Dylan was its poet laureate, "Like a Rolling Stone" its anthem, Norman Mailer and Hunter Thompson its bards. Change came fast in popular music and the movies, with angry works like *Bonnie and Clyde, Easy Rider, Nashville, Shampoo,* and *Taxi Driver.* Cynicism was in our bones; noir was the new reality.

Change came more slowly to publishing. Hardback books are expensive; the people who buy them are older and cling to comfortable habits. Yet, inevitably, publishing began to reflect the changing America. The best-seller lists for the sixties and seventies continued to be dominated by familiar names writing familiar novels, but new voices emerged. Philip Roth's *Portnoy's Complaint* in 1969 and Erica Jong's

Fear of Flying four years later treated sex with a new candor and tremendous zest. Mario Puzo's *The Godfather,* the first great crime thriller, turned the genre on its ear with its portrayal of mobsters as men of respect, businessmen. Ira Levin's *Rosemary's Baby* showed that a clever writer could concoct a best seller by installing the devil in the Dakota, and Peter Benchley's *Jaws* wove a dynamite thriller out of another of our primal fears. Evil lurked out there and readers were ready to embrace it.

Crime fiction began to change too. The important crime novelists of the fifties and sixties weren't respectable like the mainstream authors who dominated the lists. Crime fiction was still déclassé. When it sold, there was usually a reason, a justification. Meyer Levin's *Compulsion* made the list in 1957, but it was a novelized version of the Leopold and Loeb "crime of the century." Being history made it acceptable. The next year, Robert Traver's *Anatomy of a Murder* made the list, helped by the fact that the author was an honest-to-God real-life judge. (I am drawing on twentieth-century sales figures compiled by *Publishers Weekly.*) In 1966, Truman Capote's *In Cold Blood,* which he called a "nonfiction novel," was third on the nonfiction list; however defined, it was an exceptional piece of reporting and writing. Its success inspired an outpouring of true-crime books that would later include Norman Mailer's novelistic look at the Gary Gilmore case, *The Executioner's Song.* Both Mailer and Capote, literary lions of the postwar era, wrote their best books when they used real crimes to provide the structure, suspense, and passion that their novels sometimes lacked.

The International Thriller Writers list of all-time top thrillers includes several that reflected the anger of the Vietnam and Watergate eras. James Dickey's *Deliverance* (1970), a quintessential literary thriller, was a southern poet's brooding look at the violence and class hatred that were tearing America apart. David Morrell's *First Blood* (1972) introduced that formidable Vietnam veteran John Rambo. In James Grady's *Six Days of the Condor* (1974), written when he was twenty-four, rival elements of the CIA are at war. In Robert Stone's *Dog Soldiers* (1974), a small-time journalist smuggles heroin from Saigon to California, encouraged by a corrupt CIA agent.

Writers kept cropping up who defied category. Richard Condon's truly subversive *The Manchurian Candidate* (1959) was a stunning satire of Cold War paranoia. The writer who called himself Trevanian (and was really Rodney Whitaker) began a series of sophisticated spy thrillers. Some of the most influential writers of the post-Vietnam renaissance included James Crumley, James Ellroy, Richard Price, and Kem Nunn. They updated the Hammett-Chandler tradition and added an angry new edge, producing outlaw fiction with a rock-and-roll beat. Crumley gave his most celebrated novel, *The Last Good Kiss* (1978), a title, a plot, and a beginning that all reflect his admiration for Chandler. Here's the opening line:

> When I finally caught up with Abraham Trahearne, he was drinking beer with an alcoholic bulldog named Fireball Roberts in a ramshackle joint just outside of Sonoma, California, drinking the heart right out of a fine spring afternoon.

Crumley claims it took him eight years to write that line, and all across America he has fans who can recite it from memory. Trahearne is an alcoholic writer whose ex-wife has hired C. W. Sughrue, Crumley's hard-drinking Montana-based PI, to find him, all of which recalls Chandler's *The Long Goodbye*. The title of another of Crumley's novels, *The Mexican Tree Duck* (1988), is his wry tribute to *The Maltese Falcon*.

Dennis Lehane, who would emerge in the 1990s as one of the best writers of his generation, calls *The Last Good Kiss* a turning point for him and many others. "That was the single most influential novel. It was a huge influence on Michael Connelly, on George Pelecanos, on me. And then all of a sudden James Ellroy came along. I remember reading *Black Dahlia* in my college dorm room and not getting off the floor all night and saying, Oh, my God! This is truly what you can do! And then all of a sudden there was a flood of people coming from everywhere writing at a level that's at a higher pitch than ever."

Richard Price, born in 1949, grew up in a housing project in the Bronx (where his father drove a cab); he attended Cornell and then the graduate writing program at Columbia, where he wrote his first novel, *The Wanderers,* about a teenage gang in the Bronx. It was published when he was twenty-four. Other ultra-realistic novels followed, including *Bloodbrothers, Clockers,* and *Freedomland,* gritty looks at young people, drugs, poverty, race, and crime. His influence on younger writers like Lehane and Pelecanos would be enormous.

Although Stephen Hunter remained stateside during his 1969–70 army duty, he went on to write more than a dozen novels that reflect a post-Vietnam focus on conspiracy, corruption, and the art of killing. His breakthrough came with his 1993 novel *Point of Impact,* which introduced Bob Lee Swagger, a southern-born marksman who was credited with eighty-seven kills in Vietnam. Twenty years later, after the CIA betrays him, he too brings the war home.

For all their innovations, few of these writers scored major commercial success. Then in 1981, the triumph of the thriller exploded into view when four crime writers were among the year's fifteen top sellers.

Martin Cruz Smith's *Gorky Park* was in fifth place and thus became one of the first best-selling American cop stories, although the cop is Russian and the crime is in Moscow. Further down the list, three more first-rate crime thrillers announced a new day: *The Third Deadly Sin* by Lawrence Sanders in eighth place (his *Tenth Commandment* had been fifteenth the previous year); ex-LA cop Joseph Wambaugh's *The Glitter Dome* at ninth; and just under the wire, at fifteenth, the veteran John D. MacDonald's *Free Fall in Crimson.*

The success of Smith, Sanders, Wambaugh, and MacDonald was only the start. All over America, a new fiction was bubbling up, gaining readers and respectability. It was rooted in crime and used suspense and ever-greater violence to grab the reader, but it increasingly offered first-rate writing. Soon it would carry crime fiction far beyond the boundaries that Hammett and Chandler had observed.

In Detroit, a lawyer named Scott Turow thought he could write a better novel about lawyers than the Perry Mason potboilers, and down in Mississippi a lawyer named John Grisham had the same wild notion. In Annapolis, a myopic insurance agent named Tom Clancy wanted to proclaim his admiration for the U.S. military. In Detroit, Elmore Leonard had written successful Western novels, but that market was drying up so he decided to focus his offbeat vision on cops and robbers. In California, an unhappy screenwriter named Sue Grafton was at work on a novel about a female PI, and in Chicago Sara Paretsky, who hated her insurance job, had the same plan. In Boston, a college professor named Robert B. Parker, who'd written his thesis on the novels of Hammett, Chandler, and Ross Macdonald, was out to update their tradition with a private eye who was plenty tough but also a gourmet cook, respectful of women, and highly literate—Sam Spade for yuppies.

Soon, Clancy would write the first blockbuster military thriller, Turow would write the first great legal thriller, Grisham would begin an amazing series of best sellers, Grafton and Paretsky would send forth their female private eyes, Parker would gain huge success with his Spenser novels, and Leonard would write some of the most original crime fiction ever.

A new generation of spy novelists was also emerging. In 1964, an English writer who called himself John le Carré opened the door to serious Cold War fiction with *The Spy Who Came in from the Cold.* In 1973, Robert Littell, a *Newsweek* correspondent, published his offbeat *The Defection of A. J. Lewinter,* in which both American and Soviet intelligence agents are less concerned with national security than with their careers. The next year, former CIA operative Charles McCarry answered with *The Tears of Autumn,* his meditation on the Kennedy assassination.

In 1975, a reporter named Thomas Harris published *Black Sunday,* a prophetic novel about PLO terrorists who work with an embittered Vietnam veteran to hijack a television blimp and blow up the Super Bowl, thus killing thousands, including the U.S. president. Next, Harris published *Red Dragon,* which introduced that most original, most widely known villain of modern fiction, Dr. Hannibal Lecter. As he continued the Lecter saga with *The Silence of the Lambs* and *Hannibal,* Harris became the emblematic post-Vietnam thriller writer; no other American has given us best sellers this disturbing and violent.

All these writers were reinventing American crime fiction in the post-Vietnam era. The private-eye novel had spawned a big, dark, sometimes frightening offspring, the modern thriller. Let's look more closely at two great originals who emerged in the 1970s, Lawrence Sanders and Elmore Leonard. Between them, these two very different writers did much to give the emerging thriller a new and unpredictable voice.

COMMANDMENTS AND DEADLY SINS

One day in the 1980s a friend gave me a paperback copy of Lawrence Sanders's *The Seduction of Peter S* and said, "You have to read this!" She was right. *Peter S* was a wry tale about an out-of-work New York actor who starts a male brothel for rich matrons. At first he is wildly successful but there are complications, such as the mob moving in. I was soon searching the used-book stores for everything I could find by Sanders, whose first ten novels I had unaccountably missed. I read them one after another, savoring their richness and variety. *Peter S* had been, for Sanders, light comedy; his best novels were the *Deadly Sin* and *Commandment* series, big, dark, gothic, and utterly unlike what anyone else was writing.

Lawrence Sanders was the pen name of Lesley Andress (1920–98), a magazine editor who in the late 1960s sold a dozen stories about an insurance investigator to *Swank,* one of the *Playboy* imitators that had replaced the pulps as an outlet for crime fiction. His first novel, *The Anderson Tapes,* was published in 1970, when he was fifty. The novel tells the story of a mob robbery through a series of tape recordings. It won the Mystery Writers of America's Edgar award for best first novel of the year and became a Sean Connery film.

Sanders's next novel, *The First Deadly Sin,* appeared in 1973, and nothing in *The Anderson Tapes* had prepared readers for the boldness of its concept or the originality of the writing. Although it stars a cop, it was not a traditional cop novel; it was, rather, one of the first modern thrillers. It announced its originality from the outset. Traditionally, crime fiction had gotten right to it. Spade meets Brigid on the first page of *The Maltese Falcon;* Marlowe visits the Sternwood mansion on page one of *The Big Sleep.* But *The First Deadly Sin* is big and discursive, some 560 pages, and there is no corpse, crime, or confrontation on page one. Instead, we meet an odd duck named Daniel Blank. Daniel is thirty-six and divorced, works for a New York publishing house, is a physical fitness nut, wears wigs over his shaved head, and favors women's underwear. We may suspect that this weirdo will wind up a killer, but that doesn't happen right away. Instead, Daniel goes to a party and meets a woman even stranger than he is.

Her name is Celia Montfort and she lives in a town house on East End Avenue with a butler who lisps and a beautiful twelve-year-old boy she claims is her brother. "Her hair was so black it was almost purple, parted in the middle, and fell loosely below her shoulders without wave or curl." Celia talks about "sex as a religious rite and a dramatic ceremony" and says that "true evil has a kind of nobility," and when they get around to sex it is unlike anything he has known before. ("Scream if you like," she said, "no one can hear.") Dan decides that she is his soul mate and has brought forth the real him: a killer.

We spend fifty-three pages getting to know this fun couple, and then we meet Captain Edward X. Delaney, Commanding Officer of the 251st Precinct, NYPD. Delaney is a big shambling man. He served five years in the army during wartime and is nearing thirty years with the NYPD. He is tough, shrewd, proud, compassionate, and, when necessary, ruthless. His beloved wife, Barbara, is dying; her pain and the frustrations of dealing with doctors are driving him half mad. Finally, after ninety-eight pages, Daniel Blank commits his first murder, driving his mountain climber's ice ax into a stranger's skull on a dark street, and Delaney must deal with a serial killer as well as with his wife's distress.

With the invention of Edward X. Delaney, Sanders, like Hammett and Chandler before him, had found his man and his voice, but it was a new kind of voice. *The First Deadly Sin* is one of the first times an American crime writer has gambled on a big, richly detailed novel as fat as anything Herman Wouk or James Michener was churning out. Most crime novels run not much more than two hundred pages. It takes great self-confidence to write two or three times that. When you ask a reader to stay with you for five hundred pages, you'd better deliver. Sanders did. He had a rare ability to create believable characters, voices we recognize, emotions we share, and thus to draw us in to his world. His books often feel less like reading than eavesdropping. Delaney is not a fantasy figure; he is, like McBain's Frank Carella and Michael Connelly's Harry Bosch, a real, believable cop. Over the course of several novels, we come to *know* this man. With Delaney, Sanders achieved a psychological depth rarely seen in crime fiction.

Sanders alternates between Delaney's methodical investigation and Daniel and Celia's growing madness—between good and evil. His portrayal of the crazed lovers is enhanced by the fact that, thanks to court decisions and a general loosening up of the culture, he can write explicitly about sex. The days are gone when Norman Mailer had to have American soldiers saying "fug" instead of "fuck."

Sanders produced novels annually into his seventies. I remember the *Deadly Sin* and *Commandment* series with pleasure, as well as *The Tomorrow File,* his venture into science fiction, and *The Case of Lucy Bending,* the fascinating (and, to some, troubling) story of a sexually precocious eight-year-old with an all-too-suggestive name. Sanders's novels were uneven, but for two decades they were never without interest. In 1992, however, he began the Archie McNally series. I read one of them with dismay; some of his fans refused to believe he had written them. The McNally books were popular, however, and continued to appear after Sanders's death, written by someone else, which neither Sanders nor we deserved. This great original came from nowhere, helped change popular fiction, and now is largely forgotten. In the scope and perversity of his novels he is unlike any other writer we've looked at. You have to go back to Wilkie Collins or forward to Thomas Harris to find anyone as sardonic, as deliciously gothic.

COWBOYS AND ROBBERS

There is a certain irony to linking Lawrence Sanders and Elmore Leonard; aside from both being wonderful writers, they could hardly be more different. Sanders wrote big, inclusive, everything-but-the-kitchen-sink novels (in fact, he included the kitchen sink, which is where Delaney liked to stand and eat the big wet sandwiches he loved), while Leonard is a minimalist. He once announced his ten rules of writing and they all had to do with leaving things out and keeping it simple. Never open a book with the weather, he said. Use only "said" to carry the dialogue—not "declared" or "exclaimed" or "snarled" or "hissed" or "whispered" or "intoned" or the other words favored by writers who think "said" is dull. Limit yourself to two or three exclamation points per book. Minimize descriptions of people and places. And, his golden rule: Leave out the parts that readers will skip.

Leave out the dull parts—what a concept! Forests saved! Books enjoyed! This revolutionary fellow was born in New Orleans in 1925 and grew up in the Detroit area. As a schoolboy he was nicknamed Dutch in honor of a baseball player named Dutch Leonard. He wrote for his high school paper, served in the navy, and in 1946 enrolled at the University of Detroit, where he began writing short stories. After graduating, he went to work for an advertising agency but he was writing in his spare time and sold his first story, a Western, to *Argosy* in 1951. His novel *The Bounty Hunters* came out in 1955, and more Western novels and stories followed. A couple sold to the movies. But the market was drying up. Cowboys were out, private eyes were in. So Leonard switched to crime fiction.

Throughout the 1970s and 1980s he published a series of wildly original novels. These were not traditional cops-and-robbers, good-guys-and-bad-guys stories. Leonard *liked* his crooks. We usually ended up rooting for them. His books were often more like comedies set among petty criminals than traditional crime novels. Books like *Fifty-two Pickup, Swag, Gold Coast, City Primeval, Split Images, Cat Chaser,* and *Stick* won him a growing audience. By the 1980s, a lot of people were waiting for Leonard's breakthrough novel. He was waiting for it too.

"I knew what I was doing," he told an interviewer. "It was a matter of the reviewers catching up." He added, "I learned by imitating Hemingway, until I realized I didn't share his attitude about life. I didn't take myself or anything as seriously as he did." Far from sharing Hemingway's considerable ego, Leonard, a recovering alcoholic, has a sweetness and a humility that help make him both an engaging writer and an attractive human being. There is no bluster to his novels, no bigotry, no moralizing, just an amused, compassionate, unblinking eye fixed on the human comedy.

Leonard eventually won best-seller status, but he never had the huge sales of a Grisham or a Grafton. He was too offbeat—segments of the mass audience would never quite get him. He had great success, however, with movies of his novels, which have included *Get Shorty* with John Travolta, *Out of Sight* with George Clooney and Jennifer Lopez, and Quentin Tarantino's near-perfect *Jackie Brown,* based on *Rum Punch.*

I recently went back and read a Leonard novel that I'd missed, 1983's *LaBrava.* I picked it at random in a used-book store and I was lucky, because it's one of his best. Leonard sets the story in Miami's funky South Beach, where an ex–Secret Service agent named Joe LaBrava, who's in his mid-thirties, falls for a fifty-something one-time movie star named Jean Shaw. The novel is most interesting for the reflections Leonard weaves in about the creative process and for his fascination with the elusive line between illusion and reality, as embodied in his fading actress.

Leonard is known for his offbeat elliptic dialogue, but it's not a key element in *LaBrava.* About the only tricks he plays are to have people say things like "I should a let you." Rather, the novel is memorable for the twin portraits of LaBrava and Jean Shaw, who are revealed less by their talk than in their thoughts. LaBrava left the Secret Service after he learned he loved photography. He has become friendly with eighty-something Maurice Zola, an ex-gambler who owns a South Beach hotel. Zola is a delightful old scamp who says things like "I spent most of my dough on booze, broads, and boats and the rest I wasted."

LaBrava lives in Zola's hotel and the older man has been helping him sell his photos. He also introduces his young friend to Jean Shaw who, it develops, LaBrava had fallen for upon seeing her in a movie when he was twelve. Jean has gotten mixed up with a dangerous redneck named Richard Nobles, and it looks like LaBrava will have to eject this thug from her life. Eventually, there is an extortion scheme, Maurice puts up the money to save Jean, the money is stolen, and the reality of events proves not to be what it first appeared.

Leonard uses LaBrava's love of photography to comment on the nature of art and on his own work. In the opening scene, Maurice is trying to sell a gallery owner on LaBrava's pictures. When she says he's not as good as some photographers she knows, the old man shoots back that he isn't pretentious, either. "You don't see any bullshit here. He shoots barefaced fact."

A little later, Leonard tells us how LaBrava feels about photography: "He felt himself attracted to street life. It was a strange feeling, he was at home, knew the people; saw more outcast faces and attitudes than he would ever be able to record, people who showed him their essence behind all kinds of poses and trapped them in his camera for all time."

That's a writer talking, proud of his art, intoxicated by the variety and mystery of the world around him. Soon he focuses on Jean Shaw. First LaBrava observes her with perfect detachment: "He watched her take dainty bites of marinated conch, raising the fork in her left hand upside down, her moves unhurried. He watched her break off a piece of French bread, hold it close to her face, elbow resting on the table, wrist bent, staring out of the shade at ocean in sunlight, then slowly bring the piece of bread to her mouth, not looking at it, and he would see her lips part to receive the bread and then close."

Writing like that looks easy until you try it. Leonard may have rejected Hemingway's swagger but he embraces Hemingway's goal of making every word matter.

LaBrava and the actress talk about his photography. She asks if his style isn't the absence of style. He's puzzled by the question. He can only tell her, "No tricky angles," because "he didn't know if he had a style or not." She asks him what he sees when he looks at his own work and he tells her, "I wonder if I'll ever have enough confidence." And "I wonder, most of all I wonder what the people are doing now. Or if they're still like that, the way I shot them."

Is Leonard hinting that one of the best writers in America might lack confidence? Yes, that's what good writing is about, getting up every day and wondering if you can get it right just once more. And being so deep in your fantasy that you wonder sometimes if the people you've written about are more real in their lives or in your art. Earlier, Leonard said that he was waiting for the reviewers to catch up with what he was doing. Here he is giving them clues.

Jean and LaBrava go to bed. For him, this is a fantasy come true. For her, it's simply the way she controls men. His thoughts are jumbled: "He had to stop thinking if he was going to be overwhelmed. He had to *let* himself be overwhelmed." And, "The idea of it, the anticipation, the realization, was more overwhelming than the doing of it." Still, he's troubled when she says he's the best thing that could happen to her, because he remembers that from one of her movies, a line she'd spoken to Robert Mitchum.

Leonard widens his examination of illusion and reality when he introduces Franny, a young artist who supports herself by selling beauty potions to aging South Beach matrons. One of her most popular items is Bio-Energetic Breast Cream, which will allegedly add "bounce and resiliency" to sagging breasts. In fact, as Franny confides to LaBrava, you've either got bounce or you don't. But that reality doesn't stop women from embracing the illusion that the potion will bring back the glories of their youth. In Leonard's South Beach, everyone feeds on dreams.

Halfway through the novel, Leonard shows us what LaBrava does not yet know, that Jean Shaw, far from being helpless, is conspiring with Richard Nobles to steal $600,000 from her dear friend Maurice Zola. The scheme follows the plot of one of her movies. Near the novel's end, Jean has stolen the money and killed Nobles. LaBrava can't prove it and doubts that the FBI can either. Indeed, he offers to help cover up her crime if she will give Zola back his money. "She said, 'Would you do that for me, Joe?' Got sad stars in her eyes and said, 'What a guy.' " By then, LaBrava doesn't know if she's quoting from a movie or not. He has to struggle to keep hold of reality. She still has the magic that first seduced him at age twelve, even after she announces that she is going to marry poor Maurice, whom she'll probably push off the balcony one night.

At its most interesting level, *LaBrava* is a meditation on art and illusion, but at a more basic level we have a woman who gets away with murder and persuades a former Secret Service agent to help her cover it up. It's not a family-values sort of message that will make a writer as rich as Tom Clancy, but, if you have a taste for the perverse, Leonard is hard to beat. In terms of originality, artistry, discipline, and sophistication, *LaBrava* and others of Leonard's best novels strike me as equal to anything Hammett, Chandler, John D. MacDonald, or Ross Macdonald ever wrote, although comparisons are complicated because they were writing conventional crime novels and he is off in the clouds, cavorting with his own sweet muse, playing his own delightful games.

In 2005, shortly before his eightieth birthday, Leonard published his fortieth novel, *The Hot Kid,* set in the Depression-era Oklahoma that Leonard could recall from his childhood. There may have been sensible law-abiding people in Oklahoma in those days, but Leonard's world is one of near-perfect ignorance and near-total amorality. Farm boys dream of robbing banks and farmers' daughters suspect that being a gun moll is a grander fate than chopping cotton.

I happened to be midway through *The Hot Kid* when I saw a dazzling production of *The Tempest* at Washington's Shakespeare Theater, and the juxtaposition (such are the perils of art) inspired a thought or two. Leonard is our Prospero, a magician who has given us inspired fun for fifty years. He floats above the action, amused; his motto is surely "What fools these mortals be." In *The Hot Kid,* Oklahoma is his version of Shakespeare's enchanted isle, a brave new world where maidens and monsters, outlaws and oilmen, strange creatures all, act out their dubious destinies. At the time I read Leonard's novel, much was being made of a postmodern extravaganza that featured a precocious nine-year-old, blank pages (for that which cannot be expressed), and a "little flip-flop book of video stills" of people jumping out of the burning towers on 9/11. In Leonard's novels we are spared postmodern pretensions in favor of old-fashioned pleasure. To paraphrase one of Hemingway's more naughty asides (about T. S. Eliot and Joseph Conrad, as I recall), I would gladly grind several of today's postmodernists into a fine powder if I could sprinkle that powder in Elmore Leonard's morning coffee and guarantee us an endless supply of his magic.

6.

Tom Clancy's Literary Offenses

Cooper's art has some defects. In one place in
"Deerslayer," and in the restricted space of
two-thirds of a page, Cooper has scored 114 offenses
against literary art out of a possible 115. It breaks
the record. —Mark Twain, "Fenimore Cooper's Literary Offenses"

Thomas L. Clancy Jr., the second child of a Baltimore postman, was a nearsighted unathletic boy who was sent to strict parochial schools and retreated into the world of books. "I never read kids' books," he once told me. "At least not the usual kids' books. I remember reading Jules Verne in the third grade. I started on Samuel Eliot Morrison in the fourth or fifth grade—he started me on military history. I read a lot of science fiction. I read every genre you can imagine."

When he began to dream of writing, Clancy's direction was not in doubt. He was a military buff, an avid fan of the space program, a gadget freak. He loved military board games and played them relentlessly. At Loyola College, a Jesuit school, he majored in English, was dropped from the ROTC because of poor eyesight, supported the war in Vietnam, and had no use for those who demonstrated against it. He also fell in love with a nursing student named Wanda Thomas. They married soon after his graduation in 1969, whereupon Clancy put aside his dream of writing and went into the insurance business in Owings, Maryland, twenty miles south of Annapolis.

When Clancy was a young man, he planned to stay young forever. Instead, he awoke to the stunning realization that he was trapped—by a family he loved, mortgages, car payments, his job, all the bonds of middle-class life. Increasingly frustrated, by the late seventies he was trying to produce fiction in his spare time. His instinct to write about the military was reinforced by life in the Annapolis area, where many people were navy or ex-navy. Soon Clancy's fictional fantasies centered on a fellow Irish-American named Jack Ryan, an ex-marine who left Wall Street to teach history at Annapolis and was also a secret agent for the CIA.

Three distinct plots were banging about in Clancy's imagination. In one, Ryan saved members of the British royal family from IRA terrorists. Another involved Ryan with a high-level spy in the Kremlin. His third idea, about a Soviet submarine commander's defection to the United States, came from a newspaper account of crewmen on a Russian frigate who tried to defect to Sweden. In Clancy's version, the frigate became a nuclear submarine, and this was the story he decided to pursue. He had never set foot on a submarine, but he talked to people who had and began reading everything he could about them.

In July 1982, after extensive research, Clancy began to write a novel that was heavy on technical detail about nuclear submarines, helicopters, radar, and weapons systems. He finished a draft in November and showed it to an editor at the U.S. Naval Institute's magazine. Buoyed by the editor's enthusiasm, Clancy pushed on and finished the novel at the end of February. Until then, his wife had seen his writing as a waste of time. "But once I read the book, I changed my mind," she told me. "Tom said he'd be happy if it would sell five thousand copies, but I told him not to worry, it'd sell a lot more than that."

At the editor's suggestion, Clancy took his novel to the Naval Institute Press. It had traditionally published naval history and textbooks, but the editors wanted to publish a novel if they could find a good one with a maritime theme. Whether a commercial publisher would have liked *The Hunt for Red October,* with its heavy emphasis on military technology—a techno-thriller, it would be called—will never be known, but the Naval Institute Press loved it. The editors asked Clancy for only minor changes and paid him a $5,000 advance. They decided on an optimistic first printing of 15,000 copies and October publication.

The Hunt for Red October was "well published," as they say in the trade. "I can't tell you how much effort we put into that book—it was our first novel too," Tom Epley, the press director, told me. At first, the publisher concentrated on the Washington audience. Advance copies went out to government officials and military figures. They persuaded *The Washington Post* to write a story about the press publishing its first novel. The book's first break came when the *Post*'s reviewer called it "breathlessly exciting." By November, *Red October* was on the *Post*'s best-seller list. Six months after publication, the novel had sold an impressive 45,000 copies.

Then came the miracle.

Nancy Clark Reynolds, a friend of Ronald and Nancy Reagan, sent a copy of *Red October* to the president for Christmas. Soon word began to circulate that Reagan loved this tale of an idealistic Soviet naval officer who risks all for freedom. In March, *Time* magazine carried a page-long article saying that Reagan had called the novel "the perfect yarn." Within weeks, *Red October* leaped onto the national best-seller lists. It eventually sold more than 365,000 copies in hardback.

Clancy never slowed down. He had become friendly with Larry Bond, a former naval officer who designed war games. The two decided to build a novel around one of Bond's games, which involved a non-nuclear world war that turns on naval engagements in the North Atlantic. In January 1985, when *Red October* didn't yet have the Reagan endorsement, they had an outline and several chapters of *Red Storm Rising*. Their agent got an offer of a $325,000 advance from Putnam. Clancy told the Naval Institute Press that if it would come within twenty percent of the Putnam offer he would stay with them, but the press declined. After the breakout success of *Red October,* the $325,000 deal was renegotiated into a three-book, $3 million contract. Bond didn't get his name on *Red Storm Rising,* but he earned more than a million dollars from it and went off to write his own books.

Clancy's third and fourth novels returned to his original plan. In *Patriot Games,* Jack Ryan saves Prince Charles and Princess Diana from terrorists, who then attack Ryan at his home in Maryland. In *The Cardinal of the Kremlin,* Ryan works to save a high-level Russian spy who has been feeding information to the CIA. In both cases, Clancy made his alter ego, Ryan, the center of attention, which he was not in the first two novels. In 1988 I read the first four novels while writing an article on Clancy for *The New York Times Magazine.* I thought *Patriot Games* was by far the best, because it had the least technical lore and the most emphasis on Ryan and his love of his family. Not everyone agreed. Some reviewers blasted Clancy for forsaking the techno-babble they had come to expect from him.

Clancy had begun an amazing run of best sellers:

1985: *The Hunt for Red October,* #13
1986: *Red Storm Rising,* #2 (behind a Stephen King novel)
1987: *Patriot Games,* #2 (also behind a Stephen King novel)
1988: *The Cardinal of the Kremlin,* #1
1989: *Clear and Present Danger,* #1 (ahead of a Stephen King novel)
1991: *The Sum of All Fears,* #2 (behind a *Gone with the Wind* sequel)
1993: *Without Remorse,* #4
1994: *Debt of Honor,* #2 (behind a John Grisham novel)
1996: *Executive Orders,* #2 (behind Grisham, ahead of King)
1998: *Rainbow Six,* #2 (behind Grisham)
2000: *The Bear and the Dragon,* #3 (behind Grisham and a *Left Behind* novel)
2002: *Red Rabbit,* #2 (behind Grisham)
2003: *The Teeth of the Tiger,* #6

From Homer to Hemingway and beyond, as long as there has been war, writers have tried to capture its drama and tragedy, but not one has done so with a commercial success equal to Clancy's. Most of the best war novels have been written by men who have known combat and had no wish to glorify it. Clancy was the opposite. He had never fired a shot in anger and his success has been based on painting a glowing picture of American militarism. By successfully expanding the thriller into military affairs, Clancy inspired a legion of imitators who are far more interested in writing the next *Hunt for Red October* than the next *A Farewell to Arms.* His imitators typically present a fearless patriot who is some sort of globe-hopping special agent, battling not only bloodthirsty terrorists abroad but spineless liberals in the White House. Having been obliged to read a few Clancy clones I will give the man credit—he did it first and he did it best.

Clancy has a genius for big, audacious plots, a passion for research, narrative skill, the mind-set of Walter Mitty, and a blissfully uncomplicated view of human nature and international affairs. Although some of us find his obsession with technology mind-numbing, it appeals to millions of readers. Many people view fiction as a frivolous pastime unless it contains some clear benefit—unless they "learn something"— and Clancy's techno-thrillers were like crash courses in modern weaponry. Of course, he did not so much write about war as about the Pentagon's fantasies of how war should be; he gave us not war but war games.

Clancy's success went against the grain of the antiwar, antiestablishment post-Vietnam fiction that emerged in the 1970s. Clancy was a Pentagon groupie. He built his career not only on military technology but on unabashed, uncritical patriotism. He started writing before the collapse of the Soviet Union, and his message was a reassuring one: the Soviets are tough but our boys are tougher; their system is so rotten that their best men defect to us; and World War III can be fought and won without nuclear weapons.

Many Americans were profoundly troubled by the fact that the United States had lost the war in Vietnam. For a time, foreign wars were out of favor. But the pendulum soon swung back. The election of Ronald Reagan in 1980 made jingoism acceptable again. And yet, as Clancy insists, it was not just Reagan who made him a success, it was the people who elected Reagan. He was a red-state red-meat writer, a scourge of the nervous Nellies who weren't eager to police the world. Given Clancy's history, many were surprised in 2004 when he spoke out against the invasion of Iraq. He admired President Bush, he said, "but even good men make mistakes." Clearly his criticism of the war reflected the views of his friends high in the military; his loyalty was to the Pentagon, not the White House.

Clancy always saw other villains than the Soviets out there. In his third novel, Jack Ryan tangles with IRA terrorists. In the fifth, *Clear and Present Danger,* by which time Ryan is deputy director of the CIA, Colombian drug czars are the enemy. In *The Sum of All Fears,* mideastern terrorists threaten to explode a nuclear weapon in the United States. In *Debt of Honor,* Ryan is White House National Security Adviser and faces a challenge from a Japanese industrialist who wants war with the United States. In the 1,300-page *Executive Orders,* after Ryan has become vice president, a terrorist crashes a hijacked airliner into the U.S. Capitol, killing the president and much of Congress and elevating Ryan to the White House.

When I interviewed Clancy in 1988, he hinted that Ryan would be president someday. The audacity of his concept was stunning. In a series of novels, Clancy has taken his alter ego, an unknown history professor, and advanced him to the presidency, all the while using him to dramatize the Cold War and other international challenges. It is, to be sure, a dumbed-down, highly ideological version of recent history, but compelling enough to win millions of readers.

There were problems with Clancy's concept. As Ryan rose ever higher in government, it was no longer possible to involve him directly in the action adventures that were Clancy's mainstay. One way Clancy dealt with this dilemma was to invent John Kelly, aka Mr. Clark, an ultraviolent CIA assassin who became known as Ryan's dark side and was featured in several novels. On the home front, Clancy's stock villains included liberals, hippies, and Ivy Leaguers. In time, many of Clancy's readers began expressing impatience with books they found too long, too preachy, too jingoistic, and sometimes just too silly.

Clancy started out as a lonely dreamer and wound up a conglomerate. One of his recent books, in addition to listing the novels mentioned here, also listed eight novels in the "Tom Clancy's Op-Center" series and five novels in the "Tom Clancy's Net Force" series, both "created by Tom Clancy and Steve Pieczenik"; five more novels in the "Tom Clancy's Power Plays" series ("created by Tom Clancy and Martin Greenberg"); and nine more books of nonfiction on military topics. Obviously Clancy doesn't write all those books. He would do well just to read them.

In *Red Rabbit* and *The Teeth of the Tiger,* Clancy continued to deal with the problem of what you do when your hero has become president and can't run around zapping bad guys anymore. In *Red Rabbit,* he finessed the issue by basing his story on a 1981 KGB plot to assassinate the pope. This took Clancy back to the golden age when Ronald Reagan, Margaret Thatcher, and Pope John Paul II were all new to office—and the young Jack Ryan, knighted by the Queen for saving Charles and Di, was working for the CIA in London. Much of the novel involves the CIA's efforts to get a good-guy KGB officer (the red rabbit of the title) out of Russia.

I saw much to admire in *Red Rabbit*. Clancy moved skillfully among a large cast of characters in Washington, London, and Moscow and developed several of them effectively. He had compiled a great deal of information, often quite fascinating, about how spy agencies operate. The "exfiltration" of the "rabbit" was suspenseful. And Clancy's writing had improved since the clunky prose and robotic dialogue of his early novels. Whether this means he has applied himself diligently to mastering the art of fiction or has simply surrounded himself with skilled collaborators, I have no idea, but why look gift horses in the mouth? For the most part, the novel read well.

Yet there were problems, often quite maddening. It is perhaps too much to expect Clancy to mute his political views (Reagan good, media bad; Thatcher good, bureaucrats bad), since they are so basic to his success, but they became tiresome. Perhaps ten percent of the novel was devoted to beating up on the Communists—their hypocrisy, their inefficiency—and few readers would disagree, but must he beat the dead horse at such length so long after the Soviet empire has ceased to be?

Another of Clancy's literary offenses is that if he likes a phrase, he never stops using it: Characters endlessly tell us it's time "to get the hell out of Dodge," that something "is above my pay grade," that someone "is no day at the beach," and so on. It is fine if he has an energetic research staff, but must we be told not once but twice that the Hungarian language is called Indo-Altaic and three times that Kim Philby, during his years in Moscow, drank excessively even by Russian standards? Also, Clancy has Ryan indulge in endless profanity, apparently to remind us that (even if the Brits insist on calling him Sir John) good old Jack Ryan is still one hell of a fellow. Did we really have to be told, at the end of one scene, that "Ryan headed off to the men's room to dump some of his liquid lunch"?

I thought *Red Rabbit* was one of Clancy's better efforts, but serious editing, weeding out 50 to 100 pages of Clancy's excesses, would have improved it. The fact that I rather liked *Red Rabbit,* while his increasingly restive readers on Amazon.com gave it only two stars, is no surprise. I liked the novel because, by Clancy's standards, it is relatively modest and plausible. But many of Clancy's fans want more cosmic tales of nuclear showdowns, and by those standards *Red Rabbit* was a dud.

In *The Teeth of the Tiger,* Clancy tried another strategy for breathing life into the franchise. He kept Jack Ryan offstage, an ex-president writing his memoirs, and built the novel around Ryan's son, Jack Junior, also known as Ryan the Younger, and his cousins, the twins Dominic and Brian Caruso: one an FBI agent and the other a marine. The novel opens with FBI agent Dominic shooting a pedophile in cold blood and, having thus proved his mettle, being recruited for an antiterrorism hit squad. His brother too is recruited. The more scholarly Jack Junior, fresh out of Georgetown University, signs on as an analyst for the covert operation.

In the novel's strongest episode, sixteen Saudi terrorists slip across the Mexican border and carry out attacks in the American heartland that kill hundreds of people. One of the attacks is in a Charlottesville, Virginia, shopping mall. Brian Caruso happens by and helps police wipe out the terrorists. In one bizarre scene, Brian, confronting a dying terrorist, dashes to a nearby store and returns with a football, which he forces into the man's hands. "Hey, raghead. I've got something for you. I want you to carry this to hell with you. It's a football, asshole, made from the skin of a real Iowa pig." Apparently this touch of pork will block the man's journey to paradise.

Aside from that moment of pure Clancy, the shopping-mall scene is a realistic look at a terrorist attack. Clancy has never shied away from violence if it suits his dramatic purposes. But the novel soon goes downhill as the Caruso brothers are sent to Europe to kill terrorist leaders. The twins are the Hardy Boys grown up; they kill when duty demands it but are fun-loving lads at heart. They say things like this, when an intended victim shows up with a companion:

"Who's wog number two, I wonder?"
"Nobody we know, and we can't freelance. You packin'?"
"Bet your bippy, bro. You?"
"Hang a big roger on that."

We are deep in Clancy Country, where the natives communicate in a bewildering mixture of spook speak, military jargon, and bureaucratic buzzwords. Lesser mortals are called pukes ("those White House pukes") or weenies ("those computer weenies") and terrorists are mutts and wogs and ragheads. (Not since Raymond Chandler has a major American writer so shamelessly pandered to prejudice, and not since Chandler has one been in such urgent need of an editor.) We are endlessly told that when things get "hinky" (suspicious), an agent with a "good nose" (good instincts) can "twig" (figure out) a way to whack the mutts. Reporters are "newsies" when they are not "vultures on a fallen carcass." As always, if Clancy likes a word or phrase, he does not hesitate to use it twice, or twenty times, or two hundred. Someone says of the Caruso twins, "Their mom must have punched out two eggs instead of one that month" and later one of them declares, "Mom punched out two eggs that month." We are told twice that if a man is worth shooting once he's worth shooting twice, twice that there is a saying in Texas that more men need hanging than horses need stealing, twice that the terrorists didn't come to the United States to sell Girl Scout cookies, maybe fifty times that real espionage is not like the movies, and hundreds of times that e-mail messages have been encrypted or decrypted or reencrypted. The mind boggles.

When the Caruso twins aren't killing people, their passion is buzzing around Europe in expensive cars. Brian says of his twin, "He'd rather sleep with a Ferrari than with Grace Kelly," and Jack adds that "if Maureen O'Hara had been born a car" she would have been a Ferrari. Grace Kelly? Maureen O'Hara? Is Clancy living in a time warp? Does he think young men of today lust after—or have even heard of—movie stars from the 1950s? Clancy is a self-described nerd, and his efforts to be hip are a wonder.

Clancy's terrorist leaders are cartoon characters, as arrogant and hypocritical as they are bloodthirsty. They scorn the decadent West but enjoy its expensive prostitutes, wines, and luxury hotels, and they regard the zealots they send on suicide missions as fools. They are such idiots that whacking them is like swatting flies. Three times one of the Caruso brothers jabs a poisoned needle into a terrorist's butt and three times the victim obligingly drops dead on the streets of Europe. The point of this ridiculous novel seems to be Young Jack's coming of age as a warrior, so Clancy contrives to send him to Europe to assist the Caruso brothers despite the fact that (1) they don't need him, (2) he lacks training, and (3) the son of an ex-president would not be carrying out assassinations. Jack does prove himself, more or less, whereupon the novel does not so much end as announce: "to be continued." It will take additional volumes for Ryan the Younger and the Caruso Boys to rid the world of effete terrorists. Be warned.

Clancy's early novels focused on the U.S.–Soviet Cold War rivalry, and his view of it was uncomplicated. "I think we're the good guys and they're the bad guys," he told me. "Don't you?" Clancy can be both long-winded and belligerent. *The Washington Post*'s Peter Carlson wrote that interviewing him was like "being chained to a bar stool in some VFW hall and forced to listen to the world's biggest barroom blowhard." There is some truth in this, but when I interviewed Clancy in 1988 he mostly exhibited a boyish exuberance.

Clancy was living then on eighty acres overlooking the Chesapeake Bay, where he was building a new dream house to replace the earlier dream house he'd built in the first flush of success. He took me for a ride around the property in his latest toy, a four-wheel-drive GM Jimmy. "I told the agent, Don't tell me what it costs, just buy it," he said of the property. We passed an unused swimming pool ("I want an indoor pool") and skirted some steep cliffs overlooking the bay, which recalled the cliffs down which Jack Ryan fled from IRA assassins at the climax of *Patriot Games*. Clancy reflected on the moment when Ryan could have killed the terrorist who had gravely injured his young daughter. "Of all the letters I got on *Patriot Games,* not one of them said, 'He should have killed the little bastard.' Personally, I'd have done it. You harm my kids and I'll blow you away. You don't touch my kids. But I'm not Jack Ryan. He has to be in control. He plays by the rules."

He reflected on the success of his first three novels, which by then had earned him five or six million dollars. "What happened to me was pure dumb luck—I'm not the new Hemingway." Then, backtracking a bit, he added, "Of course, fortune does favor the brave. In battle you forgive a man anything except an unwillingness to take risks. Sometimes you have to put it on the line."

He spoke of his affection for soldiers. "Just treat 'em decently. Just treat 'em honestly. Reporters treat the military like drunken Nazis. They're the most loyal friends you can have. They're my kind of people. We share the same value structure." He recalled the time he drove an M1 tank and fired live 105-millimeter shells at a distant paper target: "Sixty tons, fifteen hundred horsepower, and a four-inch gun— that's sex! That was a ball! The army treats me right. Every round I've put out has been a hit—better than a hit, a pinwheel! When I was a kid I wanted to be a tanker. With a tank I am death!"

What are the lessons of Clancy's twenty-year run near the top of popular fiction? One lesson is that you don't have to write well, in stylistic terms, to sell books. To my eye and ear, Clancy's early books were clunky and reading them was agonizing. The later ones read better, probably because he has people to help him polish the prose, but he clearly does not have anyone to edit out the inane dialogue, endless repetitions, and right-wing stereotypes that blight his novels. But for aspiring writers, the lesson of Clancy is that if you have a strong, suspenseful, action-packed plot, your prose doesn't matter.

If war is politics carried on by other means, Clancy has for more than twenty years been America's leading political novelist, the rightful heir to Allen Drury, whose right-wing views he shares. As the Cold War stretched on, America was ready for a novelist who lavished praise on American soldiers, technology, and triumphalism. We can't blame Clancy for American militarism, but his books helped popularize the notion that war is easy, like video games, and that our expensive weapons would produce "shock and awe" that would rout all those ragheads out there. He was the great chronicler and champion of the Cold War, but the war on terrorism has not served Clancy as well. *The Teeth of the Tiger* was Clancy's first post-9/11 novel, his response to terrorism, and not only was it ridiculous but it didn't sell well, by the standards of his earlier books. Many war-on-terrorism novels are coming out these days, and most of them offer more plausible plans for dealing with the menace than to send the Caruso twins bopping around Europe in Ferraris, dreaming of Grace Kelly and jabbing poisoned needles into the terrorists' fat, decadent asses.

7.

Dangerous Women:

Grafton, Paretsky, Highsmith

Sue Grafton's father, C. W. (Chip) Grafton, was a Louisville lawyer who in the late 1930s wrote two mysteries about a Kentucky lawyer. Each took its title from a nursery rhyme: *The Rat Began to Gnaw the Rope* and *The Rope Began to Hang the Butcher*. After wartime service, he wrote two more mysteries. The second, *Beyond a Reasonable Doubt* (1950), told of a lawyer charged with murder who represented himself in court. It was considered the best of Grafton's novels, but he never wrote another.

His daughter Sue was born in 1940, about the time Grafton went off to military service. The first five years of her life were happy, but things fell apart when he returned from the war. Both her parents were alcoholic. Sue and her older sister grew up with a mother who spent many days reading, smoking, and drinking. At an early age, Grafton learned responsibility and discipline, along with the instinct of the child of alcoholics to put things right. "I wanted to be a good girl," she recalls. "I wanted an ordinary life."

Grafton's parents were book lovers and they made her one. In an article called "An Eye on I" she said of her early reading, "I worked my way from Nancy Drew through Agatha Christie and on to Mickey Spillane. . . . I can still remember the astonishment I felt when I leapt from the familiarity of Miss Marple into the pagan sensibilities of *I, the Jury*." She loved Jack Kerouac's *On the Road* too, but nice Louisville girls didn't go thumbing across America. Instead, the pretty, petite teenager married at eighteen. She had a daughter, Leslie, and was pregnant with her son, Jay, when she left her husband after a year of marriage. Her mother, dying of cancer, killed herself on Grafton's twentieth birthday.

Her husband took their daughter and Grafton didn't see the girl again until she was seventeen. Grafton kept her son, Jay, and married Al Schmidt, who worked in insurance. They had a daughter, Jamie. Grafton, still in her twenties, found herself in a California suburb, raising two small children and increasingly frustrated. She looked to writing as her salvation. Her first novel, *Keziah Dane,* was published in 1967 and quickly vanished. Her second, *The Lolly-Madonna War,* sold to the movies for $25,000, whereupon she took her kids and moved to Los Angeles to write.

Schmidt sued for custody of his stepson and daughter, and the case dragged on for years. Grafton was juggling screenwriting and secretarial work. She eventually had several television dramas produced but she hated Hollywood, which she saw as an endless orgy of hypocrisy and ass-kissing. She wanted out, and once again she saw novels as her escape. She started a crime novel, one that reflected not only her admiration for Hammett and Chandler but her frustrations with her ex-husband. Grafton has often said, not entirely in jest, that *A Is for Alibi,* about a woman who kills her husband, was inspired by her fantasies of killing Schmidt.

She was determined to write about a woman private eye, but it was hard to adapt the genre's traditional tough-guy persona to a woman. An early draft of *Alibi* began, "My name is Kinsey Millhone. I'm what they call a 'dick,' although the term is somewhat of a misnomer in my case." The Kinsey who eventually emerged tosses off plenty of wisecracks, but fortunately not that one.

Grafton says she picked the name Kinsey from a newspaper story because she liked it and it could be either male or female. She says Millhone caught her eye while she skimmed through the phone book. She speaks of Kinsey as "the person I might have been had I not married young and had children." She jokes that she and Kinsey are "one soul in two bodies and she got the good one." She admits that when she started her novel she wasn't even sure what a private investigator did, but she found out through interviews and reading. She chose her title because she knew publishers were interested in a series and she was too. Of course, it also echoed her father's two nursery-rhyme titles.

In the all-male world of crime fiction, the idea of a woman private eye was revolutionary. PIs were tough guys who guzzled booze, hung out with cops, and were wary of dames. The pioneering novels of Hammett and Chandler had established that women were trouble, liars and even killers, not to be trusted. Grafton, like other women of her generation, loved the novels but hated the sexist stereotypes. In the context of the feminist movement sweeping America, a woman PI was inevitable. Grafton eventually did it best, but she wasn't first.

Marcia Muller's *Edwin of the Iron Shoes* introduced PI Sharon McCone in 1977. Muller, a native of Detroit and a journalist, had two early novels rejected before Michele Slung, an editor at David McKay, liked the idea and urged Muller to try again. She did and Slung (who went on to become a well-known writer on crime fiction) published the result. The oddly named first novel did not attract much notice, and it was five years before a second followed. Since then, Muller has published a long series of Sharon McCone novels, most set in and around San Francisco. In 2004, she was named a Grand Master by the Mystery Writers of America.

By the time Grafton started her novel she had met Steve Humphrey, a good-looking welder eleven years her junior, who lived in her apartment complex. When he went to enter a graduate program in philosophy at Ohio State, she went with him. As a result her ex-husband was awarded custody of her son and daughter. In an interview with Sharon Waxman of *The Washington Post*, Grafton said, "It was death. I should've gotten on a plane and come back." Why hadn't she? "I don't know. It's what I felt I needed to do. It's not justified behavior. It's not behavior I would admire. . . . Perhaps it was my own neediness. My own process. It seemed like the choice I had to make." She kept thinking she would win her children back in court but she never did. Today, having reconciled with her children and become a doting grandmother, she told Waxman, "Having screwed up their little lives, now my job is to be there for them. I'm a much better mother now. I didn't shine at being a mother to toddlers."

Even after Grafton finished her novel, she feared it would never be published, but Marian Wood, then of Henry Holt, quickly bought *Alibi*. She is still Grafton's editor. The series built steadily, and by *G Is for Gumshoe* Grafton was a best seller and had settled into a new life. Her marriage to Humphrey has been a long and happy one. They spend most of their time on a palatial estate in Montecito (it's the nice part of Santa Barbara) but also have a mansion they've restored in Louisville. In Montecito, Grafton can garden, play with her cats, cook in her huge sun-drenched kitchen, entertain her children and grandchildren, and write in the bungalow she had built outside the main house. She jogs around Montecito and Santa Barbara, just as Kinsey jogs around Santa Teresa. Humphrey teaches philosophy part-time at the University of California at Santa Barbara. Grafton answers mail from thousands of her readers and when they say they've named their daughters Kinsey she sends a gift, hand-painted barrettes.

In the Millhone books, the complicated relationship between author and character begins with the fact that Kinsey was orphaned at age five when her parents were killed in a car crash, a traumatic episode in which young Kinsey was trapped for hours with her dead father and dying mother. Five was Grafton's age when her childhood began to fall apart. At that point the lives of the two girls—real and fictional—diverge. Whatever the difficulties of Grafton's childhood, it was a comfortable middle-class life. Kinsey, by contrast, was raised by her tough-minded Aunt Gin ("*No sniveling*") and for a time lived in a trailer. Grafton shrewdly put aside her own origins to give Kinsey a working-class childhood that would make her sympathetic to typists and waitresses and beauticians and clerks who could embrace her as one of their own.

Kinsey is a caustic, opinionated woman who holds back little, and this made her unprecedented in American crime fiction. The classic male PIs tell us little about their inner lives. We know they drink a lot and feel morally superior to the rich and smarter than cops, but we rarely know anything about their childhoods, their marriages, the pain they've suffered, the lovers they've lost. None come close to Kinsey in the sheer volume of personal data we have on them. Sherlockians still debate where Holmes went to university, but we know the name of the bully who tormented Kinsey in the fifth grade. Sam Spade and Philip Marlowe and Lew Archer reflect an American ideal of strong, silent men who never apologize and never explain. Kinsey is the opposite. She wants to share her feelings, wants to connect. In book after book, she adds new depth to her self-portrait. Women love her the way men love Travis McGee. Each is a shrewdly designed fantasy of competence and independence, one written for men, the other for women.

I took a close look at three Millhone novels, *E Is for Evidence* (1988), *M Is for Malice* (1996), and *S Is for Silence* (2005). In the first two, Kinsey becomes involved with a wealthy family and murder follows, along with dark secrets from the past. Both novels, centering on rich, troubled families, recall Ross Macdonald, but Grafton is vastly more fun to read. And while Grafton's plots dig into the past, they are never convoluted. In both books, we learn more about the men in Kinsey's life. In *Evidence,* her "second ex-husband," of whom readers previously knew almost nothing, suddenly reenters her life. In *Malice,* her sometime lover Robert Dietz reappears. Neither stays long.

Evidence begins with Kinsey finding that $5,000 in cash has been deposited to her checking account. A mistake, she thinks, but it turns out to be part of a plot against her. On the novel's third page, she identifies herself for first-time readers: "I'm female, twice divorced, no kids, and no close family ties. I'm a private detective by trade." She adds that she is thirty-two. Kinsey does not age like the rest of us. When Grafton created her, both were in their thirties. Today Grafton is in her sixties and Kinsey (born in 1950) is still in her thirties, still living in the 1980s. Kinsey tells us of her childhood:

> By the time I reached junior high I was a complete misfit, and by high school I'd thrown in my lot with some bad-ass boys, who cussed and smoked dope, two things I mastered at an early age. In spite of the fact that I'm a social oaf, my aunt instilled a solid set of values, which prevailed in the end.

This passage is basic to the characterization: Kinsey may have been wild in her youth, may still be a bit naughty, but deep down she's a good person.

She takes an assignment from an insurance company to investigate a warehouse fire, but soon she is charged with conspiring with the president of the company to file a false claim. The mysterious $5,000 is evidence against her. Kinsey went to school with Ashley Wood, sister of the company president, Lance Wood, so she has lunch with Ashley to find out more about the family. There are five siblings and much bad blood. The novel runs only 200 pages and much of it consists of Kinsey getting to know the Wood siblings, one of whom may be trying to frame her. When she goes to visit the family home, we get this description:

> The house was enormous, done in a French Baroque style—the stucco exterior was as smooth and white as frosting on a wedding cake, roofline and windows edged with plaster garlands, rosettes, and shell motifs that might have been piped out of a pastry tube.

That's in the Chandler mode but with no mention of driving elephants through the front doors or knights saving damsels in the stained glass. Inside, she comments on the sheer magnitude of the house and contrasts it with the two-bedroom stucco bungalow she grew up in, with the pink plastic flamingo out on the lawn, which she thought was pretty classy back then.

She meets with the oldest daughter, the scary, rail-thin Ebony. They have a drink and Ebony plucks the olive from her martini and sucks on her finger: "The gesture had obscene overtones and I wondered suddenly if she was coming on to me." Again, echoes of Marlowe visiting the Sternwoods in *The Big Sleep* and Carmen sucking her thumb, but it's lower-key than Chandler—Ebony doesn't fall into Kinsey's arms or threaten to throw a Buick at her.

The picture of Ebony isn't a pretty one, but sharp, often bitchy descriptions, particularly of other women, are part of Kinsey's naughty-but-nice persona: "Her complexion was still ruddy from last night's application of an acne cure that so far hadn't had much effect"; "She wore a pale-yellow sweater about the hue of certain urine samples I'd seen where the prognosis isn't keen." There's a lot of this.

Halfway through the book, Kinsey is awakened by a knock at the door and her "second ex-husband" appears. She hasn't seen him since he walked out on her eight years earlier. "Daniel Wade is quite possibly the most beautiful man I've ever seen—a bad sign." Wade asks if he can come in. No way, Kinsey says. Eventually she agrees that he can stow his expensive guitar at her place. All this is disconcerting; he hurt her and she still finds it painful to be in his company.

Kinsey goes to the home of Olive, one of the Wood siblings, to help her and her husband, Terry, with a party. Olive picks up a parcel on the front porch and it explodes. Olive is killed and Terry and Kinsey are injured. Another murder follows, of a woman named Lyda Case, whose husband once worked for the company, and a series of revelations begin. Kinsey finds that the guitar that her ex had left in her apartment had a transmitter in it—the sorry so-and-so has bugged her apartment. Kinsey hurries to his motel to confront him and finds him there with his male lover. Despite her concerns about handsome men, Kinsey had not suspected that her ex was bisexual.

We learn that as teenagers two of the Wood siblings had an incestuous relationship. The next revelation is that fingerprints show that Lyda Case was murdered by a man named Emms who had killed someone with a letter bomb twenty years earlier. Kinsey goes home and is confronted by Terry, who has a gun and a bomb and intends to blow her to smithereens. He is the psychopath Emms, who changed his identity before he married into the Wood family.

Even with the bomb ticking, our girl tosses off wisecracks: "How nuts is he? I thought. How far gone? How amenable to reasoning? Would I trade my life for bizarre sexual favors if he asked? Oh, sure, why not?" Instead of offering sex, however, she asks questions and he tells how he's murdered several people. Finally, claiming she needs a Valium, Kinsey picks up her purse, which has her gun in it, and shoots Terry. She is scrambling out the bathroom window when the bomb explodes. She survives, Terry does not, and her landlord builds her a new apartment.

E Is for Evidence is easy reading. The portrait of the worthless ex-husband is interesting, and the final revelations are dramatic, but much of the plot is far-fetched. Kinsey doesn't solve anything; people just tell her the answers. But if you're a fan, it's an enjoyable romp. It's the character of Kinsey, much more than the plots, that sells the books.

M Is for Malice, a stronger novel, opens with the reappearance of Robert Dietz. When she finds him at her door, she says, "Well, look who's here. It's only been two years, four months, and ten days." Kinsey is a woman who keeps score. However, she decides that she now has only mild interest in him.

Before she can deal with Dietz, who wants to stay with her for a few days, she has to have lunch with her cousin Tasha, a lawyer who has a job for her. A man named Bader Malek has died, leaving an estate of $20 million. He had four sons but one of them, Guy, hasn't been seen for years. The remaining brothers want Kinsey to find him—or not find him, in which case they will inherit millions more. Kinsey locates Guy easily; he's living in a nearby town. He wants reconciliation, but his brothers are bitter about his past misdeeds. Kinsey warns him that his brothers are dangerous men. Sure enough, while Guy is sleeping at the family mansion, someone bashes his head in. The police arrest his brother Jack after blood is found on his golf shoes. Kinsey fears he's being framed.

Meanwhile, Kinsey is trying to decide what to do about Robert Dietz, a private investigator who became her lover in *G Is for Gumshoe* and then went to Germany. Theirs is a classic male-female yin-yang relationship. In one scene they try to define their terms.

"Why get enmeshed when all it means is I get to have my heart ripped out?" Kinsey demands.

Being a guy, Dietz says, "Why can't we live in the present?"

Kinsey says she doesn't want an on-again off-again relationship, then blurts out the bitter truth: "People have rejected me all my life. Sometimes it's death or desertion. Infidelity, betrayal. You name it. I've experienced every form of emotional treachery there is."

That is a remarkable outburst for the normally unflappable Kinsey, and it is not hard to find echoes of Grafton's own life in her heroine's pain: her father's absence during the war, her emotional distance from both parents as a girl, her mother's suicide, her separation from her children and her bitter custody battle. All that history must inform Kinsey's anguished cry about rejection, betrayal, and treachery. It's the bleakest moment I came across in the Millhone books and one of the most interesting.

When Kinsey goes to bed with Dietz, she describes it in prose that, for such a tough-minded woman, is quite flowery: "Something about the play of shadows infused the air with a watery element, bathing us both in its transparent glow. It felt as if we were swimming in the shallows, as smooth and graceful as a pair of sea otters tumbling through the surf."

Yuck! I preferred Kinsey's tart postcoital report on her lover's snoring: "Dietz slept like a soldier under combat conditions. His snores were gentle snuffles, just loud enough to keep me on sentry duty but not quite loud enough to draw enemy fire."

Still, it's all designed to please women readers. Liberated Kinsey deals with Dietz as an equal, and when they have sex it's not messy or frustrating but as graceful as otters at play. For a comic note, he snores. Grafton is far more sophisticated than today's chick-lit novelists, but her message can be just as reassuring to the lovelorn.

Kinsey learns that before Guy fled from Santa Teresa, he may have swindled a widow, which raises the possibility that someone in the widow's family killed him for revenge. Kinsey forces a woman working in the Malek house to admit that she is the surviving daughter of the swindled widow. She faked her death, changed her name (like the bomber in *Evidence*), took a job nursing the dying Bader Malek, and sought revenge when Guy came home.

In both *Evidence* and *Malice,* the plots serve mainly as vehicles to let Kinsey work her wiles on us. But *Malice* is different in one notable way. The earlier book was 200 pages; the later one, in my paperback edition, is 337 pages. The difference is not due to a greater complexity of plot so much as it is to the lengthy descriptions of houses, furnishings, people's faces, even a gravel pit, that Grafton lavishes on us. She clearly does not subscribe to Elmore Leonard's rule that you avoid descriptions of people and places and let the reader imagine them. But Grafton has reasons to stress descriptions: first, she's good at them; second, to many readers they lend an aura of authenticity (and the rest of us can skim); and third, insofar as she's often describing hairstyles, home furnishings, and women's clothing, they presumably interest her women readers.

Grafton's success is well known, but I think her achievement has not been fully appreciated. In terms of entertaining commercial crime fiction she ranks with John D. MacDonald and John Sandford as one of the best ever. Indeed, I think the Millhone series is one of the six or eight best any American has written, although it may be hard for some male reviewers to judge its value. Kinsey isn't tough and taciturn like the classic PIs; she's soft and feminine, although in the clutch she'll pull out her trusty H&K P7 and shoot some creep dead. The first thing men readers may notice is the "girly" stuff, Kinsey's preoccupation with her hair and her butt and her romantic frustrations. To appreciate the series, we must understand that it is not only written by and about a woman but for women. We guys can tune in if we choose, but we're not Grafton's core constituency.

Having grasped that, even the most hard-bitten male reader should

come to appreciate her storytelling skills, her consummate professionalism, and the brilliance with which, in book after book, she has built
Kinsey into one of the most beloved characters in American popular
fiction. I don't become as emotionally involved with Kinsey as I do
with, say, Michael Connelly's Harry Bosch, whose obsessions are more
akin to my own. But I recognize that, for many women readers, Kinsey
is a sister, a friend, one of those rare characters that many readers think
of as real rather than made-up.

Grafton is too cute sometimes. The moment when Kinsey, facing
death, makes a joke about distracting the madman with sex is an example. It would not be an unreasonable move in such a situation, but Kinsey doesn't do it, she just wisecracks about it. The passage in which
Kinsey tells us about her youthful fondness for profanity and weed—
but then adds that of course her Aunt Gin's solid values ultimately
prevailed—is an example of Grafton having it both ways. Kinsey agonizes from time to time but it's never the dark night of the soul for her,
never the pain of a Harry Bosch. We know she'll make a joke and move
on. Kinsey is not intended to be a profound or notably deep character
but one with universal appeal, and at that she succeeds.

I am not the first male writer to succumb to the charms of
Grafton/Millhone. In 1994, *The New Yorker*'s Anthony Lane bravely
set out to review all ten novels on the *New York Times* best-seller list.
He was mostly horrified by what he found there and vastly relieved
when he encountered Grafton's *K Is for Killer.* This is part of what he
said:

> "The victims of unsolved homicides I think of as the unruly
> dead," she [Kinsey] says on the opening page. This brought me
> up short; it is a rather beautiful sentence, all the more provoca-
> tive for being mildly archaic, and it's not a freak. Every now and
> then, in the course of a fairly ordinary murder tale, Sue Grafton
> scores a direct hit: "She was strung out on something, throwing
> off that odd crackhead body odor. Her eyes kept sliding upward
> out of focus, like the roll on a TV picture." Saul Bellow wouldn't
> be ashamed to think of that.

High praise from one of our most astute critics.
In recent years a subgenre called chick-lit has sprung up that com-

bines the romance novel with the mystery and features adorable hero-
ines who are at least as interested in shoes and shopping as they are in
solving the crimes that rather improbably come their way. Read a couple of those agonizingly cute novels—nitwit lit, I called it in an unkind
moment—and you will appreciate the balance Grafton has struck between the private-eye tradition and her goal of pleasing women readers.
And please them she does. *P Is for Peril* was the eleventh best-selling
novel in 2001 and *Q Is for Quarry* ranked seventeenth the next year;
both sold around 650,000 copies in hardback.

In *S Is for Silence,* the best of the Millhone novels I've read, Grafton
made an interesting departure. All the others are told by Kinsey in a classic first-person private-eye narrative. In *Silence,* set in 1987, Kinsey is
hired to find out what happened to a woman who vanished thirty-four
years earlier, and as before she gives us a first-person account of her investigation. But in alternating chapters Grafton also gives us a third-
person narrative, set in 1953, in which we see the soon-to-vanish woman
dealing with her husband and daughter and friends and lovers and also
those people interacting with one another. It's a bit distracting to
move back and forth between narrative voices, as well as between time
periods—that's why writers generally go one way or the other—but
those third-person chapters add a new dimension to Grafton's writing.

By using the omniscient narrator, Grafton can move among her
characters, explore their thoughts, and give them a depth that is not
possible in a first-person narrative. It also permits Grafton to give a
poignant picture of two girls of thirteen coping with the challenges of
sex and unloving parents in 1953, the same year Grafton was thirteen
herself. Those flashbacks are a hard-edged tour de force that demon-
strates, if anyone doubted it, that Grafton could write a first-rate novel
without Kinsey Millhone, if she had a mind to. The book enjoyed a
long run near the top of the best-seller lists.

In future novels, Grafton might go back to a first-person narrative
or she might try a novel entirely in the third person. I for one would
love to see it. But the important thing is that, like all the best writers of
serials, she is experimenting, seeking ways to maintain both her own
interest and that of her readers. At an age when she could be forgiven
for slowing down, Grafton declares that she's determined to carry her
"alphabet series" all the way to Z. To which even the most jaded reader
can only say: You go, girl.

PARETSKY & POLITICS

Sara Paretsky and I were once seated together when she spoke at a Book World event. It was an election year, and it didn't take us long to establish that we are both yellow-dog Democrats. In fact, Paretsky writes the most unabashedly liberal novels of any major American novelist in memory. There are plenty of right-wingers producing Clancy-style thrillers in which spineless liberals in the White House (often Harvard grads who "never married") are selling out America, but liberal voices are rare. To write ideological novels, particularly if you're a liberal, has its risks. Paretsky tells of "a reader who was so furious she covered four pages by hand, demanding to know why my books are 'infested' with political issues. 'When I buy a mystery I expect to be entertained and when you bring in all that stuff about homeless people, you aren't entertaining me.' " Paretsky, as is her practice, sent the unhappy reader back the price of the novel.

Paretsky continued, in an essay:

> I thought of writing her back to say, But mysteries are political. Peter Wimsey staunchly defends an England where everyone knows his (or her) place and is happy in it. Philip Marlowe and Sam Spade inhabit a landscape filled with explicit sexual politics. . . . Mysteries, like cops, are right up against the place where people's basest and basic needs intersect with law and justice. They are by definition political. I'm an entertainer, but the stories that come to me are almost always those of voiceless people, not those of the powerful.

Paretsky grew up in a world of conservative conformity: Lawrence, Kansas, in the 1950s. But her family was different. Her grandparents met walking a picket line, and she describes her family as "eccentric outsiders in a Protestant and Republican landscape when it came to religion or civil rights." Still, Paretsky's parents conformed with the sexual politics of the era. The only girl in a household of boys, she was expected to focus on housework and eventual marriage, not on preparing for a career. The summer she was nineteen she discovered a different world. Amid the turmoil of the late sixties, she went to Chicago to do community-service work. "Everyone around me felt powerless, the blacks denied access to jobs and decent housing, the whites living just half a rung above on the economic ladder and clinging to it in panic." She went home to Kansas for a degree in political science and then returned to Chicago. She earned an MBA, which led to ten years as marketing manager for an insurance company. She hated her job and dreamed of writing fiction. She loved detective novels but resented the way women were presented, as either evil or powerless. She conceived a smart, tough, likable woman private investigator, from a blue-collar background, called V. I. (Vic) Warshawski.

Paretsky wrote her first three novels at night, while working full time and managing a home for her husband and stepsons. It took her agent a year to find a publisher for her first novel, *Indemnity Only,* which came out in 1982, the same year as Grafton's *A Is for Alibi.* Paretsky's novel had a first edition of 4,500 copies, of which 2,500 sold to libraries. She credits that sale with persuading her publisher to buy her second, *Deadlock.* Her bosses grumbled that her writing was detracting from her corporate obligations. Suddenly her luck changed. After her third novel, *Killing Orders,* came out, Disney bought the rights to V. I. Warshawski and converted them into a terrible movie starring Kathleen Turner. The movie pained Paretsky, but the money enabled her to quit her job and write full-time. (Sue Grafton has vowed never, never, never to let Hollywood get its hands on Kinsey Millhone.)

Paretsky's novels have become ever more political. She took several years to write *Ghost Country,* a stand-alone that appeared in 1998. It's a powerful, compassionate story about homeless women in Chicago. The next year Vic was back with *Hard Time,* which dealt with police corruption, prison abuse, and immigration issues. Next she published *Total Recall,* which took on reparations for the descendants of slaves and the appearance of a supposed Holocaust survivor. Finally, in *Blacklist,* her first post-9/11 novel, Paretsky combines one plot line that involves fifties McCarthyism with another about abuses under the Patriot Act.

Paretsky's anger about the Patriot Act has been expressed in lectures as well as her books. Her speech "Truth, Lies, and Duct Tape" denounces the Bush administration's willingness to examine library records, intimidate librarians, suppress free speech, and arrest people without warrants or evidence. To Paretsky, libraries are sacred places, not to be despoiled by government agents.

THE TALENTED MS. HIGHSMITH

The shadow of Patricia Highsmith looms large over all crime fiction by American women. Highsmith (1921–95) was born in that literary hotbed, Fort Worth, but escaped to New York at an early age. She studied literature at Columbia and wrote a classic first novel, 1950's *Strangers on a Train,* which became one of Alfred Hitchcock's best movies. Highsmith was gay and she followed her initial success with *The Price of Salt,* in which two women lovers are blackmailed. She wound up publishing that novel under a pseudonym. In 1955, Highsmith introduced the charming psychopath Tom Ripley in *The Talented Mr. Ripley.* She would, over a forty-year period, produce four Ripley sequels, along with other novels and many short stories.

Highsmith spent most of her adult life in France and Switzerland. Her writing was more appreciated in Europe and her lifestyle more readily accepted. Her novels are distinguished by menace, dread, deception, sexual ambiguity, and casual violence, and there was little context for them in the America of the 1950s and 1960s. Her view of humankind was closer to Poe's than to Agatha Christie's, and she saw the crime novel as an ideal vehicle to express it. *Crime and Punishment,* she once observed, was one of the greatest novels of suspense. Recent biographies of Highsmith, and a successful new movie of *The Talented Mr. Ripley,* focused new attention on her; she is more celebrated in America today than she ever was during her life. Highsmith was ahead of her time but the times have caught up, and her influence can be seen in writers ranging from Thomas Harris to women like Val McDermid, Karin Slaughter, and Mo Hayder.

Both Highsmith and Agatha Christie, in their vastly different ways, proved that women could be masters of crime fiction, and with the commercial success of Grafton and Paretsky, thrillers by women writers have proliferated. Patricia Cornwell's series about medical examiner Kay Scarpetta has had huge sales. Donna Leon, an American who lives in Venice, writes a much-admired series about the pleasure-loving, world-weary Commissario Guido Brunetti. Alafair Burke, a lawyer and daughter of James Lee Burke, has begun a series about a female deputy district attorney. Former journalist Laura Lippman has won praise for her Baltimore-based mysteries. Nevada Barr writes a successful series about park ranger Anna Pigeon. Karin Slaughter has begun a tough-minded series about a woman doctor who confronts violence in a small Georgia town. We will get to some of these women, but first let's note that, once women proved they could write best-selling thrillers, America's lawyers were not far behind.

8.

Lawyers at Large:

Turow, Grisham, Lescroart

For many years, America's best-known fictional lawyer was Erle Stanley Gardner's Perry Mason, who rarely lost a case in a long series of courtroom dramas. Gardner was a California lawyer who turned to fiction in the 1930s and wrote 150 novels, most in three weeks or less. In the novels of Hammett, Chandler, and Cain, lawyers are generally either scheming prosecutors who try to put the hero in jail or shysters who try to keep him out—either way, objects of scorn and derision, never as heroic as a private eye. The success of Robert Traver's *Anatomy of a Murder* in 1958 was a literary curiosity— a novel-writing judge was as unlikely then as a dancing pig.

Thus, when Chicago lawyer Scott Turow set out to write a novel about lawyers, one he intended to be both serious and commercial, he had little to guide him, although he was well versed in both law and literature. After graduating from Amherst, he spent five years in Stanford's creative writing program, both as student and teacher. In 1975, he entered Harvard Law School and proceeded to write *One L,* a bestselling account of his first year there. Upon graduation, he returned to his hometown of Chicago and spent eight years as an assistant U.S. attorney before joining a private firm. In his spare time he began writing a novel about a prosecutor named Rusty Sabich who is accused of murdering his mistress. He called it *Presumed Innocent.*

Turow generally cites Saul Bellow and Dickens as the greatest influences on his writing, but when I asked about other influences, he elaborated.

I had grown up on TV shows like Perry Mason and Sherlock Holmes and, when I got older, so-called "serious" fiction. The real inklings I had that suspense could serve "serious" purposes came from Conrad, Graham Greene, and, in a contemporary setting, le Carré and P. D. James. I wrote a mystery because I wanted to make some use of my experiences as a prosecutor and because I was sick of having my "serious" efforts rejected. When I finished *Presumed Innocent,* my bet would have been that I'd fallen between the stools—too serious to be commercial, too genre to be serious. But I gave no thought about how, or whether, I was departing from what had been written about lawyers before. During the summer I was finishing the first draft, I took *Anatomy of a Murder* out of the library, started on it—I'd read it as a child—then put it aside. I can't say why except it treated lawyering and the legal system with less detachment than I liked. At the end of the day, in thinking about this question frequently as I have in the years since, I note three things about *Presumed Innocent* and the books that followed: (1) A greater emphasis on legal procedures. I tried to be scrupulously accurate, and that turned out to meet the tastes of a public increasingly curious about law. (2) A view of lawyers as fallible. Rusty is a flawed man, unlike, say, Atticus Finch of *To Kill a Mockingbird,* and that too reflects public perceptions of the legal profession. And (3) the era when this arose, the eighties, the me-decade, the time of the market *über alles.* The law, at least in the popular mind, is a repository of values that aren't determined by what's selling.

Presumed Innocent did not fall unnoticed between the stools of literature and commerce. It was a Dual Main Selection of the Literary Guild, was made into an excellent movie, and ranked seventh in sales among American novels in 1987. It is, in fact, a remarkable marriage of craft and commercialism. It makes demands on the reader, but its mixture of sex, murder, law, politics, rage, duplicity, suspense, and human weakness made it irresistible to serious readers. Turow had invented what would soon become a thriving genre, the legal thriller. Moreover, he was one of those artists—like Ernest Hemingway, like Louis Armstrong—who not only did something first but did it best. Another lawyer would follow who sold more books, but no one has written a better novel about American lawyers than Turow his first time out.

Turow's second novel, *The Burden of Proof,* ranked third in sales in 1990. It was also the best of the fifteen novels on the list, which included works by Stephen King, Jean M. Auel, Sidney Sheldon, Danielle Steel, Robert Ludlum, Jackie Collins, Anne Rice, and Judith Krantz. Turow aside, it was an undistinguished year for American fiction, but the times were still a-changing. The next year, 1991, a new name appeared on the list for the first time, a name that would soon dominate it. John Grisham was also a lawyer, but one blessed with an ability to reach a mass audience that was beyond Turow's and, for that matter, beyond that of just about anyone who ever wrote fiction in America.

UP FROM CLANTON

John Grisham was born in 1955 and grew up in Jonesboro, Arkansas, the son of a construction worker and a homemaker. The family moved to Southaven, Mississippi, in 1967, and Grisham went on to attend Mississippi State University and then law school at Ole Miss. He practiced law in Southaven for a decade, and in 1983 he was elected to the state legislature, where he served for six years. But the young lawyer had more on his mind than politics. He had come of age during painful years of racial conflict, and he was well aware of the injustice, hypocrisy, and violence around him. In court one day, he watched the anguished testimony of a twelve-year-old rape victim. The scene planted an idea: What if the girl's father had in his rage murdered the rapist? Would a jury convict him of murder? What if the father was black and the rapist white?

Grisham started rising at dawn and writing before he left for the courthouse. If he had a model, it was Harper Lee's 1960 classic *To Kill a Mockingbird,* in which Atticus Finch defends a black man accused of raping a white woman in a small Alabama town. But Grisham's *A Time to Kill* is a far harsher novel than Lee's. It opens with an almost unreadable account of the rape of the black girl by two rednecks. Soon the girl's father kills the rapists. Grisham's hero, Jack Brigance, who defends the father, is not a saintly lawyer like Atticus Finch. His very name suggests brigand and the fictional town of Clanton suggests Klan town. America's publishers were not impressed by Grisham's tale of backwoods crime and punishment. Sixteen agents declined to represent him and a dozen publishers rejected the novel before *A Time to Kill* was finally bought by Wynwood Press and given a modest first printing. Like most first novels, it sank like a stone.

Grisham, undaunted, was soon at work on a second, but this time he made an adjustment. *A Time to Kill* is a rough, often ugly story. A lot of readers would never get past that first rape scene. Grisham learned from the failure of his first novel. When he began his second, *The Firm,* he devised a more fanciful and more commercial plot: A young lawyer is hired by what appears to be a blue-chip law firm but turns out to be controlled by the mob. The novel was bought by Paramount Pictures for $600,000, whereupon Doubleday bought it for book publication. It became the nation's seventh best-selling novel in 1991.

Grisham's next, *The Pelican Brief,* starts with two Supreme Court justices being murdered and puts a beautiful young law student and a fearless young investigative reporter on the case. With these and other larger-than-life plots, Grisham became one of the mega-selling novelists of the nineties, often jousting with Clancy and King for the top spot on the annual best-seller list. His *The Brethren* led all novels in sales in 2000. Then, in *The Summons,* he seemed to change his formula. Ray Atlee is a forty-three-year-old law professor at the University of Virginia. One day he receives a letter from his ailing father to come home to Clanton and discuss the father's will. Ray must obey—this is the "summons" of the title—but he dreads the trip, because he has been estranged from his father, a judge, and he isn't anxious to see his brother, who has fallen into drug abuse.

When Ray arrives at his father's decaying mansion, he finds the older man dead and three million dollars in cash. Ray makes a snap decision to tell no one about the money, lest a scandal darken his father's good name—and lest the IRS demand a healthy cut. The rest of the novel is devoted to answering two questions: Where did the money come from and can Ray stay ahead of the people who are hot on his trail? It's not a courtroom drama, but *The Summons* is a virtual handbook on how to write commercial fiction. Grisham abides by the old rule to write what you know, for he knows plenty about the law and about Mississippi. He is also careful about what he puts into his story, which contains virtually no sex, dirty talk, or violence. You can give this novel to your maiden aunt without fear of offending. Nor does Grisham have anything to say about race relations, although he is back in Clanton, the scene of racial violence in *A Time to Kill*. This is a kinder, gentler Clanton.

What Grisham does offer is a surefire plot. Finding millions in cash is an appealing fantasy and, if it happened to most of us, we might behave as foolishly as Ray. (If he behaves sensibly, there's no novel.) Grisham tightens the suspense as Ray races about the South with the cash in his trunk and unknown parties in pursuit. He weaves in the classic themes of father-son conflict and sibling rivalry, and touches a couple of trendy bases when Ray checks out one of Mississippi's new gambling casinos and when he boards a yacht to dine with one of those southern lawyers who've grown rich off class-action lawsuits. Grisham grabs you and won't let go. That's the X factor. Anyone can cook up a sexy plot, but not one writer in thousands can produce a seamless story with close to universal appeal. *The Summons* is neither a particularly good novel nor a particularly bad one, but it goes down like candy. It was the nation's best-selling novel in 2002, around 2.6 million copies.

A year later, Grisham was back with a very different novel, *The King of Torts,* a scathing attack on lawyers who have gotten rich by winning class-action suits against the tobacco industry, pharmaceutical companies, and other corporate malefactors. These mass tort boys, as Grisham calls them, are presented as shameless, greed-crazed ambulance chasers who enrich themselves off the misery of others and whose real goal is ever-younger women and ever-larger yachts. I can't think of another major American novelist who has so relentlessly bludgeoned one professional group since Sinclair Lewis went after businessmen in *Babbitt* and fundamentalist preachers in *Elmer Gantry.*

The novel is a morality tale of sorts, centering on a broke and disillusioned young public defender in Washington named Clay Carter. He is losing his girlfriend because he has no money and little ambition. Then the devil, dressed in black and calling himself Max Pace, makes Carter an offer he can't refuse. Pace will set the young lawyer up with his own firm and bring him class-action suits that will make him rich. All this comes to pass, and we learn a lot about class-action lawsuits, but of course money doesn't bring happiness. As Carter seeks to win his old girlfriend back, Grisham wants to show us that love conquers all, but he writes better about tort law and Gulfstream jets than he does about women.

Grisham's polemic didn't appear in a vacuum. Tort law is one of the few issues that have clearly divided Democrats and Republicans in recent years, and the lawyers Grisham is attacking contribute heavily to Democratic candidates. Grisham's novel gave support to Republicans who were working to limit awards in class-action lawsuits. One of the strengths of Grisham's novels has been plots that glorify the little guy who stands up against powerful forces, but it's hard to tell a David and Goliath story with Big Tobacco and the drug companies as David. But Grisham tries.

At the end of the novel, Carter renounces wealth and even the law, and he and his true love go off to be poor and happy together. I checked the comments on Amazon.com and found a barrage of complaints from Grisham's fans. They mostly found it boring and/or confusing and the ending sappy. *Give up millions?* This is not to say the novel was a flop. *The King of Torts* was the nation's third best-selling hardback in 2003, with some 2.3 million copies sold, down about ten percent from *The Summons*.

The writer that Grisham most reminds me of is James Michener, whose best sellers began in the fifties and continued into the nineties. The two men's subject matter is dissimilar—Michener wrote long, awesomely researched historical novels—but both are great storytellers and both are middlebrows in the best sense of the word. They're intelligent without being intimidating, they don't offend, and they reach out to the largest possible audience. They are also, from all reports, very decent men, who've donated generously to various good causes. Of the megaselling novelists of recent years—a list that includes Tom Clancy, Danielle Steel, James Patterson, Stephen King, Patricia Cornwell, and not many others—Grisham is easily the best writer, no small distinction.

THE BARTENDER'S TALE

America's publishers are desperately seeking the next Grisham and so far the closest they've come is John Lescroart, who writes an excellent series about two friends, a lawyer and a detective, in San Francisco. Lescroart isn't a lawyer. His history is far more complicated than that. He graduated in 1970 from the University of California at Berkeley, where he was an English major. He wrote his first novel in college and his second soon thereafter. The problem was, he didn't try to publish them. He spent his twenties singing in a rock band in Bay Area bars, but when he turned thirty he gave that up and wrote a novel called *Sunburn,* based on his travels in Spain. Not knowing anyone in publishing, he showed it to his high school teacher, who wasn't impressed. But the teacher's wife liked it and submitted it to an annual competition for the best novel by a Californian, which it won.

Sunburn wasn't published for another four years, and then only in paperback, but Lescroart began to think he could be a writer. For the next few years he wrote unpublished novels while supporting himself at everything from computer programmer to moving man, house-painter, and bartender. One day his wife, Lisa, persuaded him to dig out his fourteen-year-old draft of *Son of Holmes* (about a French spy during World War I who may be the great detective's offspring) and send it to a publisher. Six weeks later he had his first hardback book deal. Soon two more were published, but he still wasn't making a living at it.

In 1989, at forty-one, Lescroart went body-surfing and contracted spinal meningitis from contaminated sea water. He lay near death for eleven days, and when he recovered he quit his job and returned to the Bay Area to write. *Dead Irish* in 1989 and *The Vig* in 1990 had introduced Dismas Hardy, a bartender and ex-lawyer in San Francisco. Lescroart didn't know he was starting a series, but one began to take shape with *Hard Evidence* in 1993. He paired Hardy, the lawyer, with Abe Glitsky, a homicide detective, and made them friends who are sometimes on opposite sides in court. When *The 13th Juror* became a paperback best seller, he knew that Hardy and Glitsky were a team. Lescroart says that he read *Presumed Innocent* when he started the

Hardy-Glitsky series and it had a profound influence, showing him that a novel about a lawyer could go deep into character.

Lescroart is an old-fashioned writer. The great strength of his work lies in his characterizations and his ability to set his legal battles in a believable world. Hardy and Glitsky were once young policemen together. Glitsky is a hard case—"half black and half Jewish and every inch of him scary-looking"—while Hardy is the romantic. He advanced from police work to law but "when his first marriage broke up in the wake of the accidental death of his son, he took close to a dozen years off to tend bar and contemplate the universe through a haze of Guinness stout." Eventually, Hardy sobers up, marries the admirable Frannie, and returns to the law. Don't read Lescroart's novels if you don't want to know about the two men's wives and ex-wives, their children, their friends, and assorted cops, lawyers, politicians, and criminals, because the author cares about them all. He also cares about San Francisco and describes its views and neighborhoods in loving detail.

I discovered Lescroart in 2002 when *The Oath*, a hard look at crime and corruption in a big-city hospital, turned up for review. I closed my review by comparing it with *The Summons:*

> Both men are skilled professionals who mostly write legal thrillers. The difference is that Grisham, a supremely commercial writer, keeps his focus simple, whereas Lescroart has a taste for complexity. Grisham gives us a fable about a man who finds a fortune and soon is running for his life. His book is more fun. Lescroart's is more interesting and, by my standards, a better novel, although he will be lucky to earn a tenth of the royalties of Grisham's surefire best seller.

In 2005, when Lescroart published his thirteenth Hardy-Glitsky novel, *The Motive,* his publisher claimed that he had sold ten million books worldwide. In the novel, Hardy is representing his first love from high school, who is charged with murdering her rich father-in-law and his girlfriend. We and Hardy don't know if she's guilty or not, only that she's a formidable woman who might be capable of murder. What we do know is that both the prosecutor and the lead detective in her case are far more interested in gaining a conviction than in worrying about her possible innocence. It's an important point. Defense attorneys have argued for years that the prisons are filled with innocent people, victims of ambitious, over-zealous, bigoted, incompetent, or crooked cops and prosecutors. In recent years, DNA evidence has proved that to be true in a growing number of cases.

The Motive brings us up to date on Hardy and Glitsky's personal lives. Glitsky and his wife have a child born with a life-threatening heart condition (as did Lescroart and his wife), and this becomes a major element in the book. There is one lovely scene when Hardy is fixing dinner with his family and his friend Glitsky. I want to quote it at length:

> Frannie showed up a few steps behind her daughter. Her wind-blown red hair, which she'd been growing long for some months now, fell below her shoulders, and her color was high after all day in the sun. She was wearing khaki shorts and a pink tank top, and her green eyes were sparkling.
>
> Hardy found himself struck by a sudden contentment so acute that it felt for a moment like a hot blade through his heart.
>
> The sun was low enough in the late afternoon that it made it through the picture window in the front of the house, spraying the hardwood in the dining room with an amber glow that reflected all the way up and into the kitchen. Behind him, over the sink, the window was open and a still unseasonably warm breeze tickled the back of his neck. The smell of the gumbo was intoxicating, both of the women in his family were smiling and almost too lovely to believe, and his son and best friend were working with him to make something everybody would love to eat. Everything dear to him was close, safe and protected in this room, on a perfect day.

You don't often find writing like that in thrillers, because if the writer doesn't believe it and do it well, it's going to be sappy. Even done well, it's not what many people want to read. But Lescroart believes it, and does it well, and if there are impatient readers who came just for the courtroom scenes, the author has long since decided not to worry about them.

Lescroart doesn't write about the Mafia taking over law firms or Supreme Court justices being assassinated. Hardy and Glitsky pretty much do what defense lawyers and detectives do in big cities. That's why I find Lescroart's novels superior to Grisham's. They're just as entertaining and a lot more real—and, all things being equal, reality is the place for a novelist to be.

OTHER TALENT

I want to mention five other lawyers-turned-novelists whose work I've enjoyed.

Robert Reuland is a graduate of Vanderbilt Law School and practices in New York. He has published two novels, each with bang-bang titles: *Hollowpoint* and *Semiautomatic*. Despite its title, *Semiautomatic* is notable not for violence but for subtle characterizations, moral ambiguities, and graceful prose. It is set in a Brooklyn DA's office such as Reuland once worked in and concerns a prosecutor named Andrew Giobberti who has been banished from the homicide office for bungling a case. Suddenly he's given a chance to redeem himself. Gio is suspicious of the DA's motives but agrees to work on the case with a beautiful but inexperienced young African-American lawyer. The murder case provides the plot, but the novel's great virtue is its fresh, lyrical writing.

Small grace notes enliven page after page. An old judge lusts after the woman lawyer "only in darting hooded glances." That judge, without his black robe, "is the janitor again." A juror "has the soft, indistinct features of someone who owns cats." A dying man looked bad before, but "Now he is circling the drain." A shyster lawyer's "tie has gone belly up, a dog wanting a scratch." As Gio moves about Brooklyn, remembering homicides past,

> the borough is, for me, awash in blood, and there are some blocks where I cannot shake the ghosts in certain doorways and vacant lots, on stoops and manhole covers. All around them, unaware, children play. Women push strollers and shop. Old men sit on benches where dead boys leer at them. From my car win-

dow I see them. Do the living not know, or do they forget? And if they have forgotten, how do they do it? I would like to know.

Reuland's sensibility is closer to John Updike's than to John Grisham's, but he never lets us forget that he's a lawyer, one with a touch of the poet:

> I loved standing up. I loved picking a jury, winnowing out the twelve solid citizens who could do business. I loved making an opening statement, telling my jurors how I would tear away the thin veneer of civilization that separated them from the man over there. I loved the judges who slept during testimony. I loved the defense lawyers who worked with what they had and knew the score. I loved the witnesses who hated my guts. The cops who never showed up when I needed them but, when they eventually did, would sometimes bring a cup of coffee as an apology. The families of the dead boys. The mothers and sisters and aunts who came to court dressed as if for church and looked to me with unreasonable hope and apologized sometimes.

This is a different sort of legal thriller, one for readers who understand that good writing is the biggest thrill of all.

Stephen Horn is a former Justice Department prosecutor, and his second novel, *Law of Gravity*, is a smart mix of legal thriller and sophisticated political novel. His plot turns on one simple fact: A presidential campaign is in progress. In Horn's mind, this clearly means that anything is possible, including homicide, and who among us will disagree? Senator Warren Young is the front-runner for his party's nomination, but a problem arises. One of his trusted aides vanishes in a case that might involve espionage and could derail Young's candidacy. Enter Philip Barkley, a Justice Department lawyer who is close to being fired. The attorney general offers him a deal. If he will head an investigation that finds there is no espionage, he will be rewarded with a new start in life. Barkley takes the assignment but can't follow through because there's too much evidence of espionage. Barkley is fired from Justice but continues investigating the missing Senate aide. The political novel then becomes a thriller, as witnesses turn up dead and Barkley finds killers on his trail. This is finally a novel about an honest man confronting a corrupt political establishment, and it is entirely persuasive.

By and large, one does not think of lawyers as funny, but lawyer/novelist William Lashner had me laughing out loud. Philadelphia lawyer Victor Carl, the reluctant hero of *Past Due,* Lashner's grandly entertaining fourth novel, introduces himself thusly:

> My legal practice was failing for want of paying clients and my partner was thinking of bolting to greener pastures. My last love affair ended badly, to say the least. I had been summoned to Traffic Court for a myriad of moving violations that were really, really not my fault. My mother, to whom I had not spoken in a number of years, was drinking her life away in Arizona. My father was deathly ill, awaiting the operation that would prolong, but not save, his life. And worst of all, my cable had been cut off because I had fallen behind on my bill.

Most crime-fiction protagonists are either tough guys or wise guys, and Victor Carl is in the latter camp. A client called Joey Cheaps is found with his throat cut; worse, he owed Carl $3,500. Carl sweet-talks Joey's mother into signing a contingency agreement that could enrich them both if the lawyer can find the killer and bring a wrongful-death suit. His investigation soon leads to a twenty-year-old murder case in which Joey Cheaps may have killed a drug dealer named Tommy Greeley. Tommy had many friends and lovers who might have wished him dead, including a right-wing judge, a mob boss, a biker, and an overweight lesbian. These and other bizarre characters inhabit a great spinning whirligig of a plot that threatens to take on a life of its own.

Before he turned to fiction, Lashner toiled in the Justice Department's criminal division. Somewhere along the line he read his Hammett and Chandler. When police summon Carl to identify Joey's body in the middle of the night, we think of Sam Spade called to the scene of his partner's death. So many people are in search of Tommy Greeley's long-missing suitcase, supposedly stuffed with drug money, that I renamed the novel *The Maltese Suitcase,* and when a mysterious fellow named Eddie Dean entered the story I could not but recall the ineffable Eddie Mars in *The Big Sleep*. Carl even calls someone a gunsel, a word not much heard since Hammett's heyday.

Dylan Schaffer is another lawyer blessed with a sense of humor. His daffy, delightful first novel, *Misdemeanor Man*, concerned a San Francisco public defender named Gordon (Gordo) Seegerman, who is representing a fellow charged with exposing himself in a shopping mall. Gordo's real passion, however, is not the law but Barry Manilow—or, as Gordo calls his hero, MBM, for Mister Barry Manilow. Gordo's main concern about the flasher case is to get it settled, because his Manilow cover band, Barry X and the Mandys, has an upcoming gig that MBM himself may attend. But first the lawyer must deal with the fellow who allegedly exposed himself—the wanker, Gordo calls him. In legal thrillers, of course, no case is ever simple, and the alleged flashing soon expands to encompass murder, conspiracy, and millions of dollars. Schaffer handles all this deftly, but he keeps coming back to MBM. Is it possible that Schaffer is putting us on with all this Barrymania? No. The man loves his Manilow. Indeed, his second novel was fearlessly titled *I Right the Wrongs*.

In 2005 a law professor named Kermit Roosevelt published a first novel called *In the Shadow of the Law*. Roosevelt, a great-grandson of TR, had clerked for Supreme Court Justice David Souter and then gone into private practice before becoming an assistant professor of law at the University of Pennsylvania. Some reviewers compared Roosevelt's novel to *Presumed Innocent,* but that is overly generous. Turow's novel has a brilliant plot, whereas the plot of *In the Shadow of the Law* is its weakest point. Rather, it is an extended meditation on the law and lawyers: readable, informed, sophisticated, often devastating. We take a panoramic look at a supremely avaricious blue-chip Washington firm. We meet its idealistic now-deceased founder and his son, who lives to amass more money. We linger on four young associates, graduates of top law schools who are paid $125,000 a year to be, in effect, factory workers whose product is more and more billable hours. No one has a satisfying personal life and few have any illusions.

One of the most vivid characters is a former Supreme Court clerk whom we take to be in some degree autobiographical. He loves the law—"the law itself, in its pureness and intricacy"—but is bored and repelled by its practice. He knows he will never again be as happy as he was in his days as a Supreme Court clerk. By the end of the novel he is pursing law-school teaching posts. *In the Shadow of the Law* is a caustic but probably accurate portrait of the money mania of big law firms: "You're not supposed to get work done. You're supposed to bill hours." Young people considering the law could read *In the Shadow of the Law* for its cautionary value. Those already in the profession may wonder whether to laugh or cry.

9.

Spy Masters:

McCarry, Littell, Silva, Furst

The talented American spy novelists who started to emerge in the 1970s were less likely to look for inspiration to Hammett and Chandler than to Hemingway and Fitzgerald and, most of all, to the great British spy novelists. For many years, our British brethren owned the novel of espionage and international intrigue. From John Buchan's *The Thirty-nine Steps* and Somerset Maugham's *Ashenden* to Eric Ambler's *A Coffin for Dimitrios* to Graham Greene's *This Gun for Hire* and *The Human Factor,* the Brits set the standard. Still, a milestone was reached when the writer who called himself John le Carré (real name David Cornwell) published *The Spy Who Came in from the Cold,* America's best-selling novel in 1964. Le Carré's background in British intelligence and his masterly writing skills, brought to bear on the complexities of the Cold War, made him not only the greatest of spy novelists but one of the best novelists of the late twentieth century.

Le Carré raised the bar on both sides of the Atlantic, as well as showing that first-rate spy novels could command a vast international audience. He was, if not the first novelist to appreciate the dramatic possibilities of the Cold War, the first with a talent large enough to translate that vision into a major body of work.

The other notable British spy novelist of le Carré's era was Frederick Forsyth, whose *The Day of the Jackal* appeared in 1971 and told the riveting story of a paid assassin who sets out to kill Charles de Gaulle. The authorities get wind of the plot and a nationwide game of cat-and-mouse ensues as the resourceful Jackal uses disguises, forged papers, concealed weapons, and homicide to move ever closer to his target. It's an audacious concept—we know that de Gaulle died peacefully—but Forsyth made his conceit viable with his intricate portrait of an assassin at work.

Granting the high standards set by le Carré and Forsyth, a new generation of American spy novelists soon began to produce a body of work that has surpassed that of current British writers. The four most important are Charles McCarry, Robert Littell, Daniel Silva, and Alan Furst.

SPY AND SUPERHERO

Charles McCarry was born in 1930 and spent ten years working as an undercover CIA operative in Europe, Africa, and Asia. His first novel, *The Miernik Dossier*, appeared in 1973, when he was forty-three. It introduced his spy hero Paul Christopher, who has been featured in seven novels so far. All the Christopher novels are of interest, but *The Tears of Autumn* (1974) is McCarry's masterpiece. I reread it warily, after twenty-odd years, but my fear that it would not hold up was groundless. *The Tears of Autumn* is, as I remembered it, beautifully written, a classic. What rereading did was remind me that I have one reservation about it.

I'm going to lay out the plot of *The Tears of Autumn,* both because you probably already know it and because if you don't you will, fifty or sixty pages into the novel. Soon after the November 22, 1963, assassination of President Kennedy, when many Americans blamed the Russians or Fidel Castro, Christopher figures out who was really behind the crime. It was the family of the South Vietnamese leaders Ngo Dinh Diem and Ngo Dinh Nhu, who were assassinated on November 1 in a coup that Kennedy approved. His assassination, three weeks later, was revenge. But Christopher's superiors in the White House reject his theory, which might complicate their plan to save South Vietnam from communism, so he quits the CIA and sets out to prove it on his own.

His quest takes him all around the world and exposes him to great danger, but in time he has evidence.

McCarry's years as an undercover operative serve him well. Some of the best scenes in the novel show Christopher meeting with a variety of revolutionaries, rogues, and killers who can help him. But the novel also offers an idealized portrait of the spy as patriot and superhero. Christopher is blessed not only with uncommon intelligence, physical beauty, and personal charm but with such courage that he will gladly give his life for his country or simply in pursuit of the truth. Christopher's superiority is many-sided. He published a volume of poetry in his youth. Many people believe he can read minds. Like Sam Spade and Philip Marlowe, but operating on a worldwide stage, he is fearless and charismatic; other men defer to him and women adore him.

When an arrogant Kennedy aide denounces Christopher, a CIA official replies, "Three things: first, he's intelligent and entirely unsentimental. Second, he will go to any lengths to get the truth; he never gives up. Third, he is not subject to fear." Later, this man, who is Christopher's close friend, tells him, "Your whole career has been a series of moral lessons for the rest of us. *You* won't use a gun. *You* won't betray an agent. *You* won't give support to a regime that tortures political prisoners." There is a great deal more of this, and if I didn't admire the novel so much I would grow weary of Christopher's virtues. But McCarry's idealization of Christopher is the price we pay for McCarry's silken prose and his insights into the world of spies, politics, and assassinations.

Has this paragon no weaknesses? At least one: Early in his life, he was a lousy judge of women. He married Cathy, a lovely girl but with certain failings. "She had superstitions but no ideas." "She was beautiful and wanted to be nothing else." Although Christopher "bought her jewels and clothes and read to her," she repays his travels and secrecy by taking a lover, a drug-using America-hating Italian actor and Maoist—a combination designed to make Christopher crazy. "She would come home to Christopher, still wet, and want to make love." In drawing the duplicitous sex-hungry Cathy, McCarry echoes Raymond Chandler's theme of "woman as destroyer," even as he underscores Christopher's saintly forgiveness of her. Even his name, Paul Christopher, is about as saintly as you can get.

McCarry is a classicist. Many of his European scenes could be taken from *The Sun Also Rises* or *A Farewell to Arms*. Thus:

Finally they went to Siena. Christopher wanted to be in a quiet place. For a week he thought of nothing but Molly. They walked through the old town with its thin campanile and its buildings that were the color of dry earth. The afternoons turned cold and they lay in bed, reading a novel aloud to one another. They drank hot chocolate with sweet Italian brandy in it. They woke each other often in the night. Afterward, Molly pushed her heavy hair away from her face and looked down, smiling, into Christopher's face.

Late in the novel, Christopher shares a train compartment with three nuns:

One of the nuns peeled an orange and handed it to him, with the skin arranged around the fruit like the pointed leaves of a lily. She was young, with a sensual face from which prayer had scrubbed all traces of desire. However, the pretty orange, handed across the compartment as if she were feeding a horse and was wary of its teeth, was as much a gift of flirtation as of charity.

The nun and her orange have nothing to do with the story. This glimpse of her is simply a lovely moment, lovingly described. And yet there is this subtext: Christopher is so pure, so dazzling, that even virginal nuns flirt with him.

The idealization of the hero is a convention of series novels—why keep writing about someone if he's not special?—but some writers mask it by adding imperfections to the mix. That's one reason so many fictional detectives drink and smoke too much, can't keep a wife, and so on. It is interesting to compare Christopher to le Carré's George Smiley, with his toad's face, rotund body, and ill-fitting suits. Besides being spies, the only thing the two have in common is wives who cheat on them—an occupational hazard, perhaps. Christopher pays a heavy price for finding the truth about the Kennedy assassination, but he bears his punishment stoically, for that is the code he lives by. Christopher is conceived as a mythic figure, a hero out of Arthurian legend. McCarry, a political conservative, presents his saintly spy as the finest flower of Western civilization in the mid-twentieth century. The Christopher novels are brilliant, but their flaw is that he is too good to be true. That may be one reason that they were never as commercially successful as le Carré's novels about Smiley, an ungainly hero who in his imperfections is so much more like the rest of us.

McCarry says that Paul Christopher's reaction to the Kennedy assassination was very much his own. When Diem and Nhu were killed, with White House approval, he thought there could be unforeseen consequences, and after Kennedy was assassinated it came to him that it might have been in retaliation for the deaths in Saigon. Unlike Christopher, McCarry didn't try to prove his theory. But after he'd left the CIA and written *The Miernik Dossier,* he proposed to his publisher a book of nonfiction about it. "Nobody would touch that with a ten-foot pole," the publisher declared, but suggested that McCarry write it as a novel. He says he wrote *The Tears of Autumn* in fifty-six days. I once asked McCarry what he thought were the chances that his theory truly explained the assassination. "It's plausible," he said. He smiled and added, "It may be too plausible to be plausible. But it provides a motive. I always thought the question was not how it happened but why."

SPIES AS CLOWNS;
ASSASSINATION AS BLACK COMEDY

Robert Littell was born in 1935 and after college served in the U.S. Navy as a communications officer. He worked with codes, and when he began to write novels the subject continued to fascinate him. "In a certain sense, I am trying to 'decipher' things other than codes: events in the Cold War, and the CIA's behavior in particular."

The navy left Littell with a serious case of wanderlust. He worked for *Newsweek* for eighteen months in the early 1960s, then quit to drive from Paris to Moscow. He returned to *Newsweek* in 1965 and spent five years traveling in the Soviet Union and its satellite states. He came to believe that the Soviet system was rotting from within and all the United States had to do to win the Cold War was sit tight. It disturbed him that his country too often mirrored Soviet tactics.

In 1970 I quit *Newsweek* again to try my luck at novel writing. I moved to a small house in France with $10,000 in the bank and two young children, figuring I had one year to make it work. I finished *Lewinter* and sent it to my then agent in New York. He read it and in effect fired me. I showed the book to a cousin who was then editor in chief of a major publishing house; he read it and suggested I go back to my journalism. As an absolute last resort I showed it to Ben Barzman, a neighbor of mine who was one of the blacklisted Hollywood screenwriters. He and his wife, Norma, read the manuscript, then called me and said, "What's the problem? The book is terrific." Ben showed it to a French publisher, who bought the book for $500. On the strength of the French sale I got a new agent in America, who sold the book to Houghton Mifflin. The book was published to great reviews and actually hit the bottom of *The New York Times* best-seller list for an hour or two. But it was enough to launch me on a career of novel writing. I've been at it ever since.

There are four Littell novels I admire most: *The Defection of A. J. Lewinter* (1973), *The Sisters* (1986), *The Company* (2002), and *Legends* (2005). *Lewinter* and *The Sisters* can be considered together, in that each takes a surreal look at the world of espionage. *The Company*, by contrast, is a fictionalized history of the CIA during the forty-odd years of the Cold War. Then Littell made an impressive return to the surreal with *Legends*.

Littell doesn't necessarily accept my terminology. "I'm not sure I would agree with the word 'surreal.' I think they are probably 'super-real,' in the sense that they try to show that part of the iceberg that is underwater and never seen; the reality of the clandestine world that is hidden from the general public's view." He did agree when I compared certain of his novels with Joseph Heller's *Catch-22:* "It is surely the great book out of World War II and its black humor—its black vision of what war is really about—influenced a whole generation of readers, including me. I suppose you could say that I *try* to treat the Cold War the way Heller treated World War II."

In the opening scene of *The Defection of A. J. Lewinter,* the title character, an American engineer who works on the MIRV missile system, is in Tokyo, supposedly for a professional conference. He eludes the CIA agent who is following him and takes a cab to the Russian embassy. "Lewinter had lived through the moment a hundred times in his imagination, but it had never occurred to him that the guard wouldn't speak English." Trying to control his emotions, he tells the guard with the "obstinate Slavic face," "Listen, I've got to speak to the *ambassador*. . . . I'm an American-ski."

Already the novel has veered into farce: Peter Sellers or Woody Allen could be Lewinter. Finally "a small, brooding Armenian" appears.

"I want to go to the Soviet Union," Lewinter explains.

" 'It is misfortunate,' the Armenian said, 'but the visa department completes at five. Re-try tomorrow after nine.' "

A KGB official, Pogodin, is summoned. "I want to give you MIRV," the desperate Lewinter cries. Whereupon:

> It suddenly occurred to Pogodin that he was dealing with an insane man. In Pogodin's world, intelligence operations were long, tedious affairs in which hundreds of people labored over scraps of information, constructing a single piece of a jigsaw puzzle that might—perhaps—fit into some larger picture. Strangers didn't walk in off the street and offer you the pot of gold at the end of the rainbow.

Finally the idealistic American, who only wants to help end the Cold War, is permitted to board a plane to Moscow. Soon he fades into the background, because this is really a novel about the rival intelligence agencies. Each side scrutinizes Lewinter's case, wondering if his highly technical information could shift the Cold War balance of power, but they are more motivated by careerism than national security. Leo Diamond, an official at the Department of Defense, thinks his handling of the case can win him an important promotion. Pogodin, the senior Russian spy on the case, is all too aware that his career rides on Lewinter's story being true and that more powerful men hope to discredit the American. In this world, truth is nothing; careers are everything. There is a moment when Diamond passes a bald man hawking newspapers and raving: "The President has run off and they can't find him. The king's men have put Humpty Dumpty together again. American troops have invaded China." Diamond, hurrying to catch a plane, "a prisoner of his own small field of vision," ignores the man's alternative reality, which is really no more bizarre than the bureaucratic hall of mirrors he himself inhabits.

In the novel's bitter ending, decent people in both countries come to grief while the spies, however cruel or inept, win ever-increasing power. *The Defection of A. J. Lewinter* is a devastating look at the incompetence and inhumanity of the careerists who purport to protect us.

The Sisters is less tidy but darker, with its portrait of the Kennedy assassination not as Greek tragedy but as black comedy. Francis and Carroll are two half-mad old-timers at the CIA, better known as the Sisters, from Walt Whitman's line about "the sisters Death and Night." Various higher-ups want to retire them, but they are kept on for whatever offbeat ideas they can conjure up. The problem, although readers won't know this right away, is that they have concocted a perfect crime, an assassination of the president that cannot be traced back to them. To give the novel a certain mythic quality, Kennedy is not called Kennedy but "the prince of the realm," yet there is no doubt who is to die. Their motive is inanely political; they think Kennedy is soft on communism.

We watch this mad plot unfold. The KGB's last remaining sleeper agent in America is activated. (Meanwhile, unknown to the Sisters, Lee Harvey Oswald is also preparing to kill Kennedy, adding to the confusion.) In time, word of the plot reaches the highest level of the CIA, whereupon we find that the Sisters are not the only lunatics at large. Kennedy goes to Dallas to wave at crowds and score political points, unaware that officials of his own government intend to kill him. Almost everyone in this book, to one degree or another, is insane.

Littell's version of the Kennedy assassination is fundamentally different from McCarry's. *The Tears of Autumn* is linear, logical. Kennedy killed Diem and Nhu, so their family killed Kennedy. Tit for tat. You may not like it but it makes sense. In *The Sisters* nothing makes sense.

The Company is Littell's fictional history of the CIA's role in the Cold War. He spent one year on research and three years writing what became a 900-page novel. Its realism made it more accessible than his black comedies and it became his biggest commercial success. Actually, Littell thinks that the novel's style may be realistic but its substance— such as the Bay of Pigs and the U.S. sellout of the Hungarian revolution—makes it the blackest of comedies.

Legends may be his masterpiece. Its hero is a CIA spy who has used so many identities he no longer knows who he is. In its stunning opening chapter, a dazed naked man wearing a crown of thorns is buried alive on the orders of one of the gangsters who now rule Russia. If that chapter had come with the name of Kafka or Beckett attached, professors of literature would be hailing it as a masterpiece of postmodernism, surrealism, symbolism, or all of the above. But since the chapter is the work of a spy novelist who has been publishing for thirty-five years without winning much attention outside the genre, the literary world will most likely remain in ignorance of it. The fact remains that Littell is not simply a genre writer; like Elmore Leonard, he is above classification. No one I can think of has done a better job of portraying the insanity of the Cold War; only Stanley Kubrick's *Dr. Strangelove* comes close. Littell is a world-class novelist of the absurd, and in a rational world he would be hailed as such. But rationality is the last thing he would expect.

THE FIRST JEWISH SUPERHERO

Daniel Silva is the most conventional of these four novelists, and perhaps it is no coincidence that he sells the most books. After writing his first novel while working as a television producer and sending it to publishers "over the transom," he saw it become a best seller, as have those that followed it. His novels are not as wildly inventive as Littell's, and he is not as elegant a stylist as McCarry or Alan Furst, but his books are smart and solid, and the adventures of his Israeli assassin Gabriel Allon, who must be called the first Jewish superhero, have won an international following.

Silva grew up in Merced, California. His parents kept novels by Harold Robbins, Sidney Sheldon, Alistair MacLean, and Jack Higgins around the house. He now laughs and calls them junk, but he read them eagerly as a teenager, because they were a way, in his mind at least, to travel and escape. Today, thirty years later, after seeing much of the world, the slender, intense writer says he can go days without speaking to anyone except his wife and children, for he lives deep in the world of his imagination and writes at a frantic pace. He majored in journalism and political science at Fresno State. In 1984, when he was twenty-four, UPI offered him temporary work during the Democratic National Convention, which led to a permanent job. In 1987, on assignment in the Persian Gulf, he met Jamie Gangel, a correspondent for NBC's *Today Show*. They married and Silva left UPI to be a writer and producer for CNN in Washington.

He regarded journalism as a way to prepare himself to write fiction. In 1994 he began writing a novel about a British counterspy's search for a beautiful German agent who is trying to learn the plans for the Normandy invasion. Silva recalls that first novel as a labor of love; it was the last time he could write exactly what he wanted to without the pressures of success.

He had no agent and sent the manuscript for *An Unlikely Spy* cold to major publishing houses. After several houses expressed interest, Silva was able to engage a major literary agent, Esther Newberg, who sold the novel to Villard, a subsidiary of Random House, for what he calls "a very generous advance." The publisher ordered a first printing of 150,000 books, exceptional for a first novel. *An Unlikely Spy* was a Book-of-the-Month Club selection and spent five weeks on *The New York Times* best-seller list in 1996.

Having set his first novel in the past, Silva put his second very much in the here and now. *The Mark of the Assassin* concerned terrorists using surface-to-air missiles to bring down a commercial airliner off the coast of Long Island; it was suggested by the 1996 crash of TWA Flight 800. Silva has a CIA agent named Michael Osbourne investigate the attack, and soon Osbourne is battling not only terrorists but powerful forces in Washington. The novel, another best seller, was followed by a second Michael Osbourne thriller in which he is up against both IRA terrorists and a Washington-based conspiracy of right-wing politicians and arms merchants.

Despite the success of the two Osbourne thrillers, Silva was dissatisfied. For one thing, he didn't like the culture of the CIA or want to keep writing about it. For another, he thought Osbourne, as he had presented him, didn't have an "other side," a life outside his work. His next character came to him one day on a train from London to Paris. He was reading a London newspaper and his eye fell on two related stories. One said that the Israelis were cracking down on militant Palestinians to keep them from derailing the peace process. The other story told how Mossad, the Israeli intelligence agency, was in chaos because of two major scandals.

The idea of writing about an Israeli intelligence agent who struggles to protect his country while also combating incompetence in the home office intrigued Silva. As a correspondent in the Middle East he had been fascinated by the violence, tragedy, and raw passions there. Moreover, Silva, raised Catholic, had converted to Judaism when his and Gangel's twins were born, and that had heightened his interest in Israel.

If Silva was going to create an Israeli intelligence agent, he wanted him to have an "other side," but what was it to be? As he pondered this, he had another epiphany. "Jamie and I were walking down the street in Georgetown and she said, 'Don't forget we're having dinner with David Bull tonight.' " David Bull was one of the world's leading art restorers. "I was stopped in my tracks—I thought, 'Of course, he's an art restorer.' " Bull agreed to help him, and Silva began spending time at the National Gallery of Art. Bull also introduced Silva to a British art dealer who became the model for a recurring character in the series that emerged.

Silva proceeded to write *The Kill Artist* (2000), which introduced Gabriel Allon, art restorer and undercover assassin, and put him on the trail of a Palestinian assassin who is trying to destroy the peace process. Allon, we learn, is the son of an Auschwitz survivor and was an art student when Black September terrorists killed Jewish athletes at the Munich Olympics in 1972. Because of the skills he demonstrated during his military service, he was recruited to join the team that proceeded to assassinate members of Black September. Allon himself killed six of them, an experience that left him emotionally shattered. Worse, the terrorists retaliated by planting a bomb in Allon's car that left his son dead and his wife in a mental institution.

Silva never intended *The Kill Artist* to be the start of a series. It happened, however, that after its publication he signed with a new publisher. "They asked me if I had an idea for my next novel. I told them I wasn't sure. They said, 'We want you to turn Gabriel Allon into a continuing character.' I said, 'You're crazy.' I didn't think the world was ready for a Jewish superhero."

Silva relented, in part because he'd come to like Allon more than he expected. He wrote *The English Assassin,* in which Allon goes to Zurich to restore a painting for a Swiss banker. He finds the banker dead and his art collection missing. Most of the art had been stolen by the Nazis from wealthy Jews. Allon's search for the missing paintings expands to indict the Swiss for using their neutrality in World War II to hide their role as Hitler's bankers and bagmen.

Silva says, "When I started writing about this Israeli art restorer/assassin, something clicked—in my mind and with the public. I'm still amazed at how successful these books have been." He felt that Gabriel, with his career as art restorer, his tragically damaged wife, and the girlfriends who come and go (being his girlfriend is a dangerous pastime), had the "other life" he wanted. He also found that he could use Gabriel to tell many stories that interested him. Silva began to see Allon as an action hero who could also be a fully realized character. The Tom Clancy side of spy novels—the gadgets, the weaponry—is of little interest to him. "I am so utterly bored with tradecraft—I can't tell you. I am far more interested in art restoration."

His Allon novels continued to explore what Silva has called "the unfinished business of the Holocaust." In *The Confessor* the election of a pope leads to an examination of the Vatican's alleged wartime collaboration with the Nazis and to the present-day conflict between conservatives and reformers in the church. In *A Death in Vienna,* Allon goes to the Austrian capital to find out who killed an old Jew who investigated Holocaust crimes. The trail leads to a Nazi war criminal who escaped after the war and to the role of other nations, including the United States, in protecting Nazi war criminals.

In these novels, Silva takes important historical issues, which have been closely examined by historians, and brings them to a larger audience. It is not necessary to be Jewish to appreciate the novels, but they proved to have a ready-made audience. Silva received hundreds of e-mails, perhaps thousands, from Jews who thanked him for the Allon novels. These people, he says, feel that Israel is misunderstood, even hated, by much of the world and appreciate a sympathetic account of the challenges it faces. Yet Silva by no means gives a one-sided account of the Middle East conflicts. "I don't deny the humanity and aspirations of the Palestinian people," he says. "I feel sorry for the ordinary Palestinian. His leaders have let him down, over and over."

After the three-novel cycle of post-Holocaust issues, Silva changed his focus in *Prince of Fire.* In the opening scene, a truck filled with explosives destroys the Israeli embassy in Rome. Ari Shamron, the aging leader of Israeli intelligence, calls upon Allon to track down the person responsible. Shamron is Allon's friend, mentor, and surrogate father. Allon learns who masterminded the Rome attack, and because he is the son and grandson of Palestinian terrorists, Silva uses him to give a capsule history of fifty years of conflict.

In *Prince of Fire,* Silva presents both Shamron and Allon as mythic figures. The indomitable Shamron embodies sixty years of the Jewish struggle and Allon is assuming similar status. "In a way, Allon *is* Israel," Silva says. Near the end of the novel, Shamron tells Allon he will be the intelligence agency's next director of operations—his old job—and gives his blessing. "I know you'll do it. You have no choice. Your mother named you Gabriel for a reason. Michael is the highest, but you, Gabriel, are the mightiest. You're the one who defends Israel against its accusers. You're the angel of judgment—the Prince of Fire."

Silva's sales have grown with each of the Allon novels. According to *Publishers Weekly, The English Assassin* sold around 117,000 copies in hardcover, *The Confessor* neared 125,000, *A Death in Vienna* reached 150,000, and *Prince of Fire* passed 200,000. Despite this success, Silva has mixed feelings about devoting himself to a series. He understands the dangers of growing stale, repeating himself, or slipping into a formula. Like other successful writers, he is under pressure from his publisher to produce a book each year. His contract spells out penalties for not staying on schedule. Silva says that on the day he sent *Prince of Fire* to his publisher he started his next novel. Of course, like every good novelist, he's always looking for the Big One—the *Spy Who Came In from the Cold,* the *Day of the Jackal,* the *Mystic River*—but sometimes to reach those heights you need to slow down and let things simmer.

ALAN FURST: "I'LL WRITE THEM!"

In 2001 I reviewed a dazzling novel called *Kingdom of Shadows* by a writer previously unknown to me named Alan Furst. I began my review by saying that the novel "must be called a spy novel, but it transcends the genre, as did some Graham Greene and Eric Ambler classics. It is one of those rare novels that provide unqualified pleasure." I added, "Do yourself a favor and pick up *Kingdom of Shadows* or one of Alan

Furst's five previous novels." I soon learned that many other readers were discovering Furst's work and coming to regard him as one of the most talented novelists now active.

Kingdom of Shadows, unlike most of Furst's novels, has a relatively simple plot. It is set in Paris in 1938–39. Hitler is poised to overrun Europe, but there are still those who hope he can be stopped. One of them is Nicholas Morath, a forty-four-year-old Hungarian aristocrat and man about town. Service in the first war left him a fatalist, a hedonist, and a patriot. He operates a small advertising agency and secretly collaborates with his uncle, a Hungarian diplomat, on missions to oppose a Nazi takeover in their homeland, where brown-shirted thugs have begun a reign of terror. The novel concerns one such mission, which takes Morath home to try to rescue a prisoner from the SS.

Most of Furst's other novels have panoramic plots that encompass several years of the war and move characters all about Europe as both the war and the silent struggle between intelligence services play out. In *Night Soldiers,* a young man is murdered by fascists in Bulgaria in 1934. His brother is recruited into the Soviet intelligence service, trained in Moscow, then sent to fight in the Spanish Civil War, where he learns that he has been targeted by Stalin's purges. He escapes to Paris, where he fights with the French resistance. In *The Polish Officer,* the title character goes underground after the Germans overrun his country. In *Dark Star,* a Jewish Polish-born correspondent for *Pravda* is forced to become a spy for the NKVD. These novels combine the spy thriller, the historical novel, and often a love story, all with supremely evocative prose.

A few years ago Furst wrote in *The New York Times* about the origins of his spy fiction:

> I'd gone to the Soviet Union in 1983 to do a travel piece for *Esquire* and discovered that the country was a police state. Yes, I knew that, but I was, in some special American way, emotionally innocent of what it meant. . . . Moscow was a tense, dark city, all shadows and averted eyes, with intrigue in its very air, a city where writers should have turned out spy novels by the yard. So then, where was the Russian le Carré? Dead or in jail, if he or she existed at all. Russian writers were not allowed to write spy novels—or political novels of any sort. Fine, I thought,

I'll write them . . . historical espionage novels. Was that a genre? Not that I knew about, but it was now.

Furst has immersed himself in the history of Europe from 1935 to 1945 and transformed it into remarkable fiction. *Publishers Weekly* called him "a master of literary espionage." London's *Daily Telegraph* said, "His exquisitely wrought spy thrillers, set in the thirties and forties, have set new standards for the genre." *The Times* of London spoke of his "subtle brilliance." Charles McCarry, a hard man to impress, says, "Furst is remarkable. I have never met him and as far as I know he never had any connection to intelligence work. But he understands it. Through pure research, he has re-created something that is very close to the reality. It's a monumental achievement." McCarry included Furst's *The Polish Officer* on his list of the five best spy novels. The others were Eric Ambler's *A Coffin for Dimitrios* (1939), Richard Condon's *The Manchurian Candidate* (1959), Rudyard Kipling's *Kim* (1901), and Somerset Maugham's *Ashenden* (1928).

I want to quote from the opening pages of three of Furst's novels, as a sampling of his prose. In the first scene of *Kingdom of Shadows,* Morath returns from Hungary to Paris, makes love with his lover, Cara, and then takes a bath:

> Morath rested his foot on the gold-colored spigot, staring down at the puckered pink-and-white skin that ran from ankle to knee. Shrapnel had done that—a random artillery round that blew a fountain of mud from the street of a nameless village. He had, before passing out, managed to shoot his horse. Then he awoke in an aid station, looking up at two surgeons, an Austrian and a Pole, in blood-splattered leather aprons. "The legs come off," said one. "I cannot agree," said the other. They stood on either side of a plank table in a farmhouse kitchen, arguing while Morath watched the gray blanket turn brown.

On the first page of *Night Soldiers,* Furst tells us: "In Bulgaria, in 1934, on a muddy street in the river town of Vidin, Khristo Stoianev saw his brother kicked to death by fascist militia." He goes on to describe the Bulgarian fascists and their Romanian colleagues across the river:

Torchlight parades with singing and stiff-armed salutes. And the most splendid uniforms. The Romanians, who considered themselves much the more stylish and urbane, wore green shirts and red armbands with blue swastikas on a yellow field. They thrust their banners into the air in time with the drum: we are the Guard of Archangel Michael. See our insignia—the blazing crucifix and pistol.

They were pious on behalf of both symbols. In 1933, one of their number had murdered Ion Duca, the prime minister, as he waited for a train at Sinaia railway station.

A few paragraphs later, Furst broadens his focus:

The European continent lay in the ashes of economic ruin. The printing presses of the state treasuries cranked out reams of paper currency—showing wise kings and blissful martyrs— while bankers wept and peasants starved. It was, certainly, never quite so bad as the great famines of Asia. No dead lay bloated in the streets. European starvation was rather more cunning and wore a series of clever masks: death came by drink, by tuberculosis, by the knife, by despair in all its manifestations. In Hamburg, an unemployed railway brakeman took off his clothes, climbed into a barrel of tar, and burned himself to death.

The World at Night opens:

10 May, 1940.

Long before dawn, Wehrmacht commando units came out of the forest on the Belgian border, overran the frontier posts, and killed the customs officers. Glider troops set the forts ablaze, black smoke rolling over the canals and the spring fields. On some roads the bridges were down, but German combat engineers brought up pontoon spans, and by first light the tanks and armored cars were moving again. Heading southwest, to force the river Meuse, to conquer France.

Furst's work reminds us again of the folly of labels. Furst is simply writing as well as anyone has written in English about Europe before and during World War II. Hemingway wrote a great novel about the Spanish Civil War. Evelyn Waugh wrote his *Sword of Honor* trilogy, based in part on his experiences as an intelligence officer in Eastern Europe. Joseph Heller's *Catch-22* saw the war as black comedy. Furst's body of work, richly detailing the life-and-death war between spies and counterspies, is as compelling a portrait as we have of an epic struggle between communism and fascism and should be ranked with the work of these other celebrated novelists.

10.

Literary Thrillers, Killer Clowns, Barroom Poets, Drunken Detectives, Time Travel, and Related Curiosities

The crime novel began as a serious and straightforward affair. Cops and robbers. PIs and gunsels. Femmes fatales and double indemnity. There wasn't much room for humor or flights of fancy. But as the thriller emerged, writers began to explore new territory. Why not humor? Religion? History? Vampires? Cannibals? Indeed, why not complex characters with psychological depth? Increasingly, writers with literary skills and sensibilities began to produce variations on crime and suspense formulas, and the thriller began to expand far beyond the just-the-facts-ma'am police procedural. Lawrence Sanders was one of the first writers to explore the possibilities of the genre. Scott Turow owed more to Saul Bellow than to Hammett. Elmore Leonard danced to his own distant drummer.

The literary thriller emerged, novels that are better written and/or more ambitious in terms of characterizations and subject matter than the traditional thriller, and with it came an outpouring of quirky offbeat crime fiction. Chandler and Hammett didn't write about the Gay Nineties or the Civil War, but today's writers often devise time machines that carry us into the past—or the future. One great literary thriller, Iain Pears's *An Instance of the Fingerpost,* examines the murder of an Oxford don in the 1660s. The novels discussed here are a sampling of this many-faceted trend. They're original, inventive, surprising. The writers look back less to Spillane or Willeford than to free spirits like Ray Bradbury and Roald Dahl—or to Wilkie Collins and Poe. They take us places that didn't exist a half century ago.

Tropic of Night
Valley of Bones
By Michael Gruber

For many years, Michael Gruber made his living writing books, articles, and speeches for other people. He teamed up with his cousin, the lawyer Robert K. Tanenbaum, to produce a series—credited to Tanenbaum—about New York Assistant District Attorney Butch Karp. The Karp books are lively and fun, but Gruber tired of the ghost's anonymous life and set out to write for himself.

The result has been two terrific novels, both published after he turned sixty, that expand the boundaries of the thriller. The first, *Tropic of Night*, is distinguished by the intelligence of Gruber's writing, the complexity of his heroine, Jane Clare Doe, and the fearsome African sorcery that lies at the heart of the story. Sorcery, magic, witchcraft—by whatever name, no matter what you think about it now, you will take it more seriously after you've experienced this mind-bending novel. The story is set in Miami, where Jane is hiding from her husband, a black writer who mastered sorcery while in Africa and is now using it to kill in America. A police investigation is headed by the Afro-Cuban detective Jimmy Paz. As the killings continue, Paz and Jane join forces. The author wields his own sorcery as he lures us into the hallucinatory world of his imagination.

Gruber's second novel also challenges us to "accept the reality of an unseen world." In *Valley of Bones*, which must be called a spiritual thriller, the issue is Christian faith, as embodied in a woman who may be a saint or may simply be delusional. Either way, the tormented Emmylou Dideroff is one of the most compelling characters in recent popular fiction. A Sudanese government official is thrown from the balcony of his suite in a Miami hotel. Police arrive at the suite and find Emmylou deep in prayer. She is charged with murder. Jimmy Paz arranges for her to be sent to a mental institution for evaluation. She begins to write her "confessions," which become her life story. She has been a prostitute, then the girlfriend of a marijuana grower. Shot in a police raid, she escapes to a nunnery, where she embraces religion and talks to saints.

Jimmy Paz questions Emmylou, along with Lorna Wise, a psychologist. Lorna sees her as a "religious maniac," yet both recognize that strange things happen when they are with her. In one scene the Devil speaks through Emmylou: "My name is Legion," he snarls, while Lorna tries to keep from screaming. The conflict between science and faith rages throughout the book. In each novel, Gruber has created a strong, fascinating woman and has challenged us to accept, or at least consider, mysteries that have no scientific explanation. *Tropic of Night* and *Valley of Bones* are essential reading.

The Right Madness
By James Crumley

James Crumley's 1978 classic *The Last Good Kiss* is much admired by younger writers, who see him as the patron saint of the pull-no-punches, post-Chandler, post-Vietnam private-eye novel. Crumley was born in Three Rivers, Texas, in 1939, served in the army, worked in the oilfields, almost graduated from Texas A&I, then talked his way into the Iowa Writers Workshop. Over the years, besides producing ten novels, Crumley has taught in universities across the West, most recently at the University of Montana. *The Right Madness* is vintage Crumley: beautifully written, outrageous, and more or less unputdownable.

Crumley shares with Chandler not only a gift for lyrical prose but a penchant for plots that meander, vanish for long periods, then return to make baffling leaps. This novel opens with Crumley's hard-drinking, grizzled Montana private eye, C. W. Sughrue, playing in a softball game. It's the only wholesome event in the novel. After the game, he retires to a bar with his friend Mac, a psychiatrist, who prevails on Sughrue to find some files that have been stolen from his office. Sughrue starts shadowing Mac's patients around Meriwether, Crumley's fictional Missoula, whereupon they start dying violent deaths. Mac himself disappears and Sughrue's search for him leads to far-flung adventures. In time Sughrue kills a few people, solves the mystery, and returns to Montana to play with his cats, ingest his drugs of choice, and continue his search for the meaning of life.

You don't read Crumley for plot. You read him for his outlaw attitude, for his rough poetry, for scenes, paragraphs, sentences, moments. You read him for the lawyer with "a smile as innocent as the first martini." For "I had a handful of drinks, then climbed into the pickup to drift slowly through clear, high-altitude night sky, berserk with stars." Or you might read him for the wife who is "meaner than a tow sack full of drowning cats." Or the rape scene, unprecedented in my reading, when a six-foot Russian beauty overcomes Sughrue, ties him "naked, spread-eagled, to iron bedposts," makes certain threats to gain cooperation, and proceeds to have her way with him for several hours, whereupon the ever-philosophical Sughrue remarks, "Fear the fantasy that comes to life, my friend, fear it like death."

If you are fond of bars, you might savor Crumley's catalog of the shadowy, smoke-filled dens where his hero is most at ease: the Scapegoat, the Low Rent Rendezvous, the Iron Butterfly, the Phone Booth, Mutt's, Cactus Pete's, and the High Country. Sughrue consumes prodigious amounts of beer (Negra Modelo), tequila (Patrón), gin (Bombay Sapphire martinis), and Scotch (Lagavulin), as well as the joints (he calls them doobies) and fat lines of cocaine that admirers press upon him. If you disapprove of drink and drugs, you could have a problem with this novel. But if you like Crumley's prose, his love of the drinking life and the West, and his scorn for authority, there's no one else like him.

The Da Vinci Code
By Dan Brown

When Dan Brown's *The Da Vinci Code* arrived for review, it was just another book. As a thriller it was routine—scholar and sexy chick pursed across Europe by bad guys—but what was not routine was its all-out assault on the Catholic Church. I started my review:

> It is Dan Brown's considerable achievement to have written a theological thriller that is both fascinating and fun. *The Da Vinci*

Code takes us in hot pursuit of nothing less than the Holy Grail, which turns out to be not the legendary Cup of Christ but a trove of documents proving dramatic facts about Jesus that the Catholic Church has been suppressing for nearly two millennia. . . .

And ended it:

How much of this is fact and how much is fiction? Read the book and make up your own mind. As Charlie Brown said when asked if he believed in Santa Claus, I refuse to become involved in a theological discussion.

My little joke was intended to disarm angry Catholics who might think I was too sympathetic to Brown's mugging of their church. It didn't.

I didn't mind Brown's criticisms of the church—some of which are clearly farfetched—but neither did I anticipate what a nerve they would strike. I think the astonishing success of *The Da Vinci Code* came about because Brown, by accident or design, hit upon a brilliant two-part formula. His basic message was a scathing attack on Catholicism for centuries of alleged sexism, violence, hypocrisy, corruption, and related sins. Of course, all that has been said many times before, but mostly in nonfiction. Brown's inspiration was to present his case through the most popular form of fiction we have, the modern thriller, which enabled him to use murder, mystery, suspense, romance, chases, and related devices to hook the reader. If you were open to his basic message, as millions of people obviously were, his delivery system made the combination irresistible. It was like being offered Champagne with your chocolate truffles. Brown demonstrated that the thriller format could be used as an effective vehicle for attacking one of the world's most powerful institutions.

Life Expectancy
By Dean Koontz

Dean Koontz has published more than forty novels, most of them best sellers. I managed to ignore them all until *Life Expectancy* came along. A prepublication review in *Publishers Weekly* praised the novel and declared that, in a just universe, the literary world would pay more attention to this wildly successful storyteller. The review aroused my curiosity, so I read the book and found that *PW* was right. *Life Expectancy* is an often hilarious fable about decency adrift in a world of madness.

The novel is narrated by a latter-day Candide named Jimmy Tock. In its opening chapters, Jimmy recalls the events surrounding his birth on August 9, 1974 ("the day Richard Nixon resigned as President of the United States"), in a little hospital in rural Colorado. It turns out that Rudy Tock, a pastry chef, and wife Maddy, who does pet portraits, are not the only expectant parents that day. Konrad Beezo, a chain-smoking clown, is also awaiting the delivery of his first child. When he learns that his wife has died in delivery, Konrad pulls a gun and kills the doctor and nurse who attended her.

Chaos ensues: "Stepping out of the delivery room, Dad came face-to-face with the homicidal clown." (How can anyone resist a writer who could produce that sentence?) Dad fights off the killer, who escapes with his infant son, Punchinello Beezo. At least we think it was his infant son—you know how confusing it gets during delivery-room shootouts. Something else happened while the bullets were flying. At the moment that little Jimmy was born, his grandfather died, but not before making a prediction: his grandson would experience five terrible days in his life, and he helpfully gave the date for each.

Many adventures follow, all bizarre, most heartwarming. How you respond will depend in part on your tolerance for whimsy. But Koontz is a skillful storyteller and the adventures of the Tocks are funny, scary, and entertaining. The novel, like Thornton Wilder's great comedy *The Skin of Our Teeth,* proclaims that humankind, armed with love, courage, and dumb luck, can confront endless adversity and muddle through.

The X President
By Philip E. Baruth

It's the year 2055 and it looks like curtains for America. At home, the Allied Freemen's breakaway republic controls Nevada and the Bozeman-Billings-Boise triangle, and its rebel forces routinely shoot down government aircraft. Abroad, the Cigarette Wars, after raging for thirty years, have taken a turn for the worse and Sino-Russian armies are poised to invade the American mainland. At this dire moment, the National Security Council realizes that only one man can save America. He is, of course, Bill Clinton, who at age 109 is still at his presidential library in Little Rock, working on the authorized biography that will salvage his reputation from fifty-plus years of Republican calumny.

As president, BC (as he is always known here) pursued high-minded policies that, thanks to the law of unintended consequences, dragged America into this mess. Now, due to a breakthrough in time travel, the NSC can send emissaries back to the twentieth century to persuade the earlier BC to reject the policies that have brought the nation to the brink of catastrophe. All this is narrated by Sal Hayden, the thirty-something historian who is BC's authorized biographer. BC is a wreck, kept alive and mobile by various medical miracles, but he maintains his unmatched charm and guile.

At the government's urging, Sal returns to 1963, where she is to cultivate the young BC while he is in Washington on the Boys Nation trip that leads to his famous handshake with President Kennedy. She befriends the young BC—a sucker, even then, for a pretty face—and he readily agrees to help prevent the United States from losing World War III in 2055. *The X President* delights in many ways, but nowhere more than in its portrait of Bill Clinton: at sixteen, as president, and in extreme old age. Baruth does not slight Clinton's dark side: "The curse is this: BC's acts are his, but his consequences are yours." Yet he also understands his charisma. We glimpse him in 1995 "in all his glory, tall, broad-shouldered, silver-haired, powerful in a way that only an emperor or a single-superpower president could be powerful." Philip Baruth is an award-winning commentator for Vermont Public Radio. *The X President* is a gem.

Utopia
By Lincoln Child

In *Utopia,* Lincoln Child gives us the world's grandest theme park, called Utopia, a make-believe universe that stretches out beneath a vast golden dome in the desert north of Las Vegas. Every day, more than 65,000 men, women, and children pay $75 a head to explore its wonders. Needless to say, this paradise is in peril, as a gang of evildoers plans not only to seize its millions in cash but if necessary to bring its dome crashing down. Not only is this novel superior, sophisticated entertainment but I suspected Child of harboring serious intent, because his all-American theme park finally struck me as a parable of the American Dream corrupted by greed.

The Tutor
Their Wildest Dreams
End of Story
By Peter Abrahams

These are among the most recent of Peter Abrahams's highly inventive novels, many of which recall Lawrence Sanders with their sardonic view of human weakness and their belief in the ubiquity of evil. In *The Tutor*, Abrahams takes an old story—an evil stranger invades the home of an unsuspecting family—and makes it fresh and compelling. The stranger is Julian Sawyer, who sets out to destroy the Gardner family out of sheer malice. The hero of the piece is eleven-year-old Ruby, a lover of the Sherlock Holmes stories. When things begin to go wrong— her dog vanishes, her brother is framed on a drug charge—she applies Holmesian logic and concludes that the tutor must be the culprit. The showdown between child and monster could not be improved upon.

In *Their Wildest Dreams*, Abrahams plops a bunch of wayward Americans down in Arizona, injects them with dreams of glory, and watches with amusement as their bubbles burst. The characters include plucky but hapless Mackie, who after a bad divorce is dancing in a topless bar; her teenage daughter, who is mainly interested in sex; the Russian bar owner, who dreams of owning a theme park; and a crime writer who dreams of a best seller. Most of them become caught up in a failed bank robbery. *Their Wildest Dreams* is a bittersweet commentary on the American Dream gone sour.

In 2006, Abrahams sent forth another winner, *End of Story*, about a naïve writer who takes a job teaching prison inmates and gets herself far too involved with a talented and charismatic inmate who proves to be just as evil as the tutor in the earlier novel.

Joyce Carol Oates wrote this about Abrahams's novel *Oblivion* in *The New Yorker:*

> Although Abrahams's novels are genre-affiliated, they differ considerably from one another in tone, texture, ambition, and accomplishment. Often the prose is coolly deployed as a camera, gliding over the surfaces of things, pausing to expose vanity, foolishness, pathos. . . . Abrahams's novels are gratifyingly attentive to psychological detail, richly atmospheric, layered in ambiguity.

Stephen King calls Abrahams his favorite American suspense novelist. If both Oates and King praise a writer, he is doing something right.

The Guards
By Ken Bruen

The Irish writer Ken Bruen's novel *The Guards* would be a conventional private-eye story except that his private eye is drunk most of the time. His name is Jack Taylor, he was once a cop, and now he pursues the drinking life in Galway and takes the odd detecting job to pay his bar bill. A typical chapter ends with this barroom exchange between Jack and his best friend:

> "Want to grab some grub or just get wrecked?"
> "Wrecked sounds better."
> "Barman!"

The novel includes a murder, a bit of romance, much humor, and hints that Jack loves literature, but mainly he drinks. After one binge he undergoes two weeks of enforced sobriety. After his release, his efforts to stay sober arouse far more suspense than the murder case we have all but forgotten. The Mystery Writers of America did themselves proud by nominating this hilarious caper for an Edgar Award.

In 2006, Bruen published the even more outrageous *Calibre,* in which drunken, corrupt, incompetent London cops try to catch a serial killer who targets rude people—MANNERS PSYCHO ON LOOSE, one tabloid proclaims. Comedy doesn't get much blacker than this. Bruen is an original, grimly hilarious and gloriously Irish.

III.

FOUR MODERN MASTERS

Wherein the author declares that, of the

scores of talented people now writing thrillers,

four Americans can be called outstanding.

11.

Thomas Harris:

Learning to Love the Doctor

Thomas Harris does not do interviews. Like his most celebrated fictional creation, Dr. Hannibal Lecter, Harris avoids scrutiny. However, again like Dr. Lecter, his unusual talents have aroused curiosity, and this has led to occasional sightings of the reclusive author and to random facts entering the public record. We know that, unlike the aristocratic Dr. Lecter, Harris rose from modest origins. He was born in Jackson, Tennessee, in 1940, but the family soon moved to his father's hometown, Rich, Mississippi, where his father farmed and his mother taught high school biology. A bright and bookish lad, Harris grew up aware of Mississippi's celebrated traditions, both in storytelling and in darker realms. He knew of William Faulkner and Eudora Welty, and also of the cannibalistic killer who roamed his corner of Mississippi in the 1930s, and of his state's ugly history of lynchings and other violence against those challenging the status quo.

In 1960, Harris left Mississippi to attend Baylor University in Waco, Texas, where he was an English major by day and a reporter for the local paper at night. Baylor was in those days a resolutely Baptist institution, operated and attended by hard-shell Southern Baptists who were unalterably opposed to, among other things, smoking, drinking, and dancing. ("Why don't Baptists make love standing up?" went the joke. "Because God might think they were dancing.") If a student was known to smoke, drink, dance, or question church doctrine, his classmates would post his name on a bulletin board and urge everyone to pray for his soul.

It is not recorded whether Thomas Harris's classmates prayed for his soul, or whether he rejected the Baptist faith later in life, when he had become a connoisseur of vintage wines, gourmet meals, and exquisite cruelty, but it is a fact that the Baptist religion and Baylor itself are often mentioned, not fondly, in his novels. For example, in *The Silence of the Lambs,* the imprisoned Dr. Lecter tells Clarice Starling of one of his fellow inmates: "Sammie put his mother's head in the collection plate at the Highway Baptist Church in Trune. They were singing 'Give of Your Best to the Master' and it was the nicest thing he had." Harris liked that story so much he repeated it in *Hannibal.*

While still at Baylor, Harris began sending "macabre stories" to magazines like *True* and *Argosy.* After graduating, he escaped the South to travel in Europe and then to take a job as a reporter for the Associated Press in New York. In the early 1970s, Harris and two other reporters dreamed up the idea of a novel about PLO terrorists who conspire with a Vietnam veteran to use a television blimp to bomb the Super Bowl and kill all 80,000 football fans in attendance, including the U.S. president. Eventually Harris took over the project.

Black Sunday, published in 1975, won admiring reviews and became a first-rate movie. Later events would prove Harris's vision of terrorists inflicting mass death from the sky to have been prophetic. *Black Sunday* remains one of the best terrorism novels, but for our purposes it is only a prelude to Harris's next achievement: the creation of Dr. Lecter, who in a series of novels and the movies made from them emerged as the most celebrated killer in modern fiction and perhaps of all time.

Who are the great villains? Shakespeare gave us three: Richard III, Iago, and Edmund, the bastard son in *King Lear.* Conan Doyle fashioned Professor Moriarty, the "Napoleon of Crime," as a foil to Sherlock Holmes. In recent years our best-known fictional villains have been serial killers. In real life, of a dozen or so notables of the past half century, Ted Bundy became the star, perhaps because he was middleclass, good-looking, and once a law student. Bundy's two trials took place during the period that Harris was writing the first Lecter novel, *Red Dragon,* but he visibly influences him only in that in *The Silence of the Lambs* the killer known as Buffalo Bill, like Bundy, used a fake cast on his arm to lure women into trusting him. Dr. Lecter's persona must be considered an original creation, with perhaps a nod to Bela Lugosi's creepy but aristocratic Count Dracula. Thanks to Anthony Hopkins's portrayal in three movies, no previous fictional villain has been better known worldwide than Hannibal the Cannibal.

Harris has described the doctor's origins:

> In the fall of 1979, owing to an illness in my family, I returned home to the Mississippi Delta and remained there eighteen months. I was working on *Red Dragon*. My neighbor in the village of Rich kindly gave me the use of a shotgun house in the center of a vast cotton field, and there I often worked at night.

He adds that semiferal dogs wandered the cotton field, and he became friendly with them. At night, while he wrote, "they waited on the front porch, and when the moon was full they would sing." During this painful time, as his relative lingered, Harris struggled to build a plot around FBI investigator Will Graham. In his imagination, Harris accompanied Will Graham to the Baltimore State Hospital for the Criminally Insane, where "we encountered the kind of fool you know from conducting your own daily business, Dr. Frederick Chilton." The vain and stupid Dr. Chilton will annoy Dr. Lecter and the reader for two novels, before Dr. Lecter puts an end to him.

Thus, deep inside a world of illness, darkness, feral dogs, and maddening doctors, Harris conceived one of the most sinister characters in all fiction. The coming of Dr. Lecter was a turning point in the amount of sadistic stomach-turning violence that was acceptable in mainstream fiction. Harris's intelligence and wit made the depredations of Dr. Lecter and his other killers more or less acceptable to readers, but some of his imitators have trafficked in unadorned sadism. Harris might have said, "*Après moi, le deluge!*"—an unprecedented orgy of blood, gore, rape, flaying, dismemberment, disembowelment, necrophilia, torture, and cannibalism.

The deluge began with *Red Dragon*, published in 1981. Will Graham captures serial killers by putting himself in their heads. This power has brought him both physical and mental pain. He was almost killed in capturing Dr. Lecter (before the action of the novel begins), and he will again be close to death when *Red Dragon* ends. Graham, reluctantly lured from retirement to track a serial killer, goes to see Dr. Lecter in a hospital for the criminally insane, hoping to buy his help with such favors as a cell with a window. Dr. Lecter toys with him but secretly makes contact with the killer, tells him Graham's home address, and urges him to "Kill them all!"

We meet the killer, Francis Dolarhyde, who works in a film laboratory in St. Louis and chooses his victims by looking at home movies sent for processing. Dolarhyde has a disfiguring cleft palate ("wet and shiny") and had a really bad childhood, with a grandmother right out of the Bates Motel. He has become obsessed with William Blake's painting *The Great Red Dragon and the Woman Clothed with the Sun.* He talks to the Red Dragon and has developed a mythology wherein his slaughter of innocents is helping him *become* the Dragon.

The flaw of the novel is that Harris goes on interminably about this nutcase. The rule that less is more has rarely been better dramatized. We soon tire of Dolarhyde and his ravings. The only justification for the over-the-top characterization of Dolarhyde is that he makes the imprisoned Dr. Lecter look relatively sane, which may be what Harris intended. Dolarhyde aside, the novel is well plotted, precise, and subtle in its characterizations. Had he not chosen to write about serial killers, Harris had the skills to write literary novels—he just wouldn't have become as rich.

We learn that Dr. Lecter is a small, lithe man, that his eyes are maroon, and that he has killed at least nine people and attacked two others who survived. When Graham goes to see Dr. Lecter, Dr. Chilton tells him of an earlier incident when he attacked a nurse, blinded her in one eye, and tore out her tongue and ate it. Asked why Lecter kills, Will Graham replies that he does it because he likes it.

At the end of the novel, Dolarhyde is dead and Hannibal Lecter is still behind bars, where he clearly belongs. This is a conventional ending for a crime novel: Justice has been done. Let us also note that there is nothing admirable about Hannibal Lecter in *Red Dragon* beyond physical grace and superficial charm. He kills people for fun. He mutilated the nurse. He urged Dolarhyde to kill Graham and his family. Still, Dr. Lecter's combination of civilized manners and insane violence is fascinating; we are left wanting to know more about him. It is easy to think the novel was misconceived, with the focus on the wrong madman. Harris seems to have reached that conclusion. He has said that he did not intend to bring Hannibal Lecter back again. He wanted to write another FBI novel, one that featured a woman, so he invented FBI trainee Clarice Starling, only to find, when he started writing, that he was compelled to send Clarice to see the doctor.

It was an inspired move. *Red Dragon* had done well and became a good movie, *Manhunter,* directed by Michael Mann, with William Petersen as Graham and Brian Cox as Dr. Lecter. But neither the book nor the movie achieved the huge success that awaited *The Silence of the Lambs,* which introduced the odd couple of Dr. Lecter and young, pretty, tough, naïve Clarice Starling. When Harris replaced Will Graham with Starling, he gave his series a priceless ingredient: sex. Or, more precisely, the possibility of sex, the strange mating dance between the charming cannibal and the seemingly virginal Clarice.

There is an unlovely moment when some crude fellows speculate on whether Dr. Lecter wants to fuck, kill, or eat Clarice—or, if all three, in what order. But, on the surface at least, their relationship exists on a higher plane. Clarice offers him diversion, innocence; sex per se is neither practical nor, it seems, of interest to him. And Dr. Lecter can give Clarice something she craves far more than sex: career advancement.

The plot of *The Silence of the Lambs* is essentially the same as that of *Red Dragon.* An FBI agent—Starling this time—goes to the imprisoned Dr. Lecter, seeking help in capturing a serial killer. In *Silence,* the serial killer is one Jame Gumb, aka Buffalo Bill, who is as nutty as the Red Dragon but more succinctly presented. ("Jame" was supposed to be James but an error on his birth certificate became permanent.) Gumb has been abducting, killing, and skinning women, in order to use their skin to make clothing for himself. He was suggested by Ed Gein, who killed women in Wisconsin in the 1950s. Bodies and body parts were found in his farmhouse, along with clothing made from human skin. Gein spent the rest of his life in a mental institution and is said to have also inspired Norman Bates in *Psycho.*

The novel begins with Starling, a trainee at the FBI Academy at Quantico, Virginia, summoned by Jack Crawford, head of the Behavioral Science office. He assigns her, as part of a study of serial killers, to go interview Dr. Lecter but warns her not to answer any personal questions. At the Baltimore State Hospital for the Criminally Insane, she first meets the odious Dr. Chilton, who comes on to her; then she proceeds to her interview with Dr. Lecter. Harris adds a new detail about the doctor: He has six fingers on his left hand.

Dr. Lecter asks Clarice what an inmate down the hall, Miggs, said to her as she entered. She replies candidly. "He said, 'I can smell your cunt.' " He replies, "I see. I myself cannot. You use Evyan skin cream and sometimes wear L'Air du Temps, but not today." This proves him both a gentleman and a master analyst in the Sherlock Holmes tradition. They talk about Buffalo Bill and about Dr. Lecter himself. He tells her, "I collect church collapses, recreationally." If there's a God, he adds, he must relish the death of innocents.

Abruptly, he calls Starling a "well-scrubbed, hustling rube" and ridicules her origins in the coal-mining country of West Virginia. She urges him to fill out a questionnaire. He responds with one of his most celebrated lines. "A census taker tried to quantify me once. I ate his liver with some fava beans and a big Amarone." As Starling withdraws, Miggs flings semen in her face. Dr. Lecter calls her back and seems upset. "Discourtesy is unspeakably ugly to me," he tells her. Dr. Lecter says he will give her a gift: He tells her where to find the body of one of his victims.

Thanks to Starling's age and sex, this exchange has been far more interesting than any in the previous novel, since there could be little but antagonism between Dr. Lecter and Will Graham. It's a showy scene, and Dr. Lecter is the most likable man in it, far more so than the loathsome Dr. Chilton or the mad Miggs. Dr. Lecter is apparently intrigued by Starling. The fact that Clarice ignores Jack Crawford's advice and gives Dr. Lecter personal information is the mainspring of the plot.

The search for Buffalo Bill intensifies after he kidnaps the daughter of a U.S. senator. Clarice returns to Dr. Lecter and offers a deal: If the doctor will help them save the senator's daughter, the FBI will get him the cell with a view that he wants. Dr. Lecter plays with her, asks her worst memory of childhood. Her father's death, she says. He was a town marshal and was shot by two burglars. Dr. Lecter tells her she's been very candid and adds, "I think it would be quite something to know you in private life." This odd declaration is basic to the plot, which turns on Dr. Lecter's fascination with Clarice.

Dr. Chilton foolishly arranges for Dr. Lecter to be taken to Tennessee to meet with the senator. We meet Justice Department official Paul Krendler, who is an even bigger ass than Dr. Chilton. He too comes on to Starling and, rejected, becomes her nemesis. Starling meets with Dr. Lecter in the Memphis courthouse and demands more information about Buffalo Bill. He insists that she tell him more about her childhood. She relates that after her father's death, she went to live with relatives on a ranch in Montana, where she was horrified by the screaming of baby lambs that were about to be slaughtered. The silence of the lambs represents the peace that Clarice dreams of.

Her revelations please Dr. Lecter, but Dr. Chilton forces her to leave. The prisoner hands her back the case file on Buffalo Bill: "For an instant the tip of her forefinger touched Dr. Lecter's. The touch crackled in his eyes." That is how he remains in Clarice's memory, Harris adds, "Standing in his white cell, arched like a dancer, his hands clasped in front of him and his head slightly to the side."

Well. We should all be so vividly remembered by the women in our lives.

We arrive at Harris's double-barreled ending. First, Dr. Lecter escapes. He has fashioned a key to open handcuffs. In his Memphis cell, while listening to Glenn Gould play Bach's Goldberg Variations, "his strange maroon eyes half-closed," Dr. Lecter strikes. Two officers are giving him dinner. Harris returns to the language of Mississippi to describe the doctor's attack. He frees himself and "fast as a snapping turtle" handcuffs one of the officers. He seizes the other's face with his teeth and shakes him "like a rat-killing dog." He beats both men to death; one "shivered out straight like a clubbed fish." He listens to more Bach before making his escape. The scene is exquisite and horrible.

The second climax is more conventional. Starling tracks Jame Gumb to his home, where he is about to kill the senator's daughter. She draws her gun and tells him to put up his hands. Then, in the great tradition of crime fiction, she does something foolish that prolongs the drama. Gumb simply walks out of the room and she is too surprised to shoot him. She goes to the basement to reassure his captive. Gumb turns off the lights. He has both night-vision goggles and a gun. All he has to do is shoot Starling, who is helpless in the dark, but he too makes a conventional mistake. He hesitates, fantasizing about her hair.

When he cocks his gun, Starling recognizes the sound and fires at it in the dark, killing the monster.

Although Dr. Lecter has escaped, Starling has captured Buffalo Bill. Jack Crawford, her spiritual father, gives his blessing. She even has a date in which she may or may not—Harris is uncharacteristically coy here—have shared a bed with a young man. We see Dr. Lecter enjoying his freedom, sipping a glass of Montrachet and writing Clarice a note saying that he has no plans to pursue her, because the world is more interesting with her in it.

If we accept the novel's premise that a cultivated madman like Dr. Lecter would become obsessed with a naïve young woman like Clarice, *The Silence of the Lambs* is brilliant popular fiction. And it is easy to accept those things because the novel is so well written. With his intelligence, his attention to detail, his audacity, and his outrageous humor, Harris seduces us into accepting, even being amused by, many disgusting events. *The Silence of the Lambs* is the greatest of modern thrillers. It does not transcend the genre but defines it. More than any other single novel, it *is* the triumph of the thriller.

The novel inspired a movie that swept five Academy Awards: best picture, best director (Jonathan Demme), best actor and actress (Anthony Hopkins and Jodie Foster), and best screenplay (Ted Tally). The movie, although deserving of its awards, only begins to suggest the depth and perversity of the novel. Much had to be left out: Crawford's dying wife, for example; the fate of Will Graham, who has succumbed to alcoholism in Florida; the details of Gumb's madness. On the other hand, the movie offered amazing performances and at least one unforgettable image, after Dr. Lecter's escape, when police arrive and find one of his victims, strung up high on the cage that held him, like a crucified angel.

With Dr. Lecter at large and Starling determined to bring him in, *The Silence of the Lambs* cried out for a sequel, and in 1999, after eleven years, Harris gave us *Hannibal.*

It is an exceedingly dark, strange, even repellent novel. *Red Dragon* was Harris's warm-up, *The Silence of the Lambs* was his masterpiece, and *Hannibal* is his decadence. The madman was behind bars in the first book, he became increasingly sympathetic in the second, and now in the third he is a free man, an aesthete, and, incredibly enough, the hero. Harris kept his love-hate relationship with Dr. Lecter more or less in balance in *The Silence of the Lambs,* but in *Hannibal* he embraces the monster. In this novel, not just Dr. Lecter but wild pigs and giant eels feast on human flesh. Dr. Lecter is replaced as the villain by possibly the vilest creature ever to ooze through mainstream American fiction, Mason Verger. Meanwhile, Harris carries the Lecter-Starling relationship to a point that is not just shocking but grotesque. This is, at the very least, one of the most perverse novels ever written. The Marquis de Sade, if he had been a more talented novelist, might have written *Hannibal.*

The novel begins with Clarice, seven years after she killed Jame Gumb. Her career has not gone well. Her success on the Gumb case caused jealousy at the FBI. The Justice Department's Paul Krendler has undercut her for years. At the outset, Starling is wrongly blamed for the failure of a drug raid and her career is in trouble. News of her downfall makes the newspapers and inspires a friendly note from the elusive Dr. Lecter. Starling determines to save her career by capturing the fugitive cannibal. This leads to her meeting with Mason Verger.

He is the heir to a meatpacking fortune and has been a sadist and bully since childhood. He raped his younger sister, Margot. He worked for the bloodthirsty African dictator Idi Amin. He is a pedophile who, even bedridden, still enjoys tormenting children. He uses threats to make them cry and then mixes martinis with their tears. Dr. Lecter has been a naughty boy now and then but Harris, a man of fine distinctions, makes it clear that he does not rape children and drink their tears!

Starling goes to see this creature because he has put up a million-dollar reward for the capture of Dr. Lecter. Verger explains that he met Dr. Lecter when he was required by a court to undergo therapy. Dr. Lecter gave him powerful drugs, then broke a mirror, handed him a shard of glass, and suggested that he peel off his face. This Verger obediently did. "Mason Verger, noseless and lipless, with no soft tissue on his face, was all teeth, like a creature from the deep." He lives on a palatial estate in Maryland. His bedroom "is dark except for the glow of the big aquarium where an exotic eel turns and turns in an endless figure eight, its cast shadow moving like a ribbon over the room." This beast exists as a twin to Verger. It is impossible to say which is more disgusting.

Verger tells her of his ruined face, "I thank God for what happened. It was my salvation. Have you accepted Jesus, Miss Starling?"

She replies, "I was raised in a close religious atmosphere, Mr. Verger. I have whatever that leaves you with." An enigmatic response, to say the least. Is Clarice without religion? Or, given a chance to join in Christian fellowship with this ghastly creature, has she simply chosen to decline?

Verger is paying Paul Krendler for inside information on the Lecter investigation. Verger doesn't want Dr. Lecter turned over to the courts; he wants to capture and torture him personally. He has men in Sardinia breeding huge wild pigs, and he intends to feed Dr. Lecter to them.

The story shifts to Florence, where the curator of the Palazzo Capponi has vanished and a scholar who calls himself Dr. Fell (as in "I do not like thee . . .") has taken his place. Dr. Fell is Dr. Lecter, his identity concealed by surgery and other means. He lectures on Dante, listens to Bach and Scarlatti, sips fine wine, and dabbles. We accompany him not to the Uffizi Gallery but to an exposition of Atrocious Torture Instruments, where he glimpses a hanging starvation cage complete with a skeleton.

Dr. Lecter learns that Chief Investigator Rinaldo Pazzi of the Questura is on his trail. The inspector has a beautiful wife with expensive tastes, which leads him to make a fatal mistake. Instead of arresting the fugitive, he calls Mason Verger's hotline, hoping to win the reward. In time, the inspector confronts the cannibal, who smiles and says he's thinking of eating his wife. He overpowers the man, slices his guts open, and leaves him hanging over the Palazzo Vecchio. It is an ugly death but the Italian was stupid and greedy. By now we know that anyone who endangers the doctor's freedom will get what he—or she—deserves.

When Clarice, back in Virginia, learns in the middle of the night that Dr. Lecter has killed again, we are told that her eyes stung and she saw Dr. Lecter's face in the dark. What does this mean? Is poor Clarice carrying a torch? Is she nuts?

In one of Harris's rare comic scenes, we see Dr. Lecter flying back to America on a Boeing 747. To help him ease through customs, he has joined a package tour and is crushed into coach—steerage, Harris calls it—with obnoxious Americans. Amid the bedlam of screaming brats, obnoxious flight attendants, suspicious mothers, and smelly diapers, Dr. Lecter ceases to be a mad cannibal and becomes Everyman, suffering the indignities of modern travel. He retreats into his memory palace, a sanctuary we have not seen before. The palace is like a great museum. It has rooms for music and art, for childhood memories. Harris leads us deep into this sanctuary and shares with us the secret of Dr. Lecter's sister Mischa.

In Lithuania, in 1944, the Eastern Front has collapsed. Hannibal Lecter's parents are dead and their estate laid waste. We learn that the father was a count whose title dates to the tenth century and the mother was a high-born Italian. Deserters have seized the estate. Hannibal, age six, and his sister Mischa, a year older, are captives. The starving soldiers come for Mischa. Young Hannibal fights them in vain. He prays feverishly to see his sister again but his prayers cannot drown out reality—the sound of the ax. Eventually we are told, in one of the most lurid sentences ever written, "His prayer to see her again did not go entirely unanswered—he did see a few of Mischa's milk teeth in the reeking stool pit his captors used."

Since Mischa's death, Harris says, Dr. Lecter has not been troubled by religion, except to reflect that God's crimes far exceed his own: "God, who is in irony matchless, and in wanton malice beyond measure."

Mischa's story casts light on Dr. Lecter's obsession with Clarice. Both were orphaned. Dr. Lecter's failure to save Mischa is paralleled by Clarice's inability to save the lambs. He perhaps sees in her the woman Mischa might have become. Of course, if you poke around on the Internet, you will find students of the Lecter books who believe the Mischa story is a lie, invented by the doctor to justify his crimes.

With Dr. Lecter back in America, Starling redoubles her efforts to find him. Her work is interrupted by Krendler, who calls her "corn-pone country pussy." Naughty, naughty. Dr. Lecter would not approve.

We observe a meeting of Verger and his sister, Margo. She is a lesbian who wants Mason to donate his sperm so she and her lover can use it to have a child. If neither sibling produces an heir, the beneficiary of the Verger fortune will be the Southern Baptist Convention and Baylor University. We meet Verger's spiritual adviser, Dr. Doemling, a psychologist who holds the Verger Chair at Baylor. The impression grows that the author was not a happy camper at Baylor.

Starling goes jogging in a state park. Dr. Lecter watches, sitting on a hillside and savoring the smell of moldering leaves, a whiff of rabbit pellets, the "deep wild musk" of a shredded squirrel skin. The image of Starling running, her ponytail bouncing, enters his memory palace. He proceeds to Starling's car, sniffs its leather steering wheel, and licks it with his tongue.

What is with this guy? The flashback to Mischa perhaps aroused sympathy for the doctor, whose carnivorous habits could now be attributed to childhood trauma. He clearly has deep feelings for Clarice, but his intentions remain unclear—does he want to fuck her, eat her, or kill her? Or, for that matter, make her his bride? One of the advantages of having an insane protagonist is that he can do anything at all; logic is not an issue.

Mason Verger's Sardinians capture Dr. Lecter and take him to the Maryland estate, where he is to be fed to the starving hogs. He is tied to a wall with his arms outstretched—his positioning, twice described, suggests crucifixion. He shows no fear. We glimpse the "terrible beauty" of the wild swine.

Starling arrives to save Dr. Lecter. But she is wounded in an exchange of gunfire and he must carry her to safety. The swine, rushing to eat the dead and dying Sardinians, ignore Dr. Lecter because he does not fear them. A surviving Sardinian says he thinks the bloodthirsty hogs worship Dr. Lecter. In the confusion, Margot has her revenge on Mason, the brother who raped her as a child; she stuffs the huge, hungry eel down his throat.

Dr. Lecter takes Starling to his hideaway on the Chesapeake Bay. He nurses her back to health but uses drugs and hypnosis to keep her passive. In the doctor's rather muddled mind, Clarice is to replace Mischa in his life. One fine evening, Starling and Dr. Lecter have drinks—Lillet with a slice of orange—by the fire. She is wearing the long dinner gown and emerald earrings he bought her. He tells her passionately that if he saw her every day, forever, he would remember this moment. The mad cannibal has become Cary Grant and Clarice has morphed into Grace Kelly.

They have a guest. Dr. Lecter has kidnapped Paul Krendler and proceeds to remove the top of his skull and sautée slices of his brain. The process is explained in mouthwatering detail for the benefit of gourmets. This maddest of mad tea parties is surely the strangest scene in all of Harris. Krendler does not survive dinner, but the happy couple proceeds to dessert and coffee by the fire. Starling lets a drop of Château d'Yquem fall to her nipple, and her lover falls to his knee and lowers his mouth to her waiting breast.

We glide to Buenos Aires, three years later, where Clarice and Dr. Lecter are the most contented of lovers. "Sex is a splendid structure they add to every day." We are told that drugs and hypnosis are no longer needed. Clarice is happy—or brainwashed or something—and Dr. Lecter no longer sees Mischa in his dreams. The curtain falls on their conjugal bliss.

Harris has achieved a remarkable turnaround. The insane cannibal of the first book is, by the end of the third, an ardent and sophisticated lover, a man of taste and refinement, living in luxury with a gowned, bejeweled, passionate Starling. Although some readers and reviewers protested that Harris had gone too far, most accepted these stupendously weird developments. *Hannibal* was America's number-two bestselling novel in 1999 (behind Grisham's *The Testament*) and became a successful movie (with Julianne Moore replacing the sensible Jodie Foster).

The movie did clean things up a bit. The moviemakers could stomach the eating of Krendler's brain but not the novel's final image of the lovers happily romping in bed. Instead, they invented a bizarre ending in which Starling handcuffs them together as the police are approaching. Dr. Lecter grabs a meat cleaver and is about to chop off her hand but—sentimental fool—chops off his own hand instead and makes his escape.

If we could remove *Hannibal*'s style and sophistication and consider only its rapes and cannibalism and people-eating hogs, many of us would find it disgusting and probably unreadable. But to write well is like being blessed with a beautiful face—you can get away with almost anything. So we more or less accept what Harris hath wrought.

The novel could have been called *The Rehabilitation of Hannibal Lecter*—or, given its religious overtones, *The Resurrection of Hannibal Lecter*. By contrasting Dr. Lecter with seriously disgusting fellows like Dr. Chilton, Paul Krendler, and Mason Verger, Harris has made his cannibal look good. It was Harris's genius to create, in Hannibal

Lecter, a villain who, for all his faults, has traits that most of us can identify with. Dr. Lecter loathes stupid, rude, annoying people, as we all do. But he rises above our petty inhibitions and kills them. He acts out our fantasies of ridding the world of the boss or landlord or ex-spouse or bureaucrat who surely deserves his or her fate.

If we can forget about that nurse whose tongue he ripped out and ate, Dr. Lecter has come to seem a fairly reasonable fellow. He loves the beautiful things in life: Bach, Florence, Montrachet. Of course, he also loathes the unjust God who let his sister be eaten by human beasts—the kind of louts he now is pleased to kill and eat in revenge. Harris's portrayal of a God "in wanton malice beyond measure," a God who brings down churches on those who worship him, is an indictment of religion in the tradition of Voltaire.

By the end of *Hannibal*, Harris had subverted the traditional crime novel, which would have ended with Starling, the officer of the law, capturing the serial killer. Instead, he captures her. The story demands another installment. Will Clarice regain her senses and bring the madman to justice? That would be the conventional next step, but we have no reason to expect Harris to be conventional. Harris's upcoming *Hannibal Rising* is billed as a prequel, focusing on our hero from ages sixteen to twenty. We can only wait patiently for Harris's next revelations in the tender tale of Hannibal and his Clarice.

12

George Pelecanos:

Bulletins from the Front

George Pelecanos's father was born in Greece and brought to Washington as an infant. After serving in World War II, he opened the Jefferson Coffee Shop, a lunch counter and carryout on 19th Street between M and N, in a part of downtown Washington thickly populated by lawyers and lobbyists. The future writer, born in 1957, was by the summer of 1968 working for his father. He took a bus to work each day, starting near his home in Silver Spring, Maryland, just across the district line, and riding down Seventh Street, past storefronts that had been burned out a few months earlier in the riots that followed the assassination of Dr. Martin Luther King Jr. He found himself studying the people on the bus, wanting to know more about their lives. His job that summer was to make deliveries to offices around Dupont Circle. "On my runs I made up stories, serial-style, complete with music, to pass the time," he later wrote. "I would space the stories out so they would climax at the end of the week. I thought I was making movies, but I was writing my first books."

Pelecanos grew into a rebellious teenager. "My teen years consisted of Rec Department baseball, beer and fortified wine, girls, marijuana, pickup basketball, muscle cars, Marlboros, rock and funk concerts at Fort Reno and Carter Barron, and stock-boy positions at now-shuttered retailers like Sun Records at Connecticut and Albemarle. Yes, I wasted a lot of time. And yes, it was a lot of fun." He wasn't much of a reader, but he loved R & B and soul music and movies like *The Wild Bunch* and *The Dirty Dozen*. He drifted through the nearby University of Maryland and then in his senior year took a course taught by Charles C. Mish called Hard-Boiled Detective Fiction. The course was controversial, because writers like Hammett, Chandler, and Cain were not considered literature by many in the English department. But for Pelecanos their angry, gritty novels were a revelation, because they described the world as he knew it. Years later, he wrote:

> Peripherally, the stories were about crime; specifically, they dissected American society and human politics from the level of the street. . . . For the first time I knew, with the shock of recognition that only the most fortunate experience, what I wanted to "do." How to get there was the question.

It was a question that took more than ten years to answer. His teachers told him he had natural writing talent, but he had never taken a writing class, he didn't know any writers, and the ones he read about all seemed to have gone to Ivy League colleges and to spend their summers at places like the Hamptons that were unknown to him. He spent his twenties at a series of dead-end jobs: he bartended, sold TV sets and CD players, and hustled women's shoes at a trendy Connecticut Avenue shop, earning a seven-percent commission and finding it a great way to meet girls. He dedicated his nights to the pursuit of sex, booze, drugs, and music that moved him. All the while he was reading voraciously, particularly writers like James Crumley, Newton Thornburg, and Kem Nunn, whose work mirrored his own edgy, rebellious outlook.

In 1985, this hard-drinking, Marlboro-smoking, long-haired Greek American with less than sterling prospects married a beautiful blonde named Emily Hawk. ("He was very unusual," Emily told a *Washington Post* reporter. "The way he dressed. He had this brown corduroy suit, very large hair, and a goatee." "She couldn't take her eyes off me," Pelecanos added, deadpan.) Marriage settled him down, and by 1989 he had become the manager of a string of retail electronics stores. The problem was that he hated his life. At thirty-two, he thought he had to take his shot at what he wanted. With Emily's support—she was working and they had savings—he quit his job and began to write a novel. He was encouraged by the punk rock movement, which proclaimed that anyone could pick up a guitar and play. He spent much of 1989 alone in a dimly lit room, writing in longhand, not knowing if anyone would ever read his words. To help with expenses, he took a job at a bar.

At the end of 1989 he had a draft of *A Firing Offense,* but he didn't know what to do with it. He heard that St. Martin's Press would accept unagented manuscripts, which was a polite word for the mostly unreadable novels that came in "over the transom," landed in "the slush pile," and were read, if at all, by the most junior editors. He mailed off his manuscript and he and Emily went backpacking in New Zealand and Australia; he jokes now that he assumed his advance would be waiting upon their return. Instead, there was only silence. Confronted by the apparent rejection of his novel, he started another, telling Emily he'd take one more shot. They had by then adopted their first child, Nick, and Pelecanos wrote in the same small room where his infant son slept.

Writing wasn't the only means of advancement on his mind. Growing up in Washington's Greek-American community, Pelecanos knew all about the Pedas brothers, Jim and Ted, whose Circle Films operated a chain of theaters as well as a film production company. Their flagship was the much-beloved Circle Theater on Pennsylvania Avenue, where in the 1960s and 1970s, for a dollar, you could see double features that might include *The Red Shoes, The Battle of Algiers,* or *Shoot the Piano Player.* Pelecanos wrote Ted Pedas several times, asking for a job interview. "I thought, I'm Greek, I love movies, I want to get in on this." Finally, Pedas gave him a job. Pelecanos worked for the Pedas brothers' production company throughout the 1990s, reading scripts and co-producing and distributing their films.

Near the end of 1990 he found a message on his answering machine. Gordon van Gelder, a young editor with St. Martin's, apologized for the year-long delay and said he wanted to publish his novel. "I was shocked," Pelecanos says. "I was walking on air. I was going to be a published author. I was on my way." He did receive a $2,500 advance and see his novel published in 1992, but the reality of authorship was not otherwise glamorous.

Pelecanos had built his first novel around his own life. He calls his protagonist, the Greek-American Nick Stefanos, "my alter ego. His age is my age. He even looks like me." As Pelecanos had, Nick sells electronic goods in a store on Connecticut Avenue—Nutty Nathan's in the novel. The novel is called *A Firing Offense* because, as it opens, Nick is nearly fired for his rebellious ways. He and his fellow salesmen take pride in slipping down to the basement for a beer or a joint, in fast-talking customers into high-profit sales, and in hustling good-looking women. Early in the novel, Nick begins a torrid affair with a new woman on the sales staff. In time a man asks Nick to find his missing grandson, but for many pages the missing boy is of less concern to Nick than his new girl and getting high with his pals.

Finally, in the second half of the novel, the plot kicks in. The boy was involved in drugs, Nick travels south to look for him, and there is a violent showdown in—of all places—the Nutty Nathan's warehouse. *A Firing Offense* is a respectable piece of work that takes us deep into the lives of aimless young men. What at first seems a rather random plot comes together neatly. The novel is notable for its honesty about Nick's lifestyle, particularly if you take it as a self-portrait of the artist as a young outlaw.

The novel sold hardly at all. Pelecanos thinks libraries bought just enough copies to persuade the publisher to buy his next one. He followed with two more Nick Stefanos novels, *Nick's Trip* (1992) and *Down by the River Where the Dead Men Go* (1995), as well as a noirish stand-alone, *Shoedog,* that drew on his past as a shoe salesman. Before he wrote *Down by the River,* he and Emily visited Brazil, where they were adopting their second son, Pete. Brazil shocked Pelecanos. "It was the first time I'd seen hungry kids, kids eating out of Dumpsters. You saw their pain and you saw the murder in their eyes too. It radicalized me."

Brazil was one reason his novels became increasingly concerned with social issues. He had also been impressed by Richard Price's *Clockers,* which examined drug dealing and murder in an African-American housing project, and by earlier social realists like Horace McCoy, Edward Anderson, and John Steinbeck. "They wrote about common people," he says. "I wanted to combine that with the crime novel." He calls *Down by the River Where the Dead Men Go* "the darkest novel I've ever written or probably will ever write." Its first paragraph is vintage Pelecanos:

Like most of the trouble that's happened in my life or that I've caused to happen, the trouble that happened that night started with a drink. Nobody forced my hand; I poured it myself, two fingers of bourbon into a heavy, beveled shot glass. There were many more after that, more bourbons and more bottles of beer, too many more to count. But it was the first one that led me down to the river that night, where they killed a boy named Calvin Jeter.

That paragraph summarizes Nick's debauchery that night; the rest of the chapter spells it out, drink by drink. Nick is a bartender at the Spot, a bar on Eighth Street, Southeast, on Capitol Hill. He's divorced from his first wife and a part-time private investigator. After the bar closes, he downs shots until he's in a stupor. Ignoring protests that he is too drunk to drive, Nick sets off for home but winds up not far away, beside the Anacostia River, where he passes out. He is wakened by a car door slamming. He hears a moan, a scream, a splash.

When he awakes at dawn, Nick finds a black youth in the river and realizes he has been present at a murder. Nick tells what he knows to a detective who frequents his bar, but the police aren't interested. Nick's own investigation takes him into an ugly, violent world of gay prostitution and pornography. The novel builds to a confrontation with some pornographers who killed the boy in the opening scene. When the shooting stops, the killers are dead but that is not the end. Nick kidnaps the white businessman who bankrolled the porn operation and used it to satisfy his craving for young men. He takes the man down to the river where the youth died:

"Oh, God," he said as I drew the Browning from behind my back.

"There isn't one," I said, and shoved the barrel into his open mouth. "Remember?"

Mickey Spillane in his prime didn't get any tougher than that— vengeance is mine, saith the bartender. But the scene has a political edge too. Nick has rid the world of a corrupt businessman who otherwise would continue to exploit the poor. Nick's good deeds are overshadowed by the novel's sex, booze, and violence, but Nick is, in his way, as much a knight-errant as Marlowe or McGee.

Nick is an uncompromising portrait of a young man who is tough, charming, and out of control. There is only so far you can take such a character, and after he finished *Down by the River,* Pelecanos realized he was there. The books hadn't sold; probably more readers were frightened by Nick than would embrace him. Nick would continue to have cameo roles in Pelecanos's novels, but he would never again be the focus.

His fifth novel, *The Big Blowdown,* spanned a quarter century of Washington life from the 1930s to the 1950s. The focus is Nick Stefanos's grandfather, also named Nick, who operates a diner and comes into conflict with local gangsters. *Publishers Weekly* called it "feverishly alive . . . a darkly powerful story of the American city" and the novel won some international prizes. Still, when it was published in 1996, Pelecanos was uncertain about his future.

St. Martin's had published five of his novels, but his advances had risen only from $2,500 to $7,500. He had received some excellent reviews, but his sales were poor. On the plus side, he was increasingly respected by other writers; Michael Connelly called Pelecanos "the best-kept secret in American publishing." There were still no paperback editions of his novels in the United States, but in England Pete Ayrton was publishing them in his Serpent's Tail line of quality paperbacks.

Pelecanos was discouraged. He had a demanding job with Circle Films and was writing at night. The money didn't justify his time or the toll on his family life. "After *The Big Blowdown* I considered stopping. It wasn't fair to anybody. I'd come home and write at night. I had two young boys. I wanted to go out and throw the football with them." But the habit of writing died hard: "I finally started another novel just for a goof, just to do whatever I wanted. But it began to work out."

The novel that began as a goof became *King Suckerman* (1997). Set during the bicentennial summer of 1976, *King Suckerman* (the name comes from a blaxploitation film in the story) introduced two new heroes, Marcus Clay, a black Vietnam veteran who owns a record store, and his Greek-American friend Dimitri Karras, who divides his time between pickup basketball and small-time drug deals. The two of them blunder into a nasty confrontation with a homicidal ex-con. The story builds to the inevitable final confrontation, set against July Fourth fireworks and suggesting a far darker American reality than the official rhetoric.

Abruptly, Pelecanos's luck changed. An agent named Sloan Harris had agreed to represent him. Harris showed *The Big Blowdown* to Michael Pietsch, the top editor at Little, Brown. Pietsch didn't buy the novel but expressed interest in the writer. English reviews and sales had started a buzz; Pelecanos was beginning to happen. Pietsch read *King Suckerman* and thought it "blew the roof off—a daring book" and bought it in a two-book $85,000 deal. Pelecanos's movie agent, Alicia Gordon, sold the movie rights and he wrote a screenplay. Although never produced, it led to other film work. In 1999 he was confident enough to quit his job with Circle Films.

Pelecanos is philosophical now about those frustrating early years. "There's a reason it didn't happen—I didn't deserve it. I wasn't selling books but I was learning my craft. It was the best thing that ever happened to me. I was doing what I wanted to do and I was getting better." He is too modest. The early novels, if raw, are tough-minded and vital, noir at a high level.

Pelecanos calls *The Big Blowdown, King Suckerman, Shame the Devil,* and *The Sweet Forever* his DC Quartet. Each won Pelecanos more readers, more critical acclaim, and more money. They were increasingly panoramic portraits of the black Washington that both tourists and novelists avoid. By putting Clay at the heart of the novels, Pelecanos recognized that the city could not be understood in terms of a Greek-American protagonist; to write seriously about Washington he had to write about its black majority.

Pelecanos discourages the idea that he writes about the black experience. He knows that some black writers have complained about his success in portraying what they view as their world. As Pelecanos prefers to see it, he is a son of immigrants who is writing about class, not race. Still, he increasingly made black Washington his own. He reproduced the clothes, the talk, the music, the cars, the crime, and the conflicts with microscopic precision. He gathered material by talking to cops and riding with them at night and by talking to all the black people he could. As his books became known, ex-convicts and drug dealers began to call and volunteer their stories, and men in prison wrote him. In 2002, he began writing for *The Wire*, HBO's hard-hitting series about police and drug dealers in Baltimore. The program gave him access to young blacks who had never heard of his novels but regarded *The Wire* as the story of their lives.

As good as the Clay-Karras books are, Pelecanos was feeling his way toward something better. The result was *Right as Rain* (2001), the first of four novels, so far, featuring the black investigator Derek Strange. "He was a total creation," Pelecanos says. "I wanted to write a book abut racism in DC—I wasn't thinking of a series. I wanted to do something completely outside my life experience, to challenge myself by writing about a black man who's older than I am." The first three Strange novels—the beautifully titled *Right as Rain, Hell to Pay,* and *Soul Circus*—are, in a sense, one continuing story and ideally should be read in the order they were written. As a young man, Strange was a DC policeman, but at the start of *Right as Rain* we meet Strange in his fifties, as a private investigator, and Janine, his office manager and lover. Strange is fond of Janine and her son, Lionel, but afraid of them too: "Hell, everything about commitment scared him, but being a father to a young man in this world, it scared him more than anything else."

How to be a good man in "this world"—the world of poor, black, drug-ravaged, crime-ridden Washington—is the theme of the Strange novels. By the time the chapter ends, we know that Strange is independent, good-humored, a skilled investigator, and a man's man. He likes a beer now and then. He goes to church occasionally, coaches a Pee Wee football team, and tries to help young black youths stay out of trouble. He loves Janine but he loves his freedom more. He relishes his visits to a young Chinese woman in a massage parlor. As he sees it, love and sex are entirely different things. Unlike Nick Stefanos, Strange is a contented man. That fact gives the Strange novels an entirely different tone. The Stefanos novels focused on Nick's anger and frustration; the Strange novels focus on the anger and frustration of the world he lives in.

Early in *Right as Rain*, Strange visits Leona Wilson, a black woman whose policeman son, while in plain clothes, was shot and killed by a white officer in a case of mistaken identity. The white officer, Terry Quinn, resigned from the force, but Mrs. Wilson is not satisfied. She wants Strange to prove that Quinn was at fault. We meet Quinn, now working in a bookstore. Then Pelecanos shows us Earl and Ray Boone, father and son, ignorant, murderous white racists who run a drug operation from their rural home. They drive into Washington with two bricks of heroin and several guns and meet with a black drug dealer named Cherokee Coleman. Coleman is surrounded by armed men and both sides would gladly kill the others if their dealings were not so profitable.

Throughout his novels, Pelecanos provides a chilling look at the drug dealers and killers who terrorize parts of Washington. His drug czars and their stoned gun-happy teenage enforcers are far more frightening than most fictional killers because they are so true to life—they're urban nightmares. For those of us who live in the pleasant confines of Northwest Washington, Pelecanos's novels are like dispatches from a war zone we could drive to in twenty minutes but in fact never see. Pelecanos portrays young men who realize that "the life" will end with them dead or in prison but continue in the drug culture because it seems better than flipping burgers or sweeping floors. Time after time, he shows how the most trivial insults, measured by the twisted "honor" of their culture, inspire revenge and tragedy.

In *Soul Circus,* Strange works for the defense lawyers representing Granville Oliver, who is on trial for his life. Strange knows that Oliver has killed people and has poisoned the community with crack, but he resents the fact that the white prosecutors are seeking the death penalty, even though Washington's voters have rejected it. Strange sees the federal government's determination to execute Oliver as pure racism.

In one stunning scene in *Soul Circus* two teenage members of a drug gang set out to kill two members of a rival gang who have fired a gun at them from a passing car. At least one of the boys doesn't want to kill, but honor requires that he prove his manhood. We move between the two sets of young men, driving around, smoking joints, drinking beer, listening to the same Missy Elliot song on their car radios. The shooting begins outside a market, and within moments all four are dead.

Maureen Corrigan, who teaches and writes about crime fiction, said of this scene in her review in *The Washington Post:*

> In the space of a couple of paragraphs toward the middle of the novel, four gang members suddenly die in bloody, balletic sequence, and you find yourself reeling from the senselessness of their deaths, the waste of their stupid lives. Ditto for the ending of this superb novel, which shoves readers into an unwanted audience with the awful silence at the center of things.

Pelecanos shows more of the black community, of course. There are good people, black and white, policemen, parents and grandparents, teachers, social workers, and others who work to protect young people from the lure of the streets. The question is whether these good men and women can hold back the tide of drugs and violence that threatens to engulf their community.

Pelecanos has been called a writer of noir, but it may be more useful to think of him as a political novelist. He doesn't write about the whiskey-drinking white men who make the laws in offices in the Capitol and the White House and wind up rich; he writes about the dope-smoking, crack-using black men in the ghetto who suffer the laws and wind up dead or in prison. If we accept his premise that white America has by its political decisions condemned millions of black people to poverty, prison, and early death, his is an overwhelming indictment. Pelecanos's scorn for "official" Washington is seen in the fact that he never mentions it. Except as an occupying army, eager to put black people in prison, political Washington is irrelevant to his characters' lives. I quoted earlier Pelecanos's praise of private-eye novels that portrayed "human politics from the level of the street." Pelecanos writes about human politics, street politics.

After Pelecanos changed publishers, his fortunes rose. His recent novels have sold in the 20,000 range in hardback in America, and millions more in paperback around the world. In the summer of 2006, Pelecanos's fourteenth novel, *The Night Gardener,* became his first hardback best seller with its appearance on the *New York Times* list after an outpouring of rave reviews. His advances have risen from $75,000 to $150,000 to $500,000 per book. And yet his novels have not sold as well as those of many less talented writers. Considering the excellent reviews his books receive, he has to wonder why readers are resisting them. Perhaps they don't want to read about poor blacks, or they try one and find the drug dealers and random violence not to their liking. The reality of black America is one many readers prefer to ignore.

In his fourth Derek Strange novel, *Hard Revolution,* we go back in time and meet him, first as a boy, then, in 1968, as a young man. We learn that his father was a short-order cook in a diner owned by a Greek-American and his mother did housework. Derek became a policeman even though other blacks accused him of selling out to the white man. As a young cop he didn't mind smoking a joint at a party, and he found it impossible to settle down with one woman when so many were available. At the end of the novel, after the riots that followed Dr. King's death, with Washington in flames, Strange arranges the death of the man who killed someone dear to him. It's a powerful novel, both in terms of Strange's story and in its account of the riots. "It's a sensational novel," says his editor, Michael Pietsch. "It should have won the National Book Award for best novel of the year."

After *Hard Revolution*, Pelecanos wrote a stand-alone, *Drama City*. The novel focuses on Lorenzo Brown, who was a drug dealer as a young man but after eight years in prison is determined to go straight. It also concerns his parole officer, Rachel Lopez. Through Brown's job as an inspector for the Humane Society, Lopez's work with other ex-convicts, and the NA and AA meetings that both attend, Pelecanos portrays dozens of decent, often troubled people who are trying to make sense of their lives. The story also involves two rival drug gangs and a young sociopath who kills for one of them, but *Drama City* is primarily a celebration of the people who get up each day and go to work and try to meet life's challenges.

After *Drama City*, Pelecanos took some time off to write for *The Wire* and to do two segments of a miniseries set in World War II. But eventually he would have to decide what came next. Should he return to Derek Strange? Or should he strike out in a new direction, perhaps with a white protagonist? Pelecanos has, in effect, written three series—about Nick Stefanos, Marcus Clay, and Derek Strange. He starts them and then leaves them after three or four books because he fears that one ongoing series would inevitably decline in quality.

Pelecanos once wrote of his work: "All of the novels, to some degree, attempt to humanize and illuminate the lives of people who are typically underrepresented in American fiction. I mean to leave a record of this town, to entertain, and to provoke discussion. My method is simple: to present the world as it is, rather than the way readers want it to be." Both in his novels and in his work with *The Wire*, Pelecanos has gone a long way toward meeting his goals. He and Richard Price and others are writing in the Steinbeck tradition of those who care about dispossessed Americans. The question is whether the people who write about fiction understand the power and importance of his uncompromising bulletins from the front.

13.

Michael Connelly:

Death Is My Beat

Michael Connelly's paternal grandfather built houses in the suburbs around Philadelphia. As a young man, Michael's father, also named Michael, dreamed of being an artist and enrolled at the Philadelphia Institute of Art but dropped out in the early 1950s and joined his father as a builder so he could marry. His son Michael was born in 1956, the second of six children, and by the age of nine or ten was helping his father on construction projects. In the mid-1960s, a downturn in the region's economy wiped out the business. The novelist still remembers a man posting a foreclosure notice on the front door of the family home.

For a time, his father went into the car-rental business. In April 1968, passing through Washington, DC, he was caught in the riots that followed the assassination of Dr. King. Connelly abandoned his car and took refuge in a diner. He was in his mid-thirties and had recently broken a smoking habit that began when he was twelve. Shaken, he bought a pack of cigarettes and returned to smoking. He died of smoking-related cancer at age sixty, shortly before his son's first novel was published. As a successful novelist, Connelly drove around one of his father's subdivisions, Coldbrook Farms, and took pride in his father's craftsmanship and the pleasant world he'd helped create. "For years," he says, "I have felt I am sort of living out my father's unfulfilled artistic dream."

Later in 1968, the family moved to Fort Lauderdale. The next summer, when Michael's mother went to her job, she would drop him and two younger brothers at Holiday Park to amuse themselves as best they could. It was hot, and one day they noticed a sign outside the library across the street: NOW AIR CONDITIONED. The boys took refuge inside but the librarians wouldn't let them just sit; they had to read. "This is where I first started reading mysteries," Connelly recalls. "From the Hardy Boys, which I had never read, to Mickey Spillane. I remember hiding a paperback of Spillane inside a more appropriate book for a thirteen-year-old and being caught by a librarian, who took it from me and said, 'Maybe next summer.' I've often wished I could go back and thank those librarians for making me read—and read crime novels in particular."

When Connelly was sixteen he was working as a dishwasher at a beach hotel. Driving home one night he saw a bearded man running down the street. As Connelly watched, the man stripped off his shirt, wrapped something inside it, stuffed the package in a hedge, and then, wearing a T-shirt, entered a biker bar called the Parrot. Connelly pulled the shirt out of the hedge and found a gun. He called his father, who called the police. The police came to their house and told Connelly that a man had been shot in a robbery. He was the only witness. Detectives questioned the teenager for four hours, then took him to a lineup to look at several men they'd pulled from the bar. Connelly was sure that none of them was the man he'd seen; the angry detectives thought he was too scared to tell the truth. The incident intensified his interest in crime. He began reading crime stories in the newspapers and all the crime novels he could. But he wasn't yet thinking he could write about crime.

Connelly's father had gone to work for a big developer and the boy worked summers on its construction projects. When he entered the University of Florida, he was a Building Construction Sciences major but he hated classes like Introduction to Concrete. "I carried a failing average and sought almost nightly respite in the bars, bookstores, and movie theaters of Gainesville." One night he wandered into a showing at the Student Union of Robert Altman's quirky version of Raymond Chandler's *The Long Goodbye*. Connelly had not read Chandler, but he loved the movie. He watched it again the next night and within a week had read all of Chandler's novels. By then Connelly knew what his dream was—to be a crime novelist like Chandler.

"When I told my father of this dramatic shift," he recalls, "he was completely supportive. He had seen his career as a painter slip away and didn't want to discourage his son. I came upon the plan of enrolling in journalism school, learning the craft of writing as a reporter, and using the job to get into the world I wanted to write about in fiction—the world of police and crime."

After graduating in 1980, he worked for papers in Daytona Beach and Fort Lauderdale. One day he returned to the station house where he'd been questioned as a sixteen-year-old and talked to the same gruff detective, who still blamed him for not identifying the gunman. In 1986, the thirty-year-old Connelly and two other reporters wrote a long piece on the survivors of an airline crash. The story was a finalist for a Pulitzer Prize and helped him land a job as a police reporter for the *Los Angeles Times*. He had never been to Los Angeles before he sought the job. To him, it was Raymond Chandler's town.

Crime Beat, a collection of Connelly's journalism published in 2006, makes clear that even his early reporting was distinctively novelistic. The first piece in the book, about the discovery of a body in Fort Lauderdale, is filled with details that later turned up in his novels. As a police reporter in Los Angeles, he endlessly filed away details about the street cops, the detectives, the Parker Center brass, and the FBI agents who swooped in on high-profile cases. In the riots that followed the acquittal of the white policemen in the Rodney King case, he found himself confronting a black mob. A young black man in a LOVE T-shirt helped him escape. That experience, combined with his father's escape from the DC mob in 1968, would surface in one of his novels.

While still in Florida, Connelly had written two novels that he thought weren't good enough to show anyone. By his mid-thirties he was a star reporter, but his dream of writing fiction seemed to be slipping away. Then one day he saw a listing for a double feature of Altman's *The Long Goodbye* and *Chinatown*, Roman Polanski's elegant neo-noir from 1974. He went to see them and soon after that he started writing *The Black Echo* (1992), his first published novel.

In his introduction to *Crime Beat*, Connelly tells of going to a crime scene and seeking information from a detective he knew whom he'd never seen show emotion. Connelly was studying him to get details for his fictional detective, Harry Bosch. The detective came out of the house and told Connelly a mother had shot her three young children and then herself. "He had to walk away from me and I think I saw him wipe a tear out of his eye. I understood in that moment some of the difficulty, danger, and nobility of the job. And I knew I had something more to give to Harry Bosch."

We first meet Bosch on the second page of *The Black Echo*. The scene begins:

> Harry Bosch could hear the helicopter up there, somewhere, above the darkness, circling up in the light . . . he felt the terror build and he moved faster, crawling on scraped and bloody knees. . . .

This is a nightmare, based on Harry's memories of Vietnam; the horror of that war is central to Connelly's portrait of his angry, troubled detective. In the next paragraph the phone rings and awakens Harry. It is 8:53 on a Sunday morning. Harry has been asleep in a chair, fully dressed. The TV is on. Paperback novels, crumpled cigarette packs, and beer bottles are scattered around. Harry suffers from insomnia and often drinks himself to sleep in the chair.

The call summons him to a murder scene. A body has been found in a drainpipe near the Mulholland Dam, not far from Harry's home. Harry is angry. Why wasn't he called sooner? He fears that the first cops to arrive have mucked up the evidence. Harry looks in the mirror and sees red-rimmed forty-year-old eyes, gray in his curly hair. The detective stands a few inches short of six feet and is built lean, Connelly tells us, and his brown-black eyes seldom reveal his emotion.

Harry lives in the Hollywood Hills in a small one-bedroom house that is built out over the edge of a steep hill. The house embodies the precariousness of Harry's life. He made his down payment on the house with money from a film studio that made a movie about one of his cases, and he could afford it because the only things he spent money on were food, drink, and jazz. Harry's love of jazz is reflected throughout the series, as he spends solitary nights listening to the likes of John Coltrane, Stan Getz, and Frank Morgan. Once, listening to Art Pepper's rendition of "You'd Be So Nice to Come Home To," he reflects on how Pepper attacked the song: "It was the only way he knew how to play, and that relentlessness was what I liked best about him. It was the thing that I hoped I shared with him."

When Connelly first visited the *LA Times,* an editor showed him a story about some criminals who entered the city's underground storm-water system and tunneled up into a bank vault. That provided the plot of *The Black Echo.* At the crime scene that Sunday morning, Harry recognizes the dead man, Billy Meadows. They were "tunnel rats" together in Vietnam, young men with the dangerous job of exploring the Vietcong tunnel systems. The book's title comes from those tunnels: "Each one was a black echo. Nothing but death in there." The first chapter carries Harry through that long Sunday; before it ends he suspects that Meadows has taken part in a recent robbery that involved tunneling into a bank. Harry forms an uneasy alliance with the FBI, which is also investigating the bank robbery.

He meets FBI agent Eleanor Wish, who will become important in his life. Harry admires her beauty but notes coldly, "She looked hard-shell and maybe a little weary for so early in the day, the way lady cops and hookers get." Soon he is sleeping with Eleanor Wish, but the FBI is otherwise hostile and even Eleanor has her own agenda. (Her name may be a warning: "Be careful what you wish for.") In Harry's world, authority is always the enemy, and that includes the FBI. In the LAPD, the enemy is top-level officials who are incompetent, gutless, and hypocritical, particularly the agents of the Internal Affairs Division who are forever trying to drive Harry from the force.

Harry clings precariously to his job, mainly because he has cracked big cases and made friends in the media. Harry persists because his mother's murder when he was a child, along with the harsh treatment he received in foster homes, left him with a deep need to make the world right. The full name his mother gave him is Hieronymus Bosch, that of the Flemish painter who portrayed a hell on earth, populated by fiends and monsters. Harry is a lone pilgrim trying to bring order to the hell of Los Angeles.

The Black Echo is a long novel, filled with police lore. Among its strengths are the complexity and sophistication of its plot. Harry realizes that a second bank robbery is coming, again via a tunnel, and he sets out to thwart it. But the larger question is who is behind these elaborate crimes. It is no surprise that the masterminds are people in authority.

Connelly wrote *The Black Echo* before he tried to sell it. He was able to hire the agent he wanted, Philip Spitzer, James Lee Burke's agent. Connelly recalls, "I was fortunate because Spitzer immediately took the long view and planned and positioned me for a long haul." Of course, Spitzer could do that because Connelly had given him an exceptional novel. "He didn't demand big money from prospective publishers. He demanded a plan. I accepted a deal with Little, Brown and they printed a first edition of 17,000 copies." The book won an Edgar for best first novel of the year. Connelly has had the same agent and editor ever since. The editor, Michael Pietsch, later signed George Pelecanos.

In Connelly's second novel, *The Black Ice* (1993), a police detective is found in a cheap motel with his head blown off, an apparent suicide. It should be Harry's case but the higher-ups take him off it, arousing his suspicions. Harry is drawn to the dead cop's wife and begins an affair with her. In time, the cop's death proves to be far more sinister than suicide.

After these two novels, it was clear that Connelly was a serious, ambitious writer. His writing is always solid and occasionally lyrical, but it does not glitter like his hero Raymond Chandler's. He says of Chandler:

> It was his prose and his marvelous way of evoking Los Angeles—a place I had never been—that drew me to his work. Also, his depiction of a man alone against the odds and the system. Maybe because I was at the right age but I found it intoxicating and inspiring. I read the books over and over and whereas before when I read mysteries I fantasized that I was the detective on the case, winning the day and vanquishing evil, with Chandler I fantasized that I was the writer behind that wonderful prose. Of course, Chandler is not perfect. His plots are confusing and don't always add up. His views of women and race and homosexuality are of that time and ill-informed. But what holds up is the prose. What holds up is the city. Riff after riff on Los Angeles and the hopeful yet cynical view of it are wonderful and still hold up today. In chapter 13 of *The Little Sister* we are taken on a four-page ride around Los Angeles. Marlowe getting

some air. The chapter has nothing to do with the plot. It is just Chandler describing the city. He could just as easily be describing contemporary Los Angeles. When you can pull that off that is art and that is why I was and am so inspired by his work. One of my writing rituals is to read chapter 13 before starting every Bosch book.

The promise of Connelly's early novels was more than fulfilled by his fourth and fifth, *The Last Coyote* and *The Poet*. As *The Last Coyote* begins, Harry's life has fallen apart. The detective's widow has walked out on him. He's drinking too much. An earthquake has damaged his house and the building inspector says it must be demolished, although Harry is still furtively living there. Worst of all, he has been suspended from the LAPD for roughing up a superior officer and ordered to undergo psychiatric testing. In time the psychiatrist wins his respect, and Harry admits to her that he is haunted by his mother's murder in 1961, when he was eleven.

Harry's mother, Marjorie Lowe, was a call girl and at times worked the streets of Hollywood. Her body was found in an alley there. Someone had killed her with a blow to the head. No arrest was made. Harry was in a foster home but his mother was trying to regain custody. Harry knew she loved him, whatever her demons. With the psychiatrist's help, Harry realizes the mystery of his mother's death has defined his life and that he must learn the truth and avenge her.

Harry's investigation leads to his mother's best friend, Meredith Roman. She tells him that not long before she died his mother had been dating a prominent political figure. Even thirty years later, Harry smells a cover-up. He learns, along the way, who his father was, and meets him on his deathbed. Harry also flies to Florida to talk to the retired cop who investigated his mother's death. There he chances to meet a painter named Jasmine, called Jazz, who becomes the new woman in his life. Harry's search for his mother's killer is the most emotionally powerful of the early novels and its surprise ending is a shocker. The last coyote of the title is of course Harry himself. There is in fact a lone coyote he sometimes glimpses in the hills near his house, scruffy and solitary, trying to survive in an increasingly hostile environment, much like Harry.

Fans of the Bosch novels got a surprise when Connelly's fifth novel arrived. Harry Bosch was nowhere to be found in *The Poet,* the first of Connelly's stand-alones. And yet *The Poet* was possibly the best novel he had written. It begins with this paragraph:

> Death is my beat. I make my living from it. I forge my professional reputation on it. I treat it with the passion and precision of an undertaker—somber and sympathetic about it when I'm with the bereaved, a skilled craftsman with it when I'm alone. I've always thought the secret of dealing with death was to keep it at arm's length. That's the rule. Don't let it breathe in your face.

That's the voice of Jack McEvoy, a thirty-four-year-old crime reporter for the *Rocky Mountain News*—and, of course, the voice of Connelly himself. At the outset, McEvoy learns that his twin brother, Sean, a homicide detective, is dead, an apparent suicide. Devastated, unable to accept that verdict, Jack launches his own investigation and discovers evidence the police have missed. His brother may have been killed by a serial killer who has murdered other detectives around the country. The murders are linked by lines of Edgar Allan Poe's poetry that the killer left at each crime scene—thus the novel's title. Jack cannot conduct a national investigation, but because he has information no one else has he is able to bargain his way into the task force the FBI launches to pursue the killer.

Jack's alliance with the task force is an uneasy one; some agents are openly hostile. However, like Harry in *The Black Echo,* Jack McEvoy soon forms a special alliance with a comely female agent; this time her name is Rachel Walling. It is unlikely that real-life female FBI agents make a habit of sleeping with reporters who cover their cases, but it's a convention of crime fiction that the brave deserve the fair, and the improbability of the romance is mitigated by the fact that Connelly writes well about sex.

The Poet ends with a double whammy. The identity of the serial killer is a total surprise and is followed by another twist: Connelly lets the homicidal "poet" escape. Connelly had recently quit the *Times* to write fiction full-time, and he was struck by how many cases went unsolved. "It dawned on me then how many people got away with mur-der. So when I wrote *The Poet* I was bothered by the contradiction of art not imitating life. All the crime novels seemed to end with the bad guy getting caught. In LA, that only happened about seventy percent of the time. This, and what was happening in the O. J. Simpson case, added up to me deciding to let the Poet slip away."

None of Connelly's previous novels had come as easily as *The Poet*. It took him less than three months to write. "I think this is because there was no middle point of having to think about what a character like Harry Bosch would do in certain circumstances. I was essentially writing about myself as a journalist, and so I knew immediately what Jack would do in any circumstance. The story just flowed out of me."

The Poet became Connelly's breakout novel. The hardback editions of his first four novels had advanced from 17,000 to 30,000, but with *The Poet* the publisher printed 60,000 and sales increased accordingly. The paperback edition made *The New York Times* list—his first official best seller. Connelly's career, slow to start but always solid, had taken off. His recent books have sold upwards of 400,000 copies in hard-back.

Harry Bosch returned in *Trunk Music,* which concerned a movie pro-ducer who is found in the trunk of his car and may have been killed by the Mafia. It was followed by a second stand-alone, *Blood Work,* which introduced Terry McCaleb, an FBI serial-killer investigator who receives a heart transplant and then pursues the killer of the woman who donated the heart.

In 2001, Connelly published one of the best Bosch novels, *A Darkness More Than Night* (the title comes from Chandler). Con-nelly was becoming increasingly innovative. He'd left Bosch to write the two stand-alones that introduced Jack McEvoy and Terry McCa-leb. (McEvoy was Connelly's mother's maiden name and McCaleb is his wife's maiden name.) All three men—Bosch, McEvoy, and McCaleb—appear in *Darkness*. The previous Bosch novels, written in the third person, show events from Harry's point of view. *Darkness* alternates between Bosch's and McCaleb's points of view. The plot turns on Mc-Caleb's suspicion that Bosch may be a murderer. The criminal who has been killed—a man Harry openly despised—was the victim of a ritual murder. A wooden owl was left at the scene. It and other evidence linked the killing to the painter Hieronymus Bosch, which led McCaleb to suspect Harry. Connelly says of the novel:

> My plan was to make the story an exploration of Harry Bosch's character and the cost of his going into the darkness. By darkness, I mean the underworld of crime and moral corruption where he toils as a cop. The philosopher Friedrich Nietzsche once wrote that when you look into the darkness of the abyss, the abyss looks into you. Probably no other line or thought more inspires or informs my work. Harry Bosch has spent most of his life looking into the abyss, into the darkness of the human soul. What has this cost him?

The novel is finally a character study of the two very different men. McCaleb, after retirement from the FBI, marriage, and the birth of his daughter, is a contented man. During the course of the novel, each man saves the other's life but at the end they are no longer friends. Not simply because McCaleb suspects Harry of murder but because Harry is willing to go further to put monsters away than McCaleb can approve. McCaleb goes back to his family and Harry goes back to the abyss.

City of Bones opens with a dog discovering human bones buried in the Hollywood Hills. They prove to be those of a child who has been brutally abused. Harry vows to find the killer. He talks to a doctor who has witnessed unspeakable child abuse. The doctor says he could not keep going without his religion and presses Harry about his faith. The detective says, "I have faith and I have a mission. Call it the blue religion."

Harry is nearing fifty and shows signs of mellowing. He has his drinking and smoking under control and has achieved an uneasy peace with his superiors. When he meets a good woman, he tries to treat her right, only to see her die a senseless death. He remains tormented, hungry for redemption. For what? someone asks him. "For everything," he replies. "Anything. We all want to be forgiven." Although Harry fears he would be lost without his badge and his mission, he quits the LAPD after he exposes the child killer.

Lost Light is a departure in two ways. First, Harry is a private citizen again. Second, for the first time he is telling his story in the first person, presumably because Connelly wants to see if that can carry him even deeper into Harry's troubled soul. Harry's retirement is not going well. He's staying up late, drinking too much, staring at the walls. He has a call from a retired cop who offers him new information on an unsolved case. Harry remembers the case well; the memory of the dead woman, her hands lifted as if in prayer, has haunted him. Revisiting the case gives him a mission but he has no badge to go with it. His investigation brings him into conflict with a top-secret FBI antiterrorism unit operating under post-9/11 rules. When Harry defies them, he is roughed up and tossed in a cell. Harry bitterly tells an FBI agent that it used to be a free country and cites Nietzsche's remark that in combating monsters we must not become monsters ourselves.

Eleanor Wish reappears. They were married for a time but she left him and has been living in Las Vegas and working as a professional gambler. He considers her his one great love and wants her back but she resists. Increasingly, Harry has been struggling to save his soul. At the end of *Lost Light,* he unexpectedly finds salvation within his grasp, when Eleanor introduces him to the daughter he didn't know he had. Connelly has been building toward this scene for a long time and I found it immensely moving. Harry has earned a shot at happiness. The novel ends with him declaring, "In that moment I knew all the mysteries were solved. That I was home. That I was saved." The question is whether Harry can be Harry and still cling to his newfound happiness.

The Narrows brings together characters and events from several earlier novels. We again encounter Rachel Walling, the FBI agent last seen in *The Poet.* In part because of her affair with Jack McEvoy, she has been exiled to South Dakota, but now she is summoned back to California because the serial killer called the Poet has resurfaced and she has personal knowledge of him. We shift to Harry's first-person narrative—Terry McCaleb is dead and his widow wants Harry to examine his death. Perhaps McCaleb's transplanted heart failed him but Harry soon suspects murder. We move between Harry's investigation of McCaleb's death and the FBI investigation of the Poet's murders in Nevada. The two investigations inevitably merge. The FBI tries to force Harry off the case. Rachel is already an outsider within the FBI and the two of them team up to find the Poet. Their partnership includes the bedroom—Connelly's protagonists are now three-for-three with sexy FBI agents.

Connelly says that his young daughter inspired him to write *The Narrows:* "As I watched my daughter grow it began to bother me that I had created a fictional world where a killer like [the Poet] could walk free. . . . I made a decision to go back into that darkness to find him. And I decided to use Harry Bosch for the job."

In *The Closers,* Connelly is back to a third-person narration and Harry is back with the LAPD. He joins a new unit that uses DNA to re-examine thousands of unsolved murder cases. Harry and his partner, Kiz Rider, a friend from years past, are given the case of a sixteen-year-old girl abducted from her home and shot to death in 1988. It may now be possible to trace the killer through blood on the gun. *The Closers* is a return to basics. After several relatively fanciful novels in which Harry pursued the Poet, wooed an FBI agent, and was reunited with his gambler wife and their child, this is a pure police procedural. Eleanor has taken herself and their daughter to Hong Kong and there is no woman in his life. Harry is focused entirely on the case, once again an avenging angel.

As I read Connelly, this is the culmination of a process that has been under way since *City of Bones.* Just before it, in *A Darkness More Than Night,* Harry's world grew about as dark as it could. Harry was suspected of murder and almost killed. With *City of Bones,* the Bosch novels begin to change. Their style is leaner, more focused. There is less detail, less description, more dialogue. The focus is more on Harry and less on the world around him. Connelly says of the relationship between himself and his character:

> Initially there was very little of me in Harry Bosch. I deliberately took things that were the opposite of me and gave them to him. Our one commonality was left-handedness. But over the years

and the books I have not been able to continue that distance. We share more and more. Fatherhood, worldview, our disappointed hopefulness for LA. After eleven books I think it would be impossible to keep a character at arm's length. At some point you put your arm around him and invite him in.

In the later novels, Harry's smoking is gone; he still thinks about cigarettes but resists them. (Connelly never smoked.) Drinking is no longer an issue. To be sure, Harry remains a fatalist. "There was no closure and there was no peace," he says in *The Closers*. "The truth did not set you free." But Harry soldiers on. He has given himself to the blue religion. His retirement was a failure. He needs his gun and his badge to be himself. Near the end of the novel, in a kind of benediction, the police chief tells him, "You are on this earth for one thing, Detective Bosch . . . to carry out your mission."

The tormented wild man of the early novels has been replaced by the avenging angel, a kind of saint. We see now that the series has an arc; the Bosch novels have become a classic story of rebirth and redemption. At the end of *The Closers,* Harry vows "to carry on the mission . . . always to speak for the dead." His vow is a dramatic reminder of how far the crime novel has come. In the drawing-room mysteries of the early twentieth century, no one really cared about the corpse on page one. It was a formality, the starting point of the puzzle that would allow author and detective to demonstrate their brilliance. That's no longer true in modern crime fiction, and nowhere is it less true than in the Bosch novels.

Have the Bosch thrillers no flaws? Not many. People who don't like the books probably find them too dark. Harry is not a barrel of laughs. The novels offer none of the comic relief that John Sandford injects into his *Prey* series. Connelly doesn't do comic relief. There is a purity to the novels, a tragic view. Death is his beat.

All novelists ask us to suspend disbelief, but there is always the question of how far we are willing to go. Connelly's plots, as with most thrillers, sometimes make demands on us. For example, in *The Poet,* we have to accept that the serial killer is the astonishing person he turns out to be. In *The Narrows* we have to accept that, when the Poet burned evidence, one scrap of paper survived to provide Harry with a crucial clue. But good writers earn our trust. We accept these and other developments because Connelly has created a world so real, so filled with credible details and believable people, that we want to believe.

In my review of *City of Bones,* I said that the Bosch novels were "the best American crime series now in progress." Several novels later, I'll go further and say that if we consider the depth and seriousness that Connelly has brought to Harry's characterization, the excellence of his plotting, the precision of his writing, his unsurpassed grasp of the police culture, and the moral gravity of his work, the Bosch novels are the finest crime series anyone has written. There is much competition: McBain, Pelecanos, Burke, Chandler, MacDonald—all have done wonderful work. But I don't think anyone else has written at such a high level for so long. For those of us who accept Harry, warts and all, there are few more affecting portraits of an angry, damaged, tormented idealist in American fiction. Connelly may have flunked Introduction to Concrete, but he has built the world of Harry Bosch with the same skill and craftsmanship that his father and grandfather brought to the houses they put up. The excellence of the twelfth Bosch novel, *Echo Park* (2006), is further proof that, as he enters his fifties, Connelly is only getting better.

14.

Dennis Lehane:

No Turning Back

Dennis Lehane was born in 1965 in Boston's Dorchester community, then a melting pot of blue-collar Irish, Polish, and Italian families. His parents were Irish immigrants. His father worked for more than thirty years at Sears, Roebuck, just a block from Fenway Park, and his mother worked in the cafeterias of the public schools. From the start Lehane was a reader. "My mother took me to a library when I was six because the nuns had told her I liked reading," he told me. "I fell in love right then and there." He told an interviewer from *January* magazine,

> I wrote since I was eight. When I was twenty, I realized I was just lousy at everything else; I had dropped out of two colleges. That's when I said, Well, this is the only thing I'm good at so I might as well take it seriously, and I went off to major in it. Writing was just not considered a viable option where I came from, so it took me time to get there. Once I did there was—honest to God—no turning back.

Lehane made his way to Eckerd College in St. Petersburg, where he earned a bachelor's degree in creative writing, and then to Florida International University in Miami, where he studied under the novelist

James W. Hall and received his MFA. He is one of the first novelists we've looked at who emerged from the thriving world of graduate school writing courses—who went to college to learn to write. His success recalls the Nashville guitarist who, asked if he could read music, replied, "Yeah, but it don't hurt mah pickin' none." Lehane is a serious student of literature, who knows all about Greek tragedy, Shakespeare, and postmodernism—but it don't hurt his writin' none. The man was born to write.

In his student days, Lehane focused on short stories. "I was twenty-four and I was broke and I had all this time on my hands. So I sat down and wrote a detective novel and—what do you know?—it sold." That's the condensed version. *A Drink Before the War* didn't sell fast. Lehane submitted it to an agent, Ann Rittenberg, who was impressed and also surprised to learn that he was so young. But there were editors who wanted changes that Lehane refused to make and editors who proposed a paperback original, which Lehane also rejected. In time Rittenberg submitted the manuscript to an editor at Harcourt, Claire Wachtel, who went around a more senior editor to buy it for an $8,000 advance.

The novel, if begun as a lark, didn't stay one; Lehane says it went through a dozen drafts before publication. The work paid off: the novel won a Shamus Award and sold a solid 10,000 copies. When Wachtel left Harcourt for Morrow, Lehane followed her, and she speaks warmly of his loyalty. "He's had all kinds of money waved at him. He just says, 'How many boats do I need?' "

Lehane wasn't thinking about publication when he wrote the novel. "I just wanted to have a little fun—I'd always loved to read mysteries. I just wrote it." And yet, having studied with people who were serious about literary fiction, he knew the implications when his thriller was readied for publication. He told a CNN interviewer, "Coming from the world I was in, writing very esoteric short fiction, I knew exactly what boundary I was stepping over. I was leaving one camp and stepping into another."

A Drink Before the War, published in 1994, opens with thirty-something PI Patrick Kenzie arriving at Boston's Ritz-Carlton Hotel to meet some politicians. Instead of wearing his usual jeans and diver's shirt, he tells us:

I picked up a dark blue, double-breasted Armani from my closet—one of several I received from a client in lieu of cash—found the appropriate shoes, tie, and shirt, and before you could say "GQ," I was looking good enough to eat.

If that reminds you of Philip Marlowe as he arrives to meet the Sternwoods at the start of *The Big Sleep*—"I was neat, clean, shaved and sober, and I didn't care who knew it"—you have a good memory. *A Drink Before the War* reads like a hip, edgy, Generation X updating of Chandler into the post-Vietnam, post–Thomas Harris world of unlimited violence. Kenzie shares Marlowe's wise-ass attitude toward the rich and powerful, and throughout this novel Lehane tosses off Chandlerisms: "a brain-dead sociopath who was only slightly bigger than Rhode Island . . . a purse you could hide Peru in . . . lonelier than an AA meeting on St. Patrick's Day."

Lehane expressed surprise when I mentioned these echoes of Chandler. He says he read Chandler when he was about eleven and hasn't reread him. As he recalls it, "I learned the tricks of the vivid (and vividly outrageous) simile and metaphor from Robert Parker. I often cringe to read *A Drink Before the War* because it's so ridiculously faux-Parker. But then Parker learned it from Chandler, so I guess I was influenced by Chandler without being aware of it."

The novel's plot brings together elements that Lehane knew growing up in Dorchester, among them gangs, racism, and political corruption, as well as the spirit of the neighborhood itself. The politicians want Kenzie and his partner, Angela Gennaro, to find a black cleaning woman, Jenna Angeline, who they say has stolen important papers. Kenzie insults the politicians, who are racist, sexist, stupid, and corrupt, but he gets the job anyway. He tracks down Jenna, a decent woman whose ex-husband, Socia, is a vicious drug kingpin who heads a teenage gang. Their teenage son, Roland, who hates his father, leads an equally lethal gang. There are many shootouts and showdowns. The two detectives are assisted by Bubba Rogowski, a hulking sociopath and arms dealer who is their friend and protector. In the end, Kenzie shoots and kills Socia and reaches a truce with Roland, who is, like Kenzie, a victim of childhood abuse.

It's a serviceable plot but less important than the characterizations, descriptions, and sociology that Lehane hangs on it. First and foremost there is the Kenzie-Gennaro relationship. This is our first glimpse of Angie:

> She had her feet propped up on the desk, a pair of black suede Peter Pan boots covering them, the cuffs of her charcoal jeans tucked into the boots. I followed her long legs up to a loose white cotton T-shirt. The rest of her was hidden behind the newspaper except for a partial view of rich, thick hair, the color of windswept tar, that fell to her olive arms . . . eyes the color of melting caramel. Eyes you'd dive into without a look back.

That paragraph makes clear that Lehane is a writer, that Angie is to die for, and that Kenzie is in love with her. We learn that Angie is married to Phil and the three of them were childhood friends, along with Bubba. Now Phil beats Angie. In the scene above, when Angie takes off her dark glasses, Kenzie sees her latest black eye. He wants to beat his old friend to a pulp—Bubba would gladly kill him—but the last time Kenzie did that Phil just beat Angie worse when he recovered. Why does this lovely, otherwise fiercely independent woman let her drunken husband use her for a punching bag? The not entirely satisfactory answer is that she loves him. Kenzie doesn't hide his continuing interest in Angie, and Lehane gets a lot of "will-they-or-won't-they?" mileage as the relationship evolves from book to book.

We learn not only that Kenzie's fireman father beat him but that Kenzie has an ugly scar on his stomach where his father, in a rage, branded him with a hot iron. Kenzie hated his father and watched without regret when he died of cancer. Yet at times Kenzie fears that he has inherited some of his father's dark side—as, for example, when he shoots Socia in cold blood. By then, he knows that Socia sexually abused his own son, so in a sense Kenzie is killing his own father.

A Drink Before the War is a promising first novel, but Lehane's second, *Darkness, Take My Hand,* vastly surpasses it. For one thing, its plot provides more suspense—a serial killer is at large and we don't know his identity until the final pages—and its writing is looser, more fluid. The plot is too complex to do more than hint at. Horrid murders in the present lead back to other horrid murders in the past. There is a vast amount of violence; to kick things off, a young woman is crucified. There are eight or ten certifiable psychopaths banging about. The identity of the killer is a mystery until the end, but it becomes clear that he knows Kenzie and is out to get him.

The level of violence is positively Shakespearean—we're talking *Titus Andronicus* here. People are burned and beaten to death. A pair of eyeballs is left in Kenzie's kitchen cabinet, along with a taunting note. A harmless young man is killed and his limbs sliced off. A killer puts a shotgun to a woman's head with one hand and threatens to bash out her child's brains with the other. A scene in which Kenzie goes to visit a master criminal in prison suggests homage to Will Graham and Clarice Starling visiting Hannibal Lecter. If Thomas Harris upped the ante for stylish slaughter, Lehane has gladly called him. Lehane agrees he was influenced by the Lecter novels but less with regard to the violence, he says, than in terms of "the psychological damage that was done to those who hunt monsters. Will Graham, in particular, who's a wonderfully flawed hero."

Lehane's third novel, *Sacred*, offers, by his standards, comic relief. Kenzie and Gennaro become involved with a rich and lethal old man and his beautiful and equally lethal daughter. Several people die but humorous scenes are tossed into the mix. "I'm Irish," Lehane says. "Humor is part of who I am. But it's a pretty dark humor." Dark indeed. In Desiree, the daughter, Lehane apparently set out to create the most gorgeous and dangerous woman in all crime noir—the ultimate femme fatale—and he may have succeeded. Kenzie and Gennaro by now are lovers—Lehane has rid us of Phil—but we fear their happiness can't last. The climax of *Sacred* follows the convention of crime fiction that the heroes, near the end, will get themselves in a seemingly hopeless fix. As always, Lehane goes for broke. Kenzie is bound hand and foot. Gennaro is buried up to her neck in the ground. The father and the daughter are competing to kill them. Not to worry—our heroes prevail. So does the author, tongue securely in cheek.

Lehane has fun in *Sacred,* but in *Gone, Baby, Gone* he is again terrifying. He has always been obsessed with child abuse, and here he devotes an entire novel to it. Kenzie and Gennaro set out to find a missing child and enter a nightmare of pedophilia. The evil of the abusers and the suffering of the innocents are all but unreadable. Near the end, Kenzie finds the room where a pedophile keeps his victims. The room is a vision of hell, filled with bare mattresses, handcuffs, riding crops, whips, and dildos. Kenzie shoots the pedophile, then finds the victim:

> I looked in the bathtub.
> I'm not sure how long I stood there, head bent, mouth open. I felt a hot wetness on my cheeks, streams of it, and it was only after that double eternity of staring into the tub at the small, naked body curled up by the drain that I realized I was weeping.

Lehane uses violence to express moral outrage. He usually shows that the abusers were themselves once victims. As a young man, he worked for a time counseling abused children. Asked if that was the source of his concern, he said,

> The short answer is that, yes, my obsession began because I worked with abused kids. But I think it probably began earlier and I just wasn't aware of it. So many of the kids I grew up with came from broken homes or abusive homes. And I left the corner every night and went back to a sane, sound home where there was a lot of love. So, like Sean Devine [in *Mystic River*], I probably suffer from survivor's guilt. Luck, nothing more, separates me from my friends who never made it out of that place, because I won the parent lottery and they didn't.

The fifth Kenzie-Gennaro novel, *Prayers for Rain,* introduces a sadistic villain who out of sheer malice drives strangers to suicide. The series had been increasingly popular. The first book sold around 10,000 in hardback; the fifth had a first printing of 60,000, was a Literary Guild selection, and sold another 300,000 copies in paperback. Lehane had a growing audience. Bill Clinton was a fan. Yet his novels were self-limiting; their violence was such that they were unlikely to reach a huge audience. Taken on their own terms, the Kenzie-Gennaro novels are dazzling. And yet they were increasingly over the top, even out of control, not in the writing but in the subject matter.

How much physical and psychic punishment could Patrick and Angie take, or Lehane dish out, or readers tolerate? How many monsters is too many? How many atrocities? Lehane had enjoyed a remarkable run. By his early thirties he was being compared to Raymond Chandler. And yet, if you admired his remarkable gifts as stylist and storyteller, you had to believe he was capable of better.

Lehane was thinking just that. "I had tired of the high body count and visceral-kicks-for-visceral-kicks'-sake that I think reached either an apotheosis or nadir, depending on your perspective, in *Prayers for Rain*, a book that it's no secret I've never been too proud of. Maybe it was just an organic side effect of getting older, but I began to question the whole idea of 'good' violence. It just didn't jibe with my experience of the world."

More than most people who write thrillers, Lehane is a student of literature. He tells his creative-writing class at Harvard,

> I'm going to talk about depth of language, about depth of character, I'm going to talk about epiphanic moments and Aristotelian logic. . . . If you don't bring some sort of music to your prose, if that isn't something you can put on the table, then please go do something else because it's the only thing that separates literature from any other art form. Hollywood can beat us in the car chases and the explosions and the high drama. All we have is language and depth of character, the ability to take you through a life.

He has cited Graham Greene as his greatest influence and says he considers himself less a crime novelist than an urban novelist "trying to follow in the tradition not so much of Chandler or Hammett but of Hubert Selby, Richard Price, Pete Dexter, William Kennedy." Music is important to him too. He says the narrative voice in *Mystic River* was influenced by Bruce Springsteen, and that he listened to the Clash, the Rolling Stones, and the Red Hot Chili Peppers, among others, while writing the novel.

He told an interviewer from bookreporter.com, "I'm attracted to classical tragedy as a form. I can do comedy and I deeply admire satire but my strength, as far as I can tell, lies in tragedy." He told another interviewer,

I'm attracted to what I think of as "fiction of mortal event," that is, fiction in which bad stuff happens and the price is high. That led me to crime fiction. I write about violence; it's what I obsess over. I can't imagine writing a book in which crime didn't happen.

The question was whether he could draw on both the street smarts of his boyhood and the literary sophistication he gained in college to write a novel about crime that moved beyond melodrama into the realm of tragedy. He began to think about a tragedy in a blue-collar Boston neighborhood—"an epic story about small-scale lives." The germ of his plot had been with him for years. For his master's thesis, he wrote a story called "Mystic River" about a cop named Sean, and there were hints of the novel-to-be scattered throughout the Kenzie-Gennaro novels. He made frequent references to the river itself—its name, to Lehane, is evocative, mysterious, magical. In *Darkness, Take My Hand,* one character ran a grocery store before he became a Mafia boss; in *Mystic River,* ex-con Jimmy Marcus runs a grocery and at the end decides to return to crime. Also in *Darkness,* two psychopaths try to lure the young Patrick and Phil into their van, suggesting the abduction that starts *Mystic River.* In one Kenzie-Gennaro novel, there is even a brief, enigmatic reference to a man being shot to death beside the Mystic, as two men are in the novel. *Mystic River* had haunted Lehane for years and at the start of the new century he was ready to confront it.

For anyone who loves fine writing, to move from the Kenzie-Gennaro novels to *Mystic River* is like leaving the funhouse and entering a world so real that it hurts. For all their lyricism, humor, and romance, the Kenzie-Gennaro books are ultimately about violence. In interviews, Lehane has stressed the writer's duty to entertain: "That's our primary job—keep 'em awake at the campfire. It's gotta be fun, gotta be exciting, gotta have some kick." The problem with the Kenzie-Gennaro books is that they're too entertaining. Lehane gives us too many kicks, slaughters too many innocents. In *Mystic River,* Lehane finally confronts the real world, where our troubles most often come not from psychopaths but from within ourselves.

The plot of *Mystic River* is well known, both from the novel and

Clint Eastwood's extraordinary movie. We meet Sean Devine, Jimmy Marcus, and Dave Boyle when they are eleven. Already, Jimmy is tough, a troublemaker. Sean is cool and watchful; he knows that he'll go to college and make something of himself. Dave is the hanger-on, "a kid with girl's wrists and weak eyes." The novel's opening section is a dark poem about these boys and the world they and Lehane grew up in. Lehane calls it East Buckingham and says it is a blend of several working-class Boston neighborhoods:

> They all lived in East Buckingham, just west of downtown, a neighborhood of cramped corner stores, small playgrounds, and butcher shops where meat, still pink with blood, hung in the windows. The bars had Irish names and Dodge Darts by the curbs. Women wore handkerchiefs tied off at the backs of their skulls and carried mock leather snap purses for their cigarettes. . . . Days, the mothers searched the papers for coupons. Nights, the fathers went to the bars.

Jimmy lives in the Flats, the poorest part of East Bucky, with a sad, silent mother and a drunken father who beats him. Yet Jimmy loves the Flats for the good times, the street parties—the way people could suddenly put aside their problems and complaints and lost-job worries and old grudges and cut loose and enjoy their lives.

Dave is kidnapped by two pedophiles and suffers four days of sexual abuse before he escapes. This scene was inspired by a real-life incident when Lehane was eleven. He and a friend got in a fight that continued until two detectives happened by, stopped the fight, and drove them home. Lehane recalls how upset his mother was. How, she asked, did he know the men were really detectives? Twenty years later, Lehane remembered the incident and took it "to the worst-case scenario." In the novel, Dave returns home and imagines himself a hero but unsympathetic neighbors see him as "damaged goods" and other kids call him a faggot. Dave is a lonely, sensitive boy, destined for more tragedy.

The story jumps forward to 2000, and we see the three men in their thirties. Jimmy had been a successful criminal in his late teens, then went to prison for two years. He has a daughter, Katie, lost her mother to cancer, took another wife, Annabeth, and has two more daughters. He runs a corner grocery in the Flats. Jimmy's life is all right until one Sunday morning his beloved Katie is found murdered. Sean, now a police detective, works the case. Dave, married and a father, comes to be suspected of the crime. In time, Jimmy murders Dave, only to have Sean prove that someone else killed Katie. As the curtain falls, Dave is senselessly dead, Jimmy plans to return to crime, and Sean vows to prove that Jimmy killed Dave, although there is little reason to think he can.

The power of the book arises from the most basic human emotions—Jimmy's love for his child and his fury at her death. There is a heartbreaking passage in which Jimmy, in a kind of prayer, tells his dead daughter that he loved her more than he had loved her mother, more than he loved her sisters, more than he loved his wife Annabeth. In the novel, this is part of an interior monologue. In the movie, writer Brian Helgeland, unwilling to lose these powerful words, injects them as dialogue.

Lehane uses all his skill to twist the reader's heartstrings. He stretches out Katie's disappearance for a hundred pages until Sean finally confirms her death. We see Jimmy's fears grow and when the news comes he explodes, wailing and fighting the police who keep him from her body. The scene is powerful in print and even more so in the film, as Sean Penn's portrayal of Jimmy's grief is seen up close and then from above in an almost unbearable image of rage and pain.

For all its moments of high drama, the greatness of the novel rests on the "depth of character" Lehane demanded of his students. We come to know Lehane's people as well as we know anyone in recent American fiction. Few are entirely likable. Only the doomed Katie, briefly glimpsed, blazes with energy and hope, qualities that rarely survive in the Flats—and she dies trying to escape. We are taken inside these people and their tortured relationships. Lehane makes us understand people who do not understand themselves.

Serious characterizations require at least three elements. First, the writer must truly know his characters. Second, knowing them, he must have the talent to bring them to life. Third, he must have the courage to slow the action and take us deep inside them, knowing that he runs the risk of losing some readers. He must trust his material, trust his talent, and trust his readers. Writing *Mystic River*, Lehane knew he would lose many Kenzie-Gennaro fans and he had no idea how many new readers would be drawn to his blue-collar tragedy.

His gamble paid off. The novel was praised as "powerful," "gripping," "brilliant," "haunting," "overwhelming," "wrenching," "disturbing," fascinating," and "a tragedy of Shakespearean proportions." Most reviewers approached it not as genre fiction but as a serious mainstream novel about American life.

Some reviewers compared the novel to Greek tragedy. If classical Greek tragedy demands a great man brought down by a tragic flaw, *Mystic River* isn't Greek; like Theodore Dreiser's novel, it is better seen as an American tragedy. Dave, raped as a child, broken as an adult, was always doomed. When he is killed for the murder he didn't commit rather than for the one he did, it is pitiful and ironic but not tragic. Sean is a smart cop with a bad marriage—Everyman, perhaps, but not a tragic figure. Finally there is Jimmy, and if he is tragic it is not because he is a great man brought down but a man both strong and weak who can't overcome the flaws—"the burdens of my nature," he calls them—that lure him back to crime. Jimmy is conflicted, in some ways sympathetic, but not tragic. We share his heartbreak when his daughter dies, but it cannot be said that suffering ennobles him.

The novel's tragedy is more encompassing. Insofar as Jimmy is tragic, it is because he lives in a world where violence can only lead to more violence, a world that has taught him to think only in terms of revenge, not of forgiveness or understanding. The tragedy is the nature of the world these people inhabit, a world of alcoholism, wife-beating, and crime, a world in which poverty, ignorance, and violence beget more poverty, ignorance, and violence, generation after generation. Lehane, the boy the nuns brought to books, managed to escape that world and, like Larry McMurtry in *The Last Picture Show*, he looks back on his childhood with love, pity, pain, and anger. The tragedy in *Mystic River* is that of people who never had a chance.

Lehane was blessed—luck of the Irish—that Clint Eastwood bought the film rights to his novel, hired a fine writer, assembled a brilliant cast, and made one of the best American movies in years. Sean Penn and Tim Robbins won Academy Awards as Jimmy and Dave, and many called Penn's performance the best since those of the young Marlon Brando. It is fascinating to read the book and then watch the movie. The novel provides vastly more detail about the lives and thoughts of the characters, while the movie offers images that give the story a new dimension. Much is condensed but not much is lost.

I came to Lehane backwards. When his novel *Shutter Island* arrived for review in 2003 I had never read him. But its strange, dark story sent me back to the earlier novels. Here's how I began my review:

> To read Dennis Lehane's *Shutter Island* is to enter a nightmare of madness, violence, and deception. To finish the novel—and it would be criminal even to hint at its ending—is to be disoriented, perhaps angered, and finally to reflect on the ability of a master storyteller to play havoc with our minds. If we could bring back Edgar Allan Poe and equip him with today's postmodern bag of tricks, he might give us a tale as unexpected and unsettling as *Shutter Island.*

Lehane knew he couldn't follow up *Mystic River* with more of the same. "So why not go 360 degrees away and play with something I've always been enamored with: the gothic. That's what I did." He called the novel "an homage to gothic, but also an homage to B movies and pulp."

Shutter Island is perverse, a trick. We read along with one set of assumptions and abruptly, at the end, we find that reality is the opposite of what we have been gulled into believing. Not all readers liked the final twist. Some were angered, some confused. Personally, I was poleaxed by the ending—and delighted, too, to have been so neatly fooled. *Shutter Island* wasn't a step forward for Lehane, but more of a holding action while he girds himself for the next big one. Such a novel is now in progress. It is set in part during the Boston police strike of 1919 and touches on other events of the period. It will, he sighs, be very long.

For now, the question is this: How good is *Mystic River*? It seems to me that, in terms of American popular fiction, it is a great novel, like *Main Street, Lonesome Dove, From Here to Eternity, All the King's Men,* and *The Grapes of Wrath.* Not many of our major writers have attempted tragedy among the working class. McMurtry portrayed cowboys, Jones gave us soldiers, Steinbeck looked at dispossessed farmers, and Dreiser's masterpiece examined a young man who tried to rise beyond his origins. *Mystic River* doesn't suffer by comparison with any of these fine novels.

Although several murders occur in *Mystic River,* it ignores the conventions of crime fiction. Sean is a cop, trying to solve a murder, but he's not the protagonist, and although he finds out who killed Katie he can't prove that Jimmy killed Dave. In the central murder, the killers are not evil—Katie's death was unintended. The novel offers no conventional love interest; the three principals are married, and of them Jimmy is the most happily married—to a working-class Lady Macbeth who wants him to return to crime. There is room for a sequel that would show Jimmy becoming a crime czar and Sean trying to bring him down. But Lehane says he plans no sequel. Insofar as *Mystic River* is a crime novel, it is one that transcends and transforms the genre, as *Hamlet* transcended and transformed the revenge plays that inspired it.

In one interview, Lehane said, "I believe that the crime novel is where the social novel went. If you want to write about the underbelly of America, if you want to write about the second America that nobody wants to look at, you turn to the crime novel."

In terms of the social novel, the big novel about America that Tom Wolfe and others have called for, Lehane has placed himself in a line that goes back to Dreiser and Steinbeck. In terms of our theme—the triumph of the thriller—*Mystic River* is a milestone. In the eighty or so years since Hammett, thousands of writers have produced crime novels that followed more or less the same formula. Some, within the confines of that formula, have been brilliant but were nonetheless limited by its demands. Lehane, having mastered the crime thriller in his early books, moved beyond it in *Mystic River.* Other writers have tried to do that and will again. But the artistic and commercial success of *Mystic River* makes it the one that changed the landscape, the novel that will inspire and challenge other writers for years to come.

IV.

TALENT, TALENT EVERYWHERE

Wherein the author praises some fine writers you may not know, castigates some less fine writers you probably do know, ponders the modern crime series, questions the infallibility of the literary establishment, and urges readers to enjoy what they damn well please.

15

Favorites

This book would have been shorter, and my life simpler, if I'd focused on just a dozen or so of the writers I hold in highest regard. But there are many, many fine writers at work today, and I would be remiss if I didn't talk about as many as I can. In this chapter, I'll look at ten, most of them American, who are particular favorites. They come to us from the usual improbable pasts. One was an actress before she started writing. One was a private investigator before he began turning his real-life adventures into fiction. Another is a Vietnam veteran whose recent best seller alleges a massive government cover-up. Another was a prizewinning reporter who took up fiction to get rich, succeeded, and now gives much of his money to charity.

The Way the Crow Flies
By Ann-Marie MacDonald

Of all the novels I've read in recent years, only Lehane's *Mystic River* impressed me as much as *The Way the Crow Flies,* Ann-Marie MacDonald's gorgeous, heartbreaking look at the human condition.

In a brief opening scene, a child lies dead in the Canadian woods. The book's first sentence is: "The crows saw the murder." Then the main narrative begins:

The sun came out after the war and our world went Technicolor. Everyone had the same idea. Let's get married. Let's have kids. Let's be the ones who do it right.

Jack and Mimi McCarthy intend to do it right. We meet them in 1962. He's an officer in the Royal Canadian Air Force. She's a loving wife and mother. Mike, twelve, is a good student and athlete, and Madeleine, eight, is a sweetheart. They have just arrived at an airbase in rural Ontario. The mystery of the dead girl we glimpsed at the outset hangs over the story, and another outrage soon unfolds. As Madeleine starts the fourth grade, her teacher has her and other girls stay after class and proceeds to abuse them. The girls, confused and frightened, keep silent. The Cuban missile crisis begins and Jack McCarthy, busy protecting his nation, is blind to the threat to his own family. By the time the events of 1962–63 have run their course, the McCarthy family has been devastated, as have others, because of one sick schoolteacher. Then MacDonald leaps forward twenty-odd years to show us Madeleine in her thirties, still trying to overcome the harm done to her at eight.

No summary can do justice to this novel, because so much depends on the beauty of its writing. More than fifty years ago, after reading William Styron's *Lie Down in Darkness*, Dorothy Parker said of the young author, "He writes like a god." I kept thinking of that when I read *The Way the Crow Flies*. The novel is not only beautifully written, it is beautiful in its conception, its compassion, its wisdom, even its anger.

The excellence of this novel is beyond dispute. The question is whether it should be considered a thriller. (The fact that my editors sent it to me to review is not conclusive.) MacDonald, an actress and playwright in her native Canada, knows how to tell a story. She could have told us about the McCarthy family without having a girl dead on the first page, but that girl is central to her storytelling strategy. We don't find out who killed her for almost seven hundred pages, and the mystery helps keep us engrossed in a very long novel. The scenes of sexual abuse are even more gripping—we are outraged; we want that bastard caught and punished. MacDonald expertly uses the tools of a thriller to grab and hold us, but her talent transcends genre.

It can be difficult, these days, to know what is a thriller, where the boundaries stop. Another example is Alice Sebold's best seller *The Lovely Bones,* the story of a teenager who is raped and murdered by a neighbor and tells her story from Heaven. The most obvious strength of the novel is the idea of a narrator speaking from the hereafter, and that is enhanced by the beauty and pathos of the dead girl's voice. But this is also the story of a crime and we are hooked in part because we hope to see the killer caught. If the girl had died in an accident—without the murder, without our demand for punishment—I doubt that the book would have found such a huge audience. Like Ann-Marie MacDonald, Sebold uses a crime and our hope of justice to draw us in.

Crusader's Cross
By James Lee Burke

James Lee Burke, the most lyrical of today's crime writers, was born in Texas in 1936 and grew up along the Texas–Louisiana Gulf Coast. He eventually settled in New Iberia, Louisiana, where many of his novels are set. After college, he worked as a reporter, English teacher, and social worker. He published his first novel in 1965, when he was twenty-nine. Five more followed between 1970 and 1986, but it was not until his first Dave Robicheaux crime thriller in 1987 that his career took off.

Burke said in an interview:

> After my first three novels, I thought I was permanently on board. But *The Lost Get-Back Boogie* was returned by the agency handling my work after about ten rejections. I was very discouraged, but then I met my current agent, Philip S. Spitzer, who was driving a cab in Hell's Kitchen and running a one-man agency at night. Philip was my cousin André Dubus's agent and I liked him immediately and thought him a stand-up no-nonsense guy. We became close friends and business partners and for the next nine years he kept *The Lost Get-Back Boogie* under constant submission, earning a total of 111 editorial rejections. LSU finally published the novel, and today it sells all over the world.

Dave Robicheaux, the hero of fourteen Burke novels, tells us this of his family history:

> Our father, known as Big Aldous Robicheaux in the oil patch, has been a good-hearted, illiterate Cajun and notorious barroom brawler. . . . My mother had long ago disappeared into a world of low-rent bars and lower-rent men. Big Aldous, our father, died in an oil well blowout when I was eighteen.

Dave served in Vietnam, then was a street cop in New Orleans and a detective in New Iberia, and he has much on his conscience:

> The unarguable fact was I had blood on my hands and during most of my adult life I had placed myself in situations that allowed me to do enormous physical injury to others, even taking their lives, without being held legally accountable for my deeds.

The third Robicheaux novel, *Black Cherry Blues* (1989), won an Edgar. Burke published a novel called *Cimarron Rose* about Billy Bob Holland, a former Texas Ranger, that also won an Edgar. Since then, Holland novels have alternated with Robicheaux novels. Burke's writing is distinguished by its lyricism, his love of the physical world, and his ability to convey both the exceptional beauty and the exceptional violence of the American South.

Crusader's Cross (2005) opens in July 1958 when Dave and his younger half brother Jimmie are working on the Gulf Coast of Texas before going off to college. While relaxing in Galveston they meet a young woman named Ida Durbin. Jimmie falls hard for her, only to learn that she works on Post Office Street, an infamous red-light district. Jimmie persuades Ida to run away with him, but before that can happen her pimp and two crooked cops spirit her away to an unknown fate. Forty years later, hearing that Ida is still alive, Dave and Jimmie set out to find her, whereupon people start trying to kill them.

The Dave Robicheaux we encounter here, in his sixties, is haunted by more than Ida Durbin. He's haunted by memories of men he killed, by a wife and mother who died violently, and by a lifetime of violent deeds that have him clinging precariously to sobriety. The novel has an autumnal quality; Dave is seeking love, seeking peace, seeking salvation, even as his angry, violent nature continues to endanger him and everyone he cares about.

Dave has retired from his job as a detective with the New Iberia sheriff's department, but the sheriff rehires him because a serial killer is at large. He runs afoul of a wealthy, corrupt family named Chalon who are somehow connected to the missing Ida. He finds time to win the heart of an ex-nun named Molly. All these plot threads, jumbled at times, are resolved in the end, but one reads the book mostly for the writing. Lyrical moments alternate with terrible violence. I wonder what impact this fierce juxtaposition has had on Burke's popularity. Readers who love shimmering prose do not always enjoy violence, and those who relish violence may grow impatient with poetry. But if you believe, as Burke does, that beauty and bloodshed go hand in hand in this life, he can touch you in ways few writers can.

Mortal Prey
Naked Prey
Hidden Prey
Broken Prey
Dead Watch
By John Sandford

John Sandford is not the best thriller writer in America, nor does he sell the most books, but among those who write first-rate thrillers he probably does sell the most books. In 2004, his *Hidden Prey* was credited by *Publishers Weekly* with 474,500 sales, compared to 267,000 for Connelly's *The Narrows*. When *Broken Prey* came out the next year it entered the *New York Times* list at number three—a letdown, since the five previous *Prey* novels had begun at number one or two, aided by first printings in the 500,000 range. It was the sixteenth chapter in the *Prey* series, which stars Lucas Davenport, a supercop reporting to the governor of Minnesota. Davenport is a latter-day Travis McGee, a big, good-looking, two-fisted dude, unaccountably transplanted from sunny Florida to the darkling plains of Minnesota, where an endless supply of ignorant armies clash by night. He never met the woman he couldn't charm or the crook he couldn't take down.

Sandford (in real life, the Pulitzer Prize–winning reporter John

Camp) concocts smart, fast-moving, often violent plots and his books are supremely entertaining. Why, then, don't I rate him at the highest level of today's thriller writers? At the risk of being churlish, it's because the *Prey* books are *too* entertaining. Their jokes and showmanship delight readers but keep the books from having the weight of novels by Connelly, Pelecanos, Burke, and others. In *Naked Prey*, Davenport meets—and eventually adopts—tough-talking twelve-year-old Letty West, who's handy with a .22 and takes no guff from anybody: a veritable Little Orphan Letty. *Hidden Prey* opens with Davenport making sport of his wife's poor driving—she has crashed into the garage door and insists she was not at fault—in a scene right out of Desi and Lucy. In *Broken Prey*, Davenport has acquired an iPod and gives us a running commentary on the all-time top hundred rock songs. He helpfully provides his full list at the end of the book; he's heavy into Dylan, Springsteen, the Stones, and ZZ Top, but—get this, guys—no Beatles!

Sandford freely concedes that Lucas Davenport was carefully engineered to make us like him. In one interview, he said of his hero, "Lucas is a composite of cops and movie stars, with the emphasis on movie stars. He certainly doesn't resemble any real cop I've ever met. I mean, he's tall, dark, handsome, rich, drives a Porsche, has killed too many people . . . give me a break."

Showmanship aside, Sandford does many things well. In *Mortal Prey*, Davenport finally gets the best of Clara Rinker, an endearing hitwoman who survived a previous novel; in one scene, in a bar, before he knew who she was, Davenport danced with the murderous Clara. In 2004, *Hidden Prey* was gloriously perverse. At a time when every other thriller writer in America was sniffing around for Islamic terrorists, Sandford put Davenport on the trail of a Russian spy ring that had persisted in northern Minnesota since the 1940s, led by an old Bolshevik who is still lethal at ninety-two.

Sandford would be better with less comic relief, even if it is good for sales. Of course, sales—money, filthy lucre—play a central, brutal role in today's publishing world. Young writers, starting out, know that if their first books don't sell, they may not get another chance. Talent doesn't always matter if you don't have the numbers. At the other extreme, famous writers worry about being "overpublished," which means failing to earn back their huge advances and running the risk of being dropped by their publishers and shunned by others. Beyond that, at a certain rarefied level of the game, successful writers can get caught up in an ego-driven need to sell more and more books.

Sandford is a big, good-natured man, who speaks with the candor one often finds in newspaper people. He spent nearly twenty years as a reporter, first for the *Miami Herald,* then for the *St. Paul Pioneer Press.* He went into fiction for a new challenge and also to make money, rarely a danger in the reporting game. He set out to be successful and he has been. Sandford has of late been receiving an advance of $4.5 million for each new *Prey* novel. His present goal is to put aside enough money to establish a foundation that will have an income of $500,000 a year to distribute. He loves archaeology, and one focus would be sending college students to the Middle East to study there.

Sandford's *Dead Watch* appeared in the spring of 2006. It's a stand-alone and his first attempt at a Washington novel. The wild and woolly plot includes an ex-senator who is decapitated, a nest of powerful gays being exposed, a governor who has a psychopath brother to do his dirty work, and a great deal of related sex and scandal. In my review, I found some good things to say about it—like all Sandford's novels it's fun to read—but concluded:

> Alas, we must also endure Sandford's excesses. After the randy widow plants a kiss on the hero's lips, he launches a monologue on kisses: "There was, in his experience, a wide variety of kisses, ranging from Air, on one end of the spectrum, to Orgasmic on the other. Included were Affectionate, Hot, Friendly, First, Promising, Intense, Good-bye for Good . . ." and so forth. A bit later, when the lovers move past the first-kiss stage, Sandford has his sophisticated sexpot toss off one of the oldest and dumbest lines you ever chortled at in high school: "Is that a gun in your pocket, or are you just happy to see me?" The man is shameless.
>
> And yet Sandford's novels also make clear that he understands the dark, violent, corrupt underside of our society—he just keeps cutting away from it for comic relief. Whenever I read Sandford I think that if he'd eliminate the cute stuff he could produce a fine, serious, hard-edged novel. He's sixty-two now and no longer broke, so why keep tap dancing and whistling "Dixie"? The problem may be that, at a certain rarefied level of

the game, once you've jousted with Clancy and Grisham and Patterson at the top of the greasy pole, it's hard to let go. In any event, if Sandford has a really good novel in him, this isn't it.

The day the review appeared I received an e-mail from Sandford—from John Camp, actually—which read in its entirety: "I'll buy you a beer sometime and tell you about it, if you don't mind seeing an aging person crying in his beer."

We haven't had that beer yet, but a few days later Sandford posted a notice on his Web site that began: "The *Dead Watch* that is currently on sale is not the *Dead Watch* that I started to write." He said that he intended to write a serious political novel about a "budding fascist" governor, but when he sent the first 75,000 words to his editor, the editor hated it. At that point, in part because his wife had a serious illness, Sandford decided to revert to the tried-and-true thriller formula. He closed by saying that he was at work on a new *Prey* novel, and some of us continue to hope that he will produce a thriller worthy of his talents.

Cold Pursuit
The Fallen
By T. Jefferson Parker

Jefferson Parker, a native Southern Californian, was a reporter in Orange County when he published his first novel, *Laguna Heat,* in 1985. It became an HBO movie and a paperback best seller. Since 1998 he has published a book a year. Two of his novels have won Edgar Awards: *Silent Joe,* which *Washington Post* reviewer Carolyn See called a masterpiece, and *California Girl.* He considers Dashiell Hammett his greatest influence, although he also credits Joseph Wambaugh's novels about the LAPD with encouraging him to write.

Parker's *Cold Pursuit* is a state-of-the-art police procedural. He set the novel in San Diego, where he had recently moved, and the new city invigorated him. The story centers on a detective named Tom McMichael as he investigates the death of a tuna fisherman who died rich. The first suspect in the murder is a woman who was caring for the old man. She is twenty-eight, and the recently divorced detective finds her captivating: "She struck him as utterly alien. She was cut from some template he had never seen before, could not recognize or easily understand." He begins an unwise affair with this woman. The dead man's granddaughter, an ex-girlfriend of McMichael's, is another complication: "Her perfume was rich and light and drilled a hole to the exact center of McMichael's brain." Parker is good with women, and his dialogue can be luminous.

The murdered man was involved in a high-stakes dispute over a new airport. McMichael thinks this may have figured in his murder, so he and his partner go to see a young billionaire who was also involved in the deal. This leads to an amazing scene. The fellow arrives at his mansion by helicopter, introduces his attractive wife, a former porn star, pets his Staffordshire terrier, and lectures the detectives on political reality. When they accuse him of conflicts of interest, he laughs, tells them that's how the system works, and urges them to buy his stock. He tells them a chilling story about how his gentle, friendly terrier, when he gave her the chance, slaughtered four coyotes. ("It was as if a thousand years ago her ancestors had learned something, and she still remembered the instructions.") He leaves the detectives for the dinner his wife has prepared, adding with a wink that dinner won't be much, "but dessert is like nothing you've ever had." The scene is a throwaway—the billionaire didn't kill anyone—but his greed and amorality are precisely what the novel is about: respectable people who are only a step or two up from the jungle. Most novelists toil for a lifetime and never write ten pages like those.

Parker's 2006 novel, *The Fallen*, concerns a decent, even idealistic young San Diego policeman named Robbie Brownlaw. At the outset, he tries to save people from a burning building and, for his troubles, is tossed out a sixth-floor window by a madman. An awning breaks his fall and he survives, but the trauma leaves him with synesthesia, a neurological condition that jumbles the senses. In this case, when people speak to him, he not only hears their words but sees their emotions emerge as colored shapes—red squares, for instance, show that the speaker is lying.

It's an interesting device but not really indicative of the novel that follows, which is another portrait of big-city crime and corruption. Brownlaw investigates the death of another policeman, who was killed while investigating municipal corruption. The plot involves films of call girls donating their services to police officials and other prominent figures, but the novel's real strength lies in Parker's fascination with the use and abuse of power. Lovers, cops, politicians, whores—everyone is fighting for power in *The Fallen,* and Parker's title surely refers to more than one unlucky cop's descent from a burning building. I think that Parker's commercial success may have been hindered because he has concentrated on stand-alones rather than a series, but he belongs in the first rank of today's crime novelists.

Night Fall
By Nelson DeMille

Nelson DeMille came home from Vietnam determined to write the big novel of that war. On the advice of an editor, he began more modestly with a detective series. He published several novels under the name Jack Cannon, then in 1978 issued his first novel as himself. *By the Rivers of Babylon,* about Middle East terrorism, was a Book-of-the-Month Club selection. Other popular successes followed, including *The Charm School* and *The General's Daughter.* In 1990, he published perhaps his best novel, *The Gold Coast,* which charted the collision between a socialite and a Mafia boss on the North Shore of Long Island and had echoes of *The Great Gatsby.*

Plum Island and *The Lion's Game* featured a wise-guy New York detective named John Corey, who returned in the best-selling *Night Fall.* In it, DeMille takes a hard look at the explosion of TWA Flight 800 off Long Island on July 17, 1996, and sees not the mechanical failure that was the official explanation of the tragedy but a government conspiracy to cover up a missile attack. To tell this story, DeMille brought back Corey, now working with an antiterrorism task force.

The novel opens with a man and a woman cavorting on a beach at dusk; they accidentally film something "rising off the water . . . a streak of incandescent reddish-orange fire." Then they see a huge fireball and burning pieces of an airplane falling into the sea. This couple is fictional but their film becomes central to DeMille's story; it's the so-called smoking gun. We move ahead five years. Corey's FBI-agent wife has become close to some of the families of the doomed plane's 230 victims, and Corey goes with her to the annual beachside memorial service. An FBI agent warns Corey not to question the official version of the explosion, but Corey, a troublesome sort, pursues the case.

DeMille gives a detailed account of the crash and the more than two hundred witnesses who described seeing the streak of light that could have been a missile, only to have their accounts dismissed by the government. Having presented the case for both a mechanical malfunction and a missile attack—either by "friendly fire" or terrorists—DeMille comes down on the side of an attack and cover-up. His novel brought to a national audience a debate that has raged on the Internet for years. *Night Fall* is a triumph of substance over style. Its writing is pedestrian, and wise-guy Corey is one of the most obnoxious characters in memory. Moreover, DeMille does not resolve his story but leaves us awaiting a sequel. Still, *Night Fall* is first-class investigative reporting in the guise of fiction, and it struck a nerve, becoming America's twelfth bestselling novel in 2004. As with *The Da Vinci Code,* a thriller is a focal point for popular discontent—with the Catholic Church in one case, with a possible government cover-up in the other.

Done for a Dime
By David Corbett

Some writers put all they have into their first novel and can never equal it. Others, gaining confidence the second time out, spread their wings and soar to unexpected heights. David Corbett is among the lucky ones. His first novel, *The Devil's Redhead,* was impressive but didn't come close to the brilliance of his second, the angry and uncompromising *Done for a Dime.* Corbett, like Hammett, was an operative for a San Francisco private investigations firm. He did that for thirteen years, and loved the work; then he began converting what he had learned into fiction. His experience left him with no illusions about cops, criminals, the legal system, or the level of corruption in our society.

In the opening pages of *Done for a Dime,* an old R & B saxophonist is shot to death in front of his home in a black neighborhood in a town north of San Francisco. Detective Dennis Murchison arrives, and we soon see that he is no saint. When he interrogates suspects he ignores their demands for a lawyer and pushes them to confess to a murder he has no reason to think they committed. And yet he is, relatively speaking, a good cop; you ought to meet his racist partner.

We learn that the old musician's death was an unintended by-product of a plan to oust black people from their homes and make millions for white businessmen and politicians. The novel is thus a portrait of corruption on a massive scale, not unlike Hammett's *Red Harvest*. A fire burns down scores of black homes and takes many lives. Murchison by then knows of the political conspiracy, but his evidence is rejected by FBI agents who, for their own reasons, prefer to blame the fire on ecoterrorists.

The ending of the novel is unexpected and powerful—and mustn't be revealed here, except to say this is in every regard a serious novel. The characters are torn by rage, grief, fear, and loneliness. Corbett examines not only racism and corruption but the failures of the human heart. The novel may be too painfully real for some readers, but it is an example of the best in contemporary crime fiction.

The Monkey's Raincoat
The Last Detective
By Robert Crais

Without Fail
One Shot
By Lee Child

Although Robert Crais grew up in rural Louisiana and Lee Child in Birmingham, England, their careers followed similar paths. Both honed their talents in television. Crais wrote for shows like *L.A. Law* and *Miami Vice;* Child put in eighteen years with Granada Television. Then Child was downsized out of his job, Crais became fed up with television, and each began to write a crime series. Crais's is about Elvis Cole, a Vietnam vet turned LA private eye; Child's features a former U.S. military policeman named Jack Reacher. If you enjoy hard-boiled blood-and-guts crime thrillers, the Elvis Cole and Jack Reacher books are state-of-the-art.

Crais's first novel, *The Monkey's Raincoat* (1987), is another updating of the private-eye novel into the post-Vietnam era. Echoing *The Maltese Falcon,* the novel opens in Elvis Cole's office as he interviews a distraught woman. In this case, her husband is missing. He may have stolen two kilos of cocaine from a rich Mexican with ties to the Mafia. Her young son is also missing. The Mexican has a small army of killers in his employ. Fortunately, Cole has the formidable assistance of ex-marine and ex-cop Joe Pike. Cole is plenty lethal, but much of the killing is delegated to Pike. "Think of him as a samurai," Cole advises. Pike is that most useful of friends, the More Dangerous Sidekick. Others include Patrick Kenzie's psychopathic pal Bubba Rogowski, Spenser's friend Hawk, and Easy Rawlins's bad-ass buddy Mouse Alexander. With friends like these, the hero is pretty much indestructible.

Early in the novel, Crais gives us some Chandler-style descriptions: a woman "with a purse the size of a mobile home," a detective with "a face like a frying pan." He finds time for sex, soon bedding both his client and her sexy, bossy friend, who "came twice before I did." After various shootouts and showdowns, our two-man army defeats the Mexican's militia and saves the boy. *The Monkey's Raincoat* was an unusually assured thriller; it won the Anthony and Macavity awards for the year's best first novel.

In Crais's ninth novel, *The Last Detective,* Cole is again searching for a kidnapped boy, but in most regards it is unlike *The Monkey's Raincoat.* Gone are the wisecracks, the Hollywood scenes, the leisurely descriptions; *The Last Detective* is all business, tightly focused on its suspenseful plot. Someone kidnaps Cole's girlfriend's young son. A man calls and says he has taken the boy in revenge for something Cole did in Vietnam. Cole knows what he's up against: "It took special training and skills to hunt humans. I had known men with those skills, and they scared me. I had been one of them." Cole learns that the kidnappers are three dangerous soldiers of fortune. All this builds to a remarkable ten-page showdown between the two sets of killers, a stunningly choreographed ballet of violence.

Lee Child's Jack Reacher is six-foot-five, weighs 250 pounds, and is expert with every imaginable weapon. The ex–military policeman moves around America with just the clothes on his back. He has no home, no car, no credit card—he's a rambling man. The first Reacher novel appeared in 1997 and the series was soon a success, at least in part because he's a great male fantasy. But the series is also popular because Child writes well and is good at explaining things—particularly weapons and the killing arts.

One Shot, the ninth Reacher novel, pits Reacher against some Russian mobsters in an Indiana town. Soon they have framed Reacher for a murder and the police are after him. At his best, Child can stir up a skillful mix of sex, violence, sadism, weaponry, deception, suspense, and nonstop action. Some of his plots are hard to swallow, but if you're a Reacher fan, if you think he's cool or sexy, you'll suspend disbelief and have a good time. "So you're cool?" a man asks. "You could skate on me," our guy declares. "You're new in town, aren't you?" a woman says. "Usually," he replies.

Both Crais and Child write modern thrillers that reflect the drift toward ever-increasing violence. In Child's *Persuader,* a confrontation ends like this:

> The Brenneke round sounded like a bomb going off and the giant slug cut Harley in half, literally. He was there, and then suddenly he wasn't. He was in two large pieces on the floor and the warehouse was full of acrid smoke and the air was full of the hot stink of Harley's blood and his digestive system and Duffey was screaming because the man she had been standing next to had just exploded.

At the end of *One Shot,* Reacher invades a house full of Russians, armed only with a knife. He finds two of them in a downstairs room and throws his knife, which buries itself in the first Russian's neck. He grabs the other in a bear hug and literally squeezes the life out of him. They've been bad boys, so he cuts both their throats "ear to ear" for good measure. All this is described in detail. "Blood soaked the tabletop and dripped to the floor. It didn't spurt."

This is a level of violence unknown in the Hammett-Chandler era. Crais and Child are far from its only practitioners, they just serve it up more stylishly than most. It's hard to say exactly when this festival of gore began. Spillane contributed to the evolution of violence in the fifties, but Harris's *Red Dragon* was the modern milestone, with its serial killer who captured, starved, killed, and skinned women, not to mention Dr. Lecter's own alarming appetites. Why all this violence? Why not? Ours is a violent species and this is a violent age. Our writers have grown bolder about holding up a mirror to our darker impulses. And readers have grown more willing to accept—and in some cases be titillated by—these horrors.

Of course, some readers find today's fictional violence repugnant. Not long ago, a friend asked me to speak to his book club, which usually examined more genteel fiction than I was there to talk about. My friend had assigned people to read writers I recommended. The results were mixed. Several people had enjoyed Lehane's *Shutter Island* and Alan Furst's novels. Then there was the couple who tried to read *Red Dragon*. They were truly shaken. "We just don't see how people can read things like this," the wife told me. Thank God they didn't reach the books where Harris uncorks man-eating hogs and Dr. Lecter prepares sautéed brains.

Writers like Crais and Child write well about violence, but ultimately it is self-limiting. The larger audience that buys Grisham and Grafton doesn't want ultra-violence. Still, a lot of men like to read about guns and shootouts and guys who are one-man armies. Cole and Reacher are artfully drawn action heroes but they aren't interesting characters, beyond their ability to kill people and toss off wisecracks. They're killing machines with attitude. I admire the best of such novels for their craft—the dialogue, the pace, the suspense, the occasional new twist in the old business of killing—but I'd be worried if I craved a steady diet of them.

The Devil's Right Hand
By J. D. Rhoades

You never know when memorable writing will pop up. *The Devil's Right Hand* is a spicy slice of redneck noir, a subgenre that seeks to combine maximum violence with minimal sentiment. The novel starts with two Southern-fried idiots, cousins DeWayne and Leonard Puryear, attempting an armed robbery that leads, tsunamilike, to an ever-widening circle of devastation. But what really stopped me was this description of how a tough old bird named Angela survived a domestic dispute wherein her husband broke both her legs with a baseball bat and set the house on fire. "How'd she get out?" someone asks. "Dragged herself out of the house on her elbows." That, by the standards of red-neck noir, is a moment of pure art, like the scene when Daisy cries over Gatsby's beautiful shirts or Chaplin's sad little smile at the end of *City Lights*.

Little Scarlet
By Walter Mosley

Several black writers have used the crime novel to explore the black experience. The most celebrated is the prolific Walter Mosley, best known for his series about the Los Angeles private investigator Ezekiel (Easy) Rawlins. The first Easy Rawlins novel, *Devil in a Blue Dress,* appeared in 1990 and was well filmed with Denzel Washington as Rawlins and Don Cheadle nearly stealing the show as his gun-happy friend Mouse. The ninth, *Little Scarlet,* appeared in 2004 and was hailed by many reviewers as the best in the series.

Mosley, who was born in Los Angeles in 1952, has set the Rawlins books there in 1948–65. *Little Scarlet* takes place in the immediate aftermath of the Watts riots of August 1965. Rawlins, who grew up poor in Louisiana and Texas, has by then become a property owner, a private investigator, and a well-known figure in Watts. Although his wife left him, he has put together what he calls "my beautiful patchwork family." It consists of the son and daughter he has adopted and Bonnie, a Guyanese woman who works as a flight attendant. However, Bonnie has confessed to an indiscretion on a recent trip. Rawlins's resentment of this fuels the attraction he feels throughout *Little Scarlet* for a young woman who pursues him.

The first sentence of *Little Scarlet* is: "The morning air still smelled of smoke." Rawlins is in his office. Out his window he can see the stores that have been gutted by fire and stripped bare by looters. National Guardsmen patrol the street. He goes downstairs and consoles Theodore Steinman, whose shoe store is in ruins. A police detective named Suggs appears. The detective offers his hand; Rawlins rejects it. But he persists, because the police want Rawlins's help.

A young black woman named Nola Payne has been found murdered in her home. (Her nickname, Li'l Scarlet, gives the book its title.) A white man who was fleeing a black mob and took refuge in her home may have killed her. The police fear that if word of the crime gets out it may start the riots all over again. Tensions are such that no one from the overwhelmingly white LAPD can investigate, so the police official asks Rawlins to do so. After some resistance, he agrees. To help him move about freely, the deputy police commissioner gives him a To Whom It May Concern letter ordering all police officers to cooperate with him.

Rawlins's search for the killer is not really Mosley's main concern. He has Rawlins reflect at length on the riots: not on the burning and looting but on the black rage and white racism that caused them and on the possibility that by opening white eyes to that rage the riots might bring progress. Time after time, Mosley gives us speeches about white injustice. Rawlins sees on the news that scientists are worried that an asteroid might collide with earth and he reflects, "To some people that space rock would have come as a blessing from God. Something sent down to earth to shake off the invisible chains and manacles holding down five people for every one that's walking around free." I don't disagree with Mosley's views, but I began to think his anger was hurting his novel. Finally, I came to accept Easy's declarations of "rage and impotence." Such passion must be respected.

I read *Little Scarlet* with an eye to how it might compare to Pelecanos's Derek Strange novels but, aside from both featuring a middle-aged black investigator, they aren't much alike. Rawlins gives us a first-person narration, which means that the story is centered on him and his thoughts, whereas Pelecanos uses a third-person narration that permits a more panoramic view of society. Beyond that, they are writing about different times and places. The LAPD in the postwar years was notorious for its racism; Mosley, having grown up there, feels its injustice in his bones. Derek Strange, by contrast, lives some forty years later in one of America's blackest cities and is a less angry man. In the Rawlins books the basic conflict is between black citizens and white authority; in the Strange books it is between law-abiding blacks and black criminals. Mosley and Pelecanos are as different in style as in substance. Mosley is a taker-outer; Pelecanos is a putter-inner. Mosley's prose is smooth and elegant, like good jazz. Pelecanos's prose is rougher, more like the raucous R & B and alt-rock that ring out in his novels. The two writers have different styles, different strengths, and different goals.

Rawlins is tolerant of the looters: their rage is justified, he says, and they have earned the spoils of war. He is equally tolerant of his friend Raymond "Mouse" Alexander, whom he calls "a serious man who had killing in his blood." It is not hard to imagine the gun-happy Mouse reborn as one of the homicidal drug czars in the Strange novels, but in Rawlins's world he is a fellow soldier in the battle against white oppression. (He is also Mosley's updating of Stagger Lee, the bad black dude of song and legend.) During the aftermath of the riots, Mouse deals in stolen goods. When police stop Mouse, Rawlins uses the letter the deputy commissioner has given him to protect his friend. He reflects, "As a rule I avoided Raymond's illegal business. I knew he was a crook, but what could I do? He was like blood to me. And that night the rules as I had always known them had been suspended. . . . So it didn't disturb me standing in the thieves' den. That was simply another step toward the other side of our liberation."

Rawlins solves the murder of Little Scarlet, and the truth he finds is deeply ambiguous. The white man didn't kill her; a black man did. Still, we see that racism caused all the disasters in *Little Scarlet,* from the man's serial killings to the riots themselves. Rawlins comes down on the side of his people: "I hated the destruction of property and life, but what good was law and order if it meant I was supposed to ignore the fact that our children were treated like little hoodlums and whores?" For all its discipline and artistry, for all its hard-boiled trappings, *Little Scarlet* is a cry from the heart.

Mosley, in the Rawlins novels, is doing something that is rare in American fiction and quite difficult in both artistic and commercial terms. He is using more or less conventional private-eye novels as vehicles for political statements that, in the context of mainstream American politics, can only be called radical. And he makes it work. If he has not had huge sales, he is read and respected. He's doing what he wants to do—what he must do—and doing it well.

More Favorites:

Brits

Those damn Brits—they write so well. From Shakespeare and Ben Jonson to Orwell and Waugh to Lennon and McCartney, who can resist them? I wanted to stick to American writers, honest I did, but I kept encountering Brit-lit I couldn't ignore. Here are some English and Scottish writers—and one Irishman—who are among my favorites. Some carry on the civilized tradition of Maugham and Greene, while others reflect the transition from Christie-style country-house mysteries to angry social realism.

Resurrection Men
A Question of Blood
By Ian Rankin

The young Scot Ian Rankin, born in 1960, is the best of the younger crime novelists now at work in Great Britain, and one of the best anywhere. He bears comparison with American contemporaries like Connelly and Pelecanos; I think of Rankin's Inspector John Rebus as Harry Bosch's dissolute Scottish cousin: middle-aged, overweight, alcoholic, gruff, a loner, a chain smoker, an enemy of all authority. A typical novel begins, "For the best part of an hour, Rebus had been trying to blink away a hangover, which was about as much exercise as he could sustain." Need I add that women find him irresistible? I persuaded a friend whose tastes run more to Anne Tyler to try one of the Rebus books. "Is this one of your violent guy novels?" she asked suspiciously. Now she's happily working her way through the Rebus novels.

Rankin was raised in a "happy working-class home" in the Scottish village of Cardenden, and as a child he loved writing stories and song lyrics. At Edinburgh University he won prizes for poetry and short fiction. His first three novels were written while he was a graduate student, and the third of them became his first published novel, *Knots and Crosses* (1987). In those days he sang in a punk rock band, and his novels are replete with references to mostly obscure rock groups. He has become, his publisher says, the best-selling British crime writer, and his success is the most dramatic example of the transition of British crime fiction from the Agatha Christie tradition to the angrier, more violent American style. A few years ago, on a trip to America, Rankin gave this blunt assessment:

> The problem, if it is a problem, with English/British crime fiction is that it comes from a certain tradition, in which well-meaning amateur or semi-professional detectives solved crimes which tended to take place on country estates or in genteel drawing-rooms. Some readers may still get a lot out of these novels, but I don't think they can be said to reflect contemporary concerns with the breakdown of society, the drug problem, terrorism, conspiracies, and corporate cover-ups. All that's happened in Britain is that crime writers have started to write about the world around them. This produces a more troubling body of work, in that evil is not always punished or even defined; good guys and bad guys have been replaced by "gray guys"; the crimes themselves are no longer bloodless (no more rare poisons or blunt instruments); and so these newer books tend to produce fewer happy endings and make the reader think harder about the big moral questions, because few spinsters or titled gentlemen are on hand these days to solve the mysteries for us.

Rankin's novels are funny, cynical, evocative, topical, demanding, gritty, and at times lyrical. He often bases his plots on real-life cases in Scotland, hoping this will add an extra degree of realism. His *Resurrec-*

tion Men finds the always troublesome Rebus (the word means "picture puzzle") back at the police academy for remedial training on how to work with others. It seems that he threw a mug of tea at his boss. Of course, this being a Rebus novel, things are not entirely what they seem. Three plot lines emerge. Two involve murders—one of an art dealer and the other of a small-time criminal—and inevitably they prove to be connected. The third plot, as in all the Rebus novels, concerns the police themselves, not just Rebus and his good friend Detective Sergeant Siobhan Clarke but eight or ten others. Rankin is fascinated by cops, and he wants us to understand why.

Rebus has done some things he's not proud of, and the novel ends with these grim thoughts:

> *I've made a pact with the devil. . . .* This was how the jobs got done: with a tainted conscience, guilty deals, and complicity. With grubby motives and a spirit grown corrupt. His steps were so shallow, as he walked toward the door, he could have been wearing shackles.

Rankin's novels feature mostly unhappy people living mostly sordid lives. But they are also skillful, serious, and wildly readable. Some writers pride themselves on graceful prose. Rankin's narratives are ragged, unruly, rough-textured. He is a hungry writer who soaks up the world around him, in all its ugliness, absurdity, and occasional beauty, and spews it out at us. He's one of those writers like Whitman or Dylan who reach out and try to embrace everything and don't worry about the occasional loose end. Edinburgh, where Rankin has lived since college, is vividly and endlessly described, made real and never prettied up. Here's a more or less typical paragraph from *A Question of Blood,* as Rebus and a colleague set out on a trip:

> Dawn had brought milky sunshine to the capital, but Rebus had known it wouldn't last. The sky had been too hazy, blurred like a drunk's good intentions. Hogan had decided they should rendezvous at St. Leonard's, by which time fully half of Arthur's Seat's great stone outcrop had vanished into the cloud. Rebus doubted David Copperfield could have pulled the trick with any more brio. When Arthur's Seat started disappearing, rain was

sure to follow. It had started before they reached the city limits, Hogan flipping the wipers to intermittent, then to constant. Now, on the M74 south of Glasgow, they were flying to and fro like the Roadrunner's legs in the cartoon.

You could cut that paragraph and not lose a thing as far as plot is concerned. Yet that rich, seemingly offhand mix of barroom humor, weather report, local color, and pop culture is basic to Rankin's rowdy genius.

Black Out
Bluffing Mr. Churchill
Old Flames
Flesh Wounds
A Little White Death
By John Lawton

Few writers have given me more pleasure in recent years than John Lawton, with his sophisticated series about Frederick Troy of Scotland Yard. In these novels, spanning twenty-plus years, Troy advances from sergeant to chief superintendent of the Yard, confronts challenges from spies, gangsters, and politicians, and copes less successfully with the often ill-chosen women in his life, as well as with his formidable family. His father fled Russia, shortened the family name to Troy, and became a press lord. Older brother Rod was a war hero, then a leader of the Labor Party, and he steers the books into the corridors of power. Twin sisters Masha and Sasha marry well and cheat endlessly; Troy thinks of them as "one dreadful woman in two bodies." Frederick, the youngest, became a cop in part to reject the British class system. He's a loner, content with his work, fond of women, but happy at home with a good bottle of wine and the sounds of Thelonious Monk, Art Tatum, Dave Brubeck, and Erroll Garner.

My favorite of the Troy novels is *Bluffing Mr. Churchill,* the earliest chronologically. It is set in London in the spring of 1941, when England was struggling to survive and we Yanks were still dithering, and it is a moving reminder that London during the blitz was the most heroic, most romantic, most dramatic moment of the unhappy twentieth century. The novel is Lawton's tribute to the courage of his countrymen when they stood alone. But not a mawkish tribute, for Lawton understands that love, wine, and laughter were never sweeter than when the bombs were falling and no tomorrow was guaranteed.

An American officer named Calvin Cormack III is sent to London to find a German spy. He joins forces with Police Inspector Walter Stilton, a huge man with "a plump, reddish, fiftyish face, framing bright brown eyes, and a big, bushy wild moustache." Stilton is Lawton's portrait of England's finest—stolid, canny, fearless. He and the American become fast friends, and just as quickly Cormack is seduced by Stilton's daughter Kitty. After their first night together, the bewildered American asks, "What happened to the famous English reserve?" Sly Kitty replies with the all-purpose catchphrase of the era: "Don't you know there's a war on?"

We learn that Troy and Kitty have been lovers and that she is trying—in vain—to use Cormack to make him jealous. Meanwhile, the elusive spy leaves corpses in his wake, America First zealots rage against FDR, and we catch glimpses of Churchill, H. G. Wells, and Lord Beaverbrook. But all this is secondary to Lawton's portrait of London under siege, a portrait all the more powerful for being as often hilarious as heartrending. Cormack has no sooner checked into Claridge's when he hears air raid sirens. He asks a maid for directions to the shelter. The baffled woman explains that isn't what people do: "The women mostly put in earplugs and go to bed, and the men use it as an excuse to gather on the ground floor and play pontoon and drink half the night." The next morning, Cormack wanders the streets ("men in blue, men in khaki, backs bent to shovels and piles of debris, half in and half out of the half-houses, twisting and wiggling through the ruins, seeking out the trapped, the living, the dying, and the dead") and comes to a "smoldering and smoking" Parliament. He speaks to an "eye-bleary and chin-fuzzy" Englishman wearing his pin-striped suit over pajamas who quotes Wordsworth ("This City now doth, like a garment, wear the beauty of the morning; silent, bare") before brushing away tears and wandering back "toward the great orange haze south of the Thames, the false dawn of conflagration. London burning."

We join a British intelligence agent who encounters his ex-brother-in-law outside his club:

"Archie, I was just going in for a snifter."

"Complete washout, old boy—the Hun put one right through the roof, through five ceilings and into the wine cellar last night."

"The swine! My God, the 1912 Margaux!"

"Broken glass and red puddles, I'm afraid."

A moving scene follows the sinking of the HMS *Hood* by the *Bismarck*. Two of the 1,400 lost sailors are Inspector Stilton's twin sons. Kitty comes to Cormack's hotel room and pleads for him to help comfort her parents. "The vicar been round. That was nice for me mum. He told her Kev and Trev was 'eroes. Me dad wouldn't talk to him. Atheist me dad is. Me mum cries all the time an' me dad puffs on his pipe and says nothin'." Cormack reluctantly visits the home and has an amazing exchange with the mother in which she rejects the vicar's pieties for her own kind of peace: "I'd much sooner remember them the way they were—a pair of scallywags looking out for the next fag and the next likely girl. . . . I don't think I believe in dead heroes." The scene recalls J. D. Salinger's great story "For Esmé—With Love and Squalor," in which one English girl's brave, silly chatter in a tearoom somehow embodies all the courage and pain of a nation at war.

After *Bluffing Mr. Churchill,* you can advance to *Black Out,* set later in the war; *Old Flames,* set during Khrushchev's visit to England in 1956; *Flesh Wounds,* in which Kitty Stilton, now the wife of a U.S. senator, returns to London and Troy's bed in 1959; and *A Little White Death,* a version of the 1963 Profumo scandal. But the two wartime novels are exceptional.

Bangkok 8
Bangkok Tattoo
By John Burdett

John Burdett, the son of a London cop and a seamstress, studied literature in college, loved D. H. Lawrence and Graham Greene, dreamed of writing, but did the sensible thing and went to law school. He wound up as a partner in a Hong Kong law firm, but in his spare time he wrote two novels that died quick deaths. Undaunted, he quit his firm and moved around the globe, seeking the right place to set a series of thrillers. He chose Bangkok, moved there, talked to cops, hung out in the red-light districts, but wasn't able to get started until a bar girl invited him to visit her and her family in a distant village. There, amid poverty, drunkenness, and brawling, he decided he'd found the real Thailand. About the time he turned fifty, he began the novel that made his name.

Bangkok 8 is narrated by the young policeman Sonchai Jitpleecheep, son of a bar girl and a long-departed American GI. In an opening scene, an American marine in a Mercedes is killed by snakes planted in the car, and Sonchai's beloved partner Pichai also dies as he investigates. Sonchai vows revenge, and we have launched our adventure into one of the most crowded, colorful, corrupt cities on earth. It helps to have visited Bangkok, but, if you haven't, Burdett will take you there. He tells us how Sonchai and Pichai became officers of the law:

> After we murdered the *yaa baa* dealer our mothers secured us an interview with the abbot of a forest monastery in the far north, who told us we were the lowest form of life in the ten thousand universes. Pichai had thrust the broken bottle into the jugular of humanity, and therefore of the Buddha himself, while I giggled. After six months of mosquitoes and meditation, remorse had gouged our hearts. Six months after that the abbot told us we were going to mend our karma by becoming cops. His youngest brother was a police colonel named Vikorn, chief of District 8. Corruption was forbidden to us, however. If we wanted to escape the murderer's hell we would have to be honest cops.

Bangkok Tattoo continues Sonchai's adventures. A CIA agent is killed in the Old Man's Club, the brothel his mother has opened for aging Viagra-powered Western tourists. In both novels, Sonchai becomes involved with American investigators, *farangs;* because he is himself half American, he views them with mingled affection and scorn. Only the latest in a long line of English writers—Somerset Maugham is the prototype—to report on the inscrutable East, Burdett says of Bangkok, his adopted city, "There's no cushion of gentility here. Life is raw. The people don't lie. You tell me a better place to be a writer." But Burdett's success also reflects the triumph of the thriller.

He had grown up loving Lawrence and Greene and might have pursued more literary fiction. Instead, his series starts with a cop trying to avenge the death of his partner (shades of *The Maltese Falcon*), who was killed by snakes planted in a Mercedes. But Burdett's talent is such that his Bangkok tales transcend their lurid subject matter and become models of colorful, wry, irresistible thrillers.

Killing the Shadows
By Val McDermid

It's always a pleasure to see a smart concept skillfully executed, and Val McDermid's novel *Killing the Shadows* does precisely that. Her plot is as nasty as it is delicious. A serial killer is stalking some of the world's leading crime writers and dispatching them with gruesome methods borrowed from their own novels. It is as if, God forbid, some bookish fiend were to kidnap Thomas Harris and, inspired by *Hannibal,* feed him to starving hogs.

McDermid tells her story through Fiona Cameron, a crime-fighting psychologist, who lives with Kit Martin, a leading English crime writer. Their idyllic life is threatened when Kit's peers start dying horrid deaths. One is picked up in a gay bar and mutilated in ways pioneered by Jack the Ripper and featured in his own best-selling *Copycat.* England's Queen of Crime is drawn, quartered, and deposited in a meat market. Worst of all, because we are privy to the killer's mind, we know that our admirable Kit Martin is next on the list, destined to die in a room painted with his own blood.

The prolific McDermid has plenty of fun with this wicked concept. She is a Scottish-born and Oxford-educated novelist who was a journalist before she turned to fiction. Her books have won numerous prizes, and this one shows why.

Dead I Well May Be
By Adrian McKinty

Adrian McKinty grew up in Northern Ireland, graduated from Oxford, and came to America in the early 1990s. He settled in Harlem, where for five years he was variously a bartender, salesman, and teacher. He now lives in Colorado. I don't know that in his Harlem days McKinty was ever an enforcer for a gang of Irish extortionists, but he nails that world in his gripping *Dead I Well May Be* (the title is from "Danny Boy"). The novel manages to be both deadpan hilarious and ultraviolent and to present its violence in prose that amounts to poetry. Did I mention that the man is Irish?

We meet Michael Forsythe in 1992 when he is nineteen and living on the dole in Belfast. After some trouble with the law he accepts a job offer from a kinsman in America, Darkey White, a businessman who dabbles in extortion. His Irish gang is in conflict with some Dominican gangs in Harlem and he needs a young man like Michael who is both smart and tough. Michael is good at the work, but then he starts sleeping with Darkey's girlfriend. Darkey, who is no fool, sends Michael on a vacation to Cancun that ends with him in shackles in a vile Mexican prison. His suffering there and his attempts to escape are spellbinding. Here is Michael, after escaping, lost in the jungle, half dead, hallucinating, and dreaming of revenge:

> Your skin is hanging from you and your hair is falling out, you are in rags caked in blood and filth. But you are a holy fool. Enthused. The Lord is in you. You are St. Anthony in the demon-filled desert. You are Diogenes mired in grime. You are the Buddha at Bodhgaya. You are a Jain priest, naked, with a broom before you to sweep away any living being that you might inadvertently step upon. You are holy because you are possessed by a vision of a future time. It is a bright vision and a tight one, compact. Simple. The truth of it has made you pure.

Michael's pure and relentless pursuit of Darkey, and a dazzling epilogue in which his past catches up with him, are memorable.

He Kills Coppers
By Jake Arnott

We first see Billy Porter, the cop-killing title character in Jake Arnott's intense *He Kills Coppers,* as a young English soldier in Malaya. Billy might have been a good soldier, but instead he returns to London and petty crime. In 1966 he and two dim-witted pals are cruising about in a stolen car. When police stop them, Billy panics, shoots three policemen dead, and sets off a national manhunt.

Billy's story is linked to those of Frank, a policeman, and Tony, a journalist. Arnott follows all three of them for twenty years, and their lives are uniformly sordid. Frank, who wanted to be an honest cop, is soon corrupted. By the 1980s, in Margaret Thatcher's England, he sees himself as part of an occupying army that is used to brutalize striking coal miners and hippies who defy a ban on the Stonehenge Festival. Tony, the gutter journalist, is a closeted, self-hating gay. One night he goes home with a man he meets in a bar and kills him. The author portrays Tony and his friends as even more miserable than the straight characters. Meanwhile, Billy Porter remains at large and becomes a legend, even as he loses touch with reality. Young toughs taunt police by chanting, "Billy Porter is our friend, he kills coppers."

Arnott, born in 1961, was a high school dropout, sometime actor, and mortuary assistant before he burst on the literary scene in 1999 with *The Long Firm,* a novel based on the Kray crime family. *He Kills Coppers* was reviewed in England as a devastating portrait of national decline. In 1956, John Osborne's angry young man in *Look Back in Anger* was named Jimmy Porter. I doubt that Billy Porter's name is a coincidence, although he is not so much angry as confused, which could be the author's point. When Ian Rankin called for British crime fiction that takes a hard look at society and its discontents, he couldn't have asked for work more powerful than this.

17

Three Young Writers:

Karin Slaughter, Peter Craig, Charlie Huston

The thriller is not necessarily the high road to instant success. Some writers strike it rich with their first novels—Clancy with *The Hunt for Red October,* Harris with *Black Sunday*—but far more build their readership over a period of years. That was the case with Grafton, Pelecanos, Connelly, Lehane, Lescroart, and countless others. Even Grisham saw his first novel flop. In this chapter I'll look at three talented American writers who are still in their thirties. One moved quickly into the realm of book clubs, six-figure advances, and international success. The other two are just happy that they've been able to quit their day jobs and write full-time while they wait for the breakout novel that may or may not come.

Blindsighted
Kisscut
A Faint Cold Fear
Indelible
Faithless
By Karin Slaughter

As the twentieth century wound down, Karin Slaughter was running Snappy Signs in Atlanta. She'd started working there while she was in college and, because she was bright, hardworking, and ambitious, she wound up owning it. But running a small business didn't satisfy her. As a child in Covington, Georgia, she'd been an avid reader and often wrote her own stories. In her mid-twenties, in her spare time, she tried her hand at historical fiction. It didn't jell and her agent suggested that crime fiction would be easier to sell. Slaughter loved writers as varied as Flannery O'Connor and the Brontë sisters, but she'd always been interested in crime too. She was a child when a much-publicized serial killer was abducting children in Atlanta, and she says now that the crime "informed my life." Many of the books she loved growing up, such as *The Great Gatsby* and *To Kill a Mockingbird,* featured violence of one sort or another. So she followed the agent's advice and began to think about a thriller.

She started with what she knew best, a small Georgia town like the one she grew up in, and came up with the idea of a woman doctor and medical examiner there. She began to read more crime fiction; she now calls Sue Grafton a "touchstone" for her and says Patricia Highsmith should be ranked with Hemingway and Fitzgerald. She educated herself on medical subjects and police procedures, and as the new millennium arrived she produced a thriller called *Blindsighted.* It quickly sold to a publisher as the first novel in a series about Dr. Sara Linton of fictional Grant County, Georgia.

In August of 2001 an advance copy of *Blindsighted* was included in a box of books the *Post* sent me for possible review. Unlike the majority of books, *Blindsighted* grabbed me. In the novel's opening scene, to please her mother, Sara attends church on Easter, figuring that "putting on pantyhose one Sunday out of the year was a small price to pay for Cathy Linton's happiness." During the service, her ex-husband, Jeff Tolliver, the local sheriff, sits down nearby, causing Sara such visible distress that her mother fears that she will surely "go to hell for thinking about sex at the Primitive Baptist on Easter Sunday."

Thus far we are in familiar territory: a peaceful southern landscape populated by mildly eccentric but ultimately good-hearted folk. But the landscape soon turns bloody. The next day, Sara hurries to a late lunch at the local diner. When she goes to wash her hands, she discovers Sibyl Adams, a professor at the local college, bleeding to death in one of the stalls. She has been bound, raped, and cruelly mutilated. She was blind, a lesbian, and—Sara's autopsy reveals—a virgin until the final moments of her life.

Those scenes—humor in church, horror at the diner—are a concise preview of the series that lay ahead. Sara Linton is a smart, attractive, sensitive woman, a loving doctor to the children of Grant County. Her family—dad a plumber, mom a homemaker—are decent hardworking people. The major problem in Sara's life is Jeff. She divorced him when she caught him with another woman, but she still loves him, works closely with him on murder cases, and can't decide whether to take him back. Slaughter maintains a nice balance with Sara—she's a well-brought-up daughter of the small-town South but she's also flesh and blood and misses the great sex she enjoyed with Jeff. Theirs is a not uncommon relationship; she's a perfectionist, he's a guy.

Slaughter combines this story of small-town romance with some of the most horrific crimes you'll find in current fiction. Near the novel's climax, the killer captures Lena Adams, a deputy sheriff and sister of the woman he killed at the outset. He drugs her, literally crucifies her—nails her hands and feet to the floor—and repeatedly rapes her.

Slaughter's violence was shocking—I wondered if a male writer could get away with it—but I never thought it was gratuitous. When the killer crucified Lena it was obvious that the author was dealing in symbolism, not sadism. Slaughter was clearly outraged by violence against women and determined to remind us how vulnerable they are, not only in rural Georgia but everywhere.

In her second novel, a nest of pedophiles is preying on children. Meanwhile, Sara continued to agonize over Jeff and we learn more about her sister, her mother, Lena's recovery from her ordeal, and other Grant County citizens, good and bad. It's a town of Tupperware and Blue Bell ice cream, a place where people gossip endlessly and don't lock their doors at night. Slaughter's ability to capture the mood of a southern town has been as impressive as the intensity of her violence; the interplay between the two distinguishes her books. By her fifth novel, *Faithless,* in which a clan of religious fundamentalists may have buried a young woman alive, it was clear that Slaughter is one of the most talented of the young Americans now expressing themselves through thrillers. She is presenting her own angry, highly personal version of social realism, a continuing battle between good and evil being fought in the not-so-sunny South she knows so well.

Hot Plastic
By Peter Craig

Peter Craig's second novel, *Hot Plastic,* was an explosion of wit, creativity, and colorful writing. It's the story of three con artists: Jerry, an old-fashioned hustler who "found any robbery unseemly if it didn't involve a phony smile and a handshake"; Kevin, Jerry's brilliant and erratic teenage son, a Holden Caulfield whom fate has placed in his father's crime school instead of Pencey Prep; and Colette, smart and sexy and not much older than Kevin, who goes from being the father's lover to the son's.

Hot Plastic is a veritable encyclopedia of crime. Kevin is capable of pulling off door-to-door scams in which he feigns a physical handicap and collects money for charities of his own invention (Swim for Braille, Bowling for Diabetes); he becomes a master pickpocket, and, since he is also a master skateboarder, he sometimes picks pockets while whizzing along at twenty miles an hour. He has a modern teenager's skills with computers that he can use in increasingly elaborate financial scams. After Jerry is sent to jail, Kevin and Colette flee to Europe, which at first seems a paradise: "No matter where they traveled, Kevin reaped wallets from the predictable herds of Americans, following them like a wolf alongside migrating caribou." But Kevin learns the hard way that Paris police are more dangerous than their American counterparts.

Craig gets it all right. The scams are fascinating, his writing is lovely, and he wins our sympathy for his thieves. What we have here, finally, is a love story. Kevin fell for Colette at fifteen, the first time he saw her, and by the time he's eighteen she's finding him pretty great too. The only possible objection to this novel would be moralistic—the author clearly loves his three con artists—but, for this reader, good prose trumps bad morals every day of the week.

Caught Stealing
Six Bad Things
Already Dead
By Charlie Huston

Charlie Huston, born in 1967, started out with two delightful novels about a trouble-prone young man named Henry (Hank) Thompson. Huston makes Thompson's accidental life of crime horrific, hilarious, and hip, all at once. If his literary godfathers include Raymond Chandler and Elmore Leonard, they also include Hunter Thompson, who would have appreciated the speed freaks, crank heads, gun nuts, Russian mobsters, greedy *federales,* and assorted geeks and psychos who populate these pages.

In *Caught Stealing,* Hank, once a high school baseball star in a little California town, gets into big trouble in New York. His problems began when he agreed to keep a friend's cat, a good deed that leads him inexorably into possession of four and a half million dollars from a bank robbery—and much bloodshed and tragedy. The Russian Mafia says the money is theirs and kills Hank's girlfriend. He kills several of them, they shoot up a bar with some of his friends in it, and when the death toll reaches double digits he skips town with the money.

Six Bad Things picks up the story with Hank living quietly as a beach bum south of Cancun. A young Russian turns up and starts asking questions. Hank disposes of the Russian, but then two *federales* start hounding him and he decides it's time to go home. The problem is the money, which weighs sixty kilos. In desperation he ships it via Fed Ex to his drug-dealer pal Tim in Las Vegas. Hank makes his way to California, but people keep following him, demanding money. He proceeds to Vegas, only to find Tim and the money gone and more vultures circling.

While in Mexico, he's become a folk hero. He's been featured on the *America's Most Wanted* TV show and someone has written a book about him called *The Man Who Got Away.* For a time he's the prisoner/partner of two psychos named Sid and Rolf. Sid, the crazier of the two, is Hank's biggest fan: "You're this totally famous dude! You've done so much with your life." Huston sweetly mingles violence with slapstick. During one showdown, a drug dealer's killer mastiff called Hitler attacks a cowboy armed with a crossbow while Sid is fumbling for the .45 that has slipped down his pants leg and Rolf and another cowboy fight over a shotgun. Meanwhile, a stripper named Sandy (it's her apartment) jumps out the window with Hank close behind. Funny stuff, but the body count keeps rising.

If you agree that noir can encompass slapstick as well as slaughter, *Six Bad Things* is major fun because Huston writes with such deadpan verve and because Hank, his self-described mad-dog killer, is so appealing—Hank is you or me, a fine fellow but with monumentally bad luck. This crazed, wildly readable series is the sort of thing Hammett might write if he were starting out today, had replaced booze with more advanced pharmacology, and was a totally cool dude.

The first two novels were billed as part of a trilogy, so when *Already Dead* arrived in 2006 I was anxious to learn the outcome of Hank's saga. Imagine my surprise to learn that Huston had put the trilogy aside and written, of all things, a vampire novel. Huston's Joe Pitt is a vampire but he's also a private eye in Manhattan. He's Sam Spade, except that his drink of choice is blood. If he can steal it from a hospital that's fine, but in a pinch he'll knock you in the head and drink yours. This is a droll, deadpan, highly inventive thriller that, if you're into vampires, is just about perfect. Among the new voices in twenty-first-century American crime fiction, Charlie Huston is, as much as anyone I can think of, where it's at.

All three of these novelists are talented, but talent doesn't pay the rent. Of the three, which one has made the big bucks? As is probably clear, it has been Karin Slaughter. Her commercial success reflects the nature of her Grant County series. As publishers evaluated Slaughter's first novel, she had strong selling points, the kind publishers understand, above and beyond the fact that she writes well. Sara Linton is a woman in her mid to late thirties, a doctor and ex-wife (and a daughter and sister) with whom many women can identify. Slaughter's plots, which reflect her outrage at violence against women and children, have a clear appeal to women. Placing the novels in the small-town South gave them regional appeal—a core constituency, in political terms. And by making Sara the local coroner, she added the autopsies that had been so effective for Patricia Cornwell and others. All these elements gave Slaughter's series the potential to be a major franchise, and as a result she began her career with a healthy advance and a publisher that aggressively marketed her books.

It didn't hurt that Slaughter is an attractive, articulate young woman who is more than willing to promote her novels at bookstores and book festivals all over the world. She's also ambitious and tough-minded. In the fall of 2002 she sent a friend some e-mails that expressed some of her fears and uncertainties. It was a tense time. *Blindsighted* had just been issued in paperback and she was concerned about its sales. Moreover, her second novel, *Kisscut,* was about to be published and she was fearful that its portrait of child abuse might offend readers or reviewers—even though the novel had already been selected by book clubs.

She said,

> I'm very concerned about the child angle in *Kisscut*. When I first wrote the book, I thought it was important to talk frankly about issues surrounding pedophilia and child abuse, but this was before the priest scandal and all those Internet pedophile rings were exposed. Who knows if people have had enough? And let's face it, it's a hard issue to read about (as it should be) and some people may be turned off by the subject matter before they even pick up the book.

She noted that one paperback house had passed on *Kisscut* because of the child abuse, and added,

> I am *very* worried that other reviewers will have the same reaction and I'll be pummeled and never get another contract again. Yes, it is a hard topic, but I think I worked equally as hard to put it in context. I cannot stand writers who write explicitly just to titillate. This is a serious issue, and I have tried very hard to write about it with compassion.

A couple of months later, on her book tour, Slaughter reported on the success of *Blindsighted* in paperback: "As of the week of the twentieth, I'll be nineteenth on the *Times* list, and the week of the twenty-seventh I'll be at fifteen, which puts me on the printed list, which means I am officially a '*New York Times* best-selling author.' I have gotten lots of calls and such from my publisher and they are all very happy, and I am just a little bit shocked. It's almost surreal for me. Like it's not me."

Later, after noting that Hollywood was skittish about the violence in *Blindsighted* ("Have they watched a movie lately, I wonder?"), Slaughter commented again on how her life was changing: "I can see where fame/money/whatever can corrupt a writer, so I'm trying to just keep my feet on the ground and work on the books and not worry about any other crap that might come along."

For all her concern that the violence in *Kisscut* might cost her readers, Slaughter continued to pull no punches in her novels. When she sat down to write, she gritted her teeth and told the truth, which is the only way to write well. And her honesty paid off, as her books continued to sell well, at home and around the world. There is every reason to think Slaughter has a long and successful career ahead of her. Her first stand-alone, *Triptych* (another wonderful title), published in 2006, is set in Atlanta and opens with the murder of a prostitute. I haven't read it yet, but my guess is that it will be darker, grittier, and perhaps even more violent than the Grant County books and may have echoes of those Atlanta murders that haunted her childhood. Perhaps, like Lehane moving beyond his Kenzie-Gennaro novels, Slaughter may step up to a new level.

The careers of Peter Craig and Charlie Huston have moved more slowly—more typically, one might say.

Peter Craig was born in 1969, grew up in Los Angeles, and from an early age knew he wanted to write. At seventeen he dropped out of high school and became obsessed with the novels of Vladimir Nabokov. "I considered him a crime writer, especially because I read him alongside Patricia Highsmith and Charles Willeford. I always thought that Nabokov played with all sorts of genres—with touches of spy novel techniques and thrillers—and that he simply wrapped everything in a massively more ornate ribbon. I became so obsessed that I decided to do everything I could to go back to school and be a writer."

He made his way to Syracuse University, where he studied writing under Tobias Wolff. Wolff helped him get into the Iowa Writers' Workshop, and he later won a James Michener–Copernicus Fellowship. He had a slew of day jobs, from teaching Spanish at a Quaker school in Iowa to working on the tarmac for United Airlines. His first published novel, the satirical *The Martini Shot* from 1998, concerned an over-the-hill movie star and an eighteen-year-old illegitimate son who comes to Hollywood to meet him. His third, *Blood Father,* focused on a Hollywood girl who gets into trouble with drug dealers and calls on the ex-convict father she's never known to save her. None of the first three novels sold well, but *Blood Father* sold to the movies and this opened the door to screenwriting jobs: "About a month later, I sold my own spec screenplay. Now my day job is basically script doctoring and other jobs like that, while I finish my fourth novel."

I asked Craig to sum up how his writing career is going.

"I guess things are going fairly well at the moment—though the publishing business is just brutal, and it's very difficult to survive in it."

Craig's mother is the actress Sally Field. I asked him how that fact had influenced his career.

"My mother really didn't have anything to do with my career at all," he replied, "though Morrow did try to use her name and celebrity to market my first book, much to my dismay. The only positive of that failed effort was that afterward I had proof that it doesn't *work*. No one wants to read a book because you're related to someone, especially if you're writing in an entirely different tone and in a different genre."

Charlie Huston's career has also been catch-as-catch-can, and he would agree that the publishing business is brutal, although he too has been doing better of late. He was born in California, decided he wanted to be an actor, and gives this account of how he started writing.

"I've been a hobbyist scribbler all my life but never made any attempt to publish. I came to New York as an actor, but after losing my agent and having my theater company collapse, I needed to stay busy while regrouping. I started writing *Caught Stealing,* not knowing exactly what it would be. I knew it was a detective story of some kind, but I had no real plans to try and write a novel. It just kept getting longer, and the longer it got, the more determined I became to finish it. Once it was done, I stuck it in a drawer. A couple years later, a friend offered to pass it to a film agent, Maura Teitelbaum of Abrams Artists. She actually sold a film option on the manuscript, and a year later she hooked me up with a literary agent, Simon Lipskar of Writer's House. He had a first offer within two weeks. Dumb luck pretty much defines my experience in the publishing business."

I asked if he had a day job.

"I was working off and on while editing *Caught Stealing* and writing *Six Bad Things,* but it's been about a year and a half now since my last day job, as a bartender. My wife and I are able to pull it off by sucking in our guts and tightening our belts. Virginia is an actress, and I tried the same game for many years, so we're used to not having a pot to piss in, but I don't advise the lifestyle for everyone."

Huston said he was editing *A Dangerous Man,* the final book in the Hank Thompson trilogy, and also planning a crime thriller set in 1983, "about a gang of teenage housebreakers who rob the wrong house and see something they shouldn't. Needless to say, chaos ensues."

I asked how he felt his writing career was going.

"Obviously, I'm grateful to be able to do this every day. It beats the hell out of bartending. The work itself I'm quite pleased with. I feel like I'm getting better at it, both the writing itself and the career aspects, but there are ups and downs. For instance, *Six Bad Things* was meant to be a hardback, but, based on sales of *Caught Stealing,* it was shifted to trade paperback original. My publisher did a great job of repackaging the book and retargeting the marketing, and the book had a second printing by the end of its first month on the shelf, but we're still dealing with quite small numbers. Truth is, the stuff I write is unlikely ever to break very far into the mainstream, it's simply too violent and vulgar, and even establishing yourself within the genre market is a task. I think it's always a struggle for a writer. Bottom line, this is going great, and I'm a lucky guy."

What about influences on his work?

"I'm pitifully read in my own genre. I've done the major noir classics—Hammett, Chandler, Highsmith, Thompson, Cain, etc.—but I didn't read my first Elmore Leonard until after I wrote *Caught Stealing.* Last week I finally read James Crumley for the first time. What I realized, reading both those guys, was how deeply influenced I'd been by them through secondary sources—primarily movies and James Ellroy, who I have read a great deal of. There were only two writers I really had in mind while writing *Caught Stealing;* one was Ellroy, the other was Cormac McCarthy. I'm still getting caught up on the literary classics. I just read my first Hemingway last year. Talk about realizing you've been influenced through secondary sources! How blind could I have been? Obviously everyone has been stealing from this guy forever, especially within noir, and I was just the last one to find out about it."

Writers are wonderful. Here are two, about the same age, both from California, one who was deep into Nabokov at seventeen, the other who didn't read Hemingway until his mid-thirties, and both of whom show exceptional promise—yet are scrambling to make ends meet.

Their lack of commercial success thus far relates not to writing talent but to subject matter. Slaughter offered publishers a highly commercial package—woman doctor, sexy ex-husband, small-town South, autopsies—whereas Huston and Craig are writing wild, funky, outsider's books about young men's concerns—sex, drugs, rock and roll, motorcycles, tattoos, violence, even vampires—and young men are not big buyers of hardback novels. Slaughter moved immediately to book clubs and best-seller lists, while both men have seen some of their books published as trade paperbacks because of their supposedly limited appeal. But both are hanging on, and they have the careers of George Pelecanos and John Lescroart, among many others, to remind them that success can barge in when you least expect it. Still, Craig is right—publishing *is* a brutal business, and for every writer who makes it big there are a thousand who don't.

18.

No More Mr. Nice Guy

The *Post* sends me more books than I can review and lets me sort them out. For the most part, I try to find the best books I can, both because I don't want to spend my time reading bad books and because I want to alert readers to good ones. As a result, I write a good many favorable reviews, which might give readers the impression that I'm a nice guy. I'm not a nice guy. I grow surly and vindictive when obliged to read a book that bores me or insults my intelligence. What's more, it makes me crazy when decent people surrender $25 for some piece of crap. Of course, if people really *like* lousy books, that's their problem, but I worry about unwary readers who might be misled by full-page ads or those you-scratch-my-back blurbs or might have seen the books on the best-seller lists and think they must be okay. They're *not* okay. They can cause permanent brain damage.

But what is good writing? What is this holy grail we're looking for? I think the ability to write exceptionally well is innate. Some people are born with it, just as Louis Armstrong and Picasso were born with inexplicable gifts. The best writers work hard, but their work builds upon instincts that cannot be taught. It enables them to produce sentences like the opening of *A Farewell to Arms* ("In the late summer of that year we lived in a house in a village that looked across the river and the plain to the mountains") or the closing of *The Great Gatsby* ("So we beat on, boats against the current, borne back ceaselessly into the past"). Of course, you don't have to be Hemingway or Fitzgerald to write well. Not long ago I was reading a novel by the British crime writer John Harvey and smiled to read his description of someone opening a bottle of wine: "The cork came free with a pleasing pop." Simple? Sure, the way Picasso's doodles are simple. The best-seller lists are filled with writers who will not in a lifetime produce so sweet a line.

Not long ago I heard from a reader who was troubled by my reviews. She had tried to diagram my sentences, she explained, and it couldn't be done. "What rules, if any, do you follow in your writing?" she asked. Her message reminded me that back in the fourth grade I hated diagramming sentences—even then, I thought it an utterly pointless exercise. I told the woman that, after many years and many books, I don't think there *are* any rules to writing except what works—and what works is subjective. What works for you may not work for me. I admire Elmore Leonard's rule about keeping it simple, but some good writers don't keep it simple. Still, when in doubt, simple is good.

Of the writers we've considered, only a handful can be called outstanding stylists—Chandler, Burke, Leonard—but that's okay. For most of us it is enough to write clearly. The process of writing is a humbling experience. You endlessly confront your limitations. I remember, in my novel-writing days, feeling like poor Christian in *Cyrano de Bergerac,* who when trying to express his love for Roxanne could only stammer "I . . . I . . . love you!" Whereas Cyrano could so effortlessly tell her, "Your name is like a golden bell hung in my heart, and when I think of you the bell swings and rings, 'Roxanne, Roxanne, along my veins, Roxanne.' " Most of us are Christian, not Cyrano: plodders, not poets. But style doesn't necessarily sell books. Most readers have no interest in elegant prose. They agree with the woman who said, "I don't want the writing to get in the way of the story." So it's fine to keep the writing plain vanilla if you have a good story to tell. But it's not fine to be deliberately dumb or dishonest or to pander to the reader's worst instincts.

The sin of most of the people I discuss in this chapter is not that they write clunky sentences, although some do, but that they treat their readers like idiots. They deal in clichés, stereotypes, cheap thrills, and ridiculous plots. Some of them can't help it—that's how their minds work—but others deliberately dumb down their work because a lot of money is made that way. Let's look at a few examples. To do so, I'm going to reprint some of my *Post* reviews. Accuse me of recycling old material if you must, but these reviews are heartfelt.

The Beach House
By James Patterson and Peter de Jonge

Years ago, I read a few chapters of James Patterson's novel *Kiss the Girls*. It concerned a man who kidnapped college girls and took them to an underground bunker, where he tormented, raped, and sometimes killed them. New arrivals were warned that any attempt to escape would be punished by immediate execution and lesser offenses by facial and/or genital mutilation. Somewhere in America, an intrepid detective was trying to find the women, but my guess was that Patterson's readers were more likely to be drooling over the horrors inflicted on the women than cheering the detective's progress. The book was sick, sexist, sadistic, and subliterate, so I tossed it and made a mental note that this was a writer to avoid at all costs.

Then Patterson's latest, *The Beach House,* arrived for possible review. I searched my soul and finally decided to read the damned thing. Why? Mostly because Patterson has been jousting with John Grisham at the pinnacle of the best-seller lists, and I wondered if this meant that he had cleaned up his act or that American taste had reached new depths of depravity. The answer is that Patterson has, to a certain extent, cleaned up his act. *The Beach House* is a dreadful novel, and it turns on sex, but at least the sex is consensual. Patterson has advanced from rape fantasies to a fantasy of class struggle in the Hamptons, where pure-hearted natives are pitted against zillionaire intruders from Manhattan who are as decadent as they are rich.

The champion of the locals is Jack Mullen, a law student of good Irish stock, who is a summer intern with "the most prestigious firm" in New York. The corporate Darth Vader he confronts is a media mogul named Barry Neubauer, who doesn't seem to be Irish and who in the opening scene is hosting a $200,000 Memorial Day party at his $40 million beach house in Amagansett. It happens that Jack's randy younger brother, Peter

Mullen (aka Peter Rabbit), is parking cars at the party. At least that is his official role. We glimpse a darker scenario when he takes a cell-phone call from a party guest who asks him to meet her on the beach. Peter strolls down to the surf, only to be greeted not by a sex-starved society matron but by three thugs who beat him to death and toss his body in the ocean.

Jack hurries home, rejects the police story that his brother drowned, and sets out to find the killers. He turns for help to his old high school buddies, who for their troubles are variously killed, beaten, and sexually abused by a ubiquitous thug with a nasty scar on his face. At the outset, Jack is wooing the zillionaire's gorgeous daughter, but we soon perceive that she is a Bad Girl, both because she is sexually aggressive (always a danger signal) and because Jack's canny high school pals don't trust her. Jack comes to his senses and replaces her with a Good Girl. We know she is good because she wears no makeup.

Jack's quest for justice gets him fired by his law firm, which represents the zillionaire, and beaten by a crooked cop. Throughout his travails, Jack can count on the support of his adorable eighty-six-year-old grandfather, who is an unending source of wisdom and home truths. One of Jack's friends is a gay hairdresser, who proves his mettle by slitting the throat of the scarfaced thug before other thugs toss him out a window. Happily, the hairdresser leaves behind photographs that reveal that poor mixed-up Peter had been having sex with the zillionaire and various of his family and friends, including the Bad Girl daughter.

For a time it seems that the corrupt zillionaire's vast wealth and power will enable him to cover up Peter's murder. He controls not only crooked cops and homicidal thugs but even the attorney general of the United States, who is glimpsed "on all fours" wearing "a studded dog collar hooked to an industrial-strength leash." But Jack has an inspiration. He, Gramps, and their truth-seeking friends kidnap the bad guys, take them to a secret hideaway, and put them on trial, with Jack as the prosecutor and Gramps as the judge. And—get this—they manage to have their kangaroo court broadcast live on national television. It's the biggest thing since O.J., and soon the zillionaire is headed for the slammer and all is right with the Hamptons.

The trouble with *The Beach House* is that it unfolds like an unspeakably dumb comic book. One can read it in hopes of lip-smacking orgies that feature corrupt zillionaires and their willowy but depraved women—except here it's a tease, because there's precious little sex—or one can skim the book in wonder at the awfulness of its prose and the absurdity of its plot. But no one with even a minimal appreciation of good writing could possibly read it for pleasure.

James Patterson is possibly the best-selling writer of fiction in America today. He is also, in my view, the absolute pits, the lowest common denominator of cynical, scuzzy, assembly-line writing. If, on a bullshit scale, people like Pelecanos and Leonard rate a perfect 0, Patterson is the other extreme, a bloated, odoriferous 10. So why is he popular? Well, he keeps things not just simple but simple-minded. He writes short sentences and short chapters and deals in stereotypes. He teases his readers with soft-core sex. He telegraphs who are the good guys and who are the bad guys—a man with a scar on his face is a bad man, a girl who doesn't wear makeup is a good girl. He panders to ignorance, laziness, and prurience.

More than any other megawriter, Patterson embodies the belief that you can sell books the way you can sell dog food. Patterson came out of advertising; he is said to have been the youngest CEO in J. Walter Thompson's history. Patterson spends a great deal of time on the design, marketing, and advertising of his books, probably more than he does on writing, now that he is surrounded by collaborators. It has been reported that when his books were not selling well on the West Coast, he set one in San Francisco to boost sales out there.

It is nice to think that, as years go by, public education will provide rising levels of taste in America, but there is evidence to the contrary. If Spillane was the most popular bad writer of the 1950s, and Patterson is the most popular bad writer today, that is not progress. The Mick, whatever his faults, wrote from the heart. Patterson is just a cynical adman grinding out dog food for fun and profit.

I enjoyed writing the Patterson review—"sick, sexist, sadistic, and subliterate" has a certain ring to it—but I didn't enjoy this next one, of a David Baldacci novel. Baldacci, a lawyer, started his career with a pretty good political thriller called *Absolute Power*. Later he wrote a sweet novel about a poor rural family during the Depression. Then one of his books came along that I thought was awful—Patterson-style awful—and it was my duty to call a turkey a turkey. It seemed to me that Baldacci, like some other novelists in this chapter, was trying to imitate Patterson, a deplorable thing to do.

Hour Game
By David Baldacci

In David Baldacci's new *Hour Game*, his fictional Wrightsburg, Virginia, emerges as the murder capital of America. It does so thanks to a fiendish serial killer who, aided by a copycat, quickly eliminates eleven citizens of little Wrightsburg. The police are predictably clueless and Wrightsburg's best hope for ending the slaughter rests with the duo of Sean King and Michelle Maxwell, ex–Secret Service agents who are now partners in crime fighting.

Maxwell is age thirty-two, a former Olympic medalist and drop-dead gorgeous. King is forty-something, a student of wine and art and blessed with the finest investigative mind Maxwell has ever encountered. They indulge in a lot of inane banter but they are not lovers, and it is just as well because the victims of the crime spree tend to be people who engage in sex, including a stripper, a young couple making out in a car on lovers' lane, and a couple who succumb to a brief affair. Baldacci's gee-whiz view of sex is suggested when one of his characters visits a local strip club called Aphrodisiac: "The shapely, barely clothed women were performing acts so lewd against the metal dancing poles that it would have caused their poor mothers to die of humiliation—after they had strangled their shameless daughters, that is." For some reason, this passage made me think of Noel Coward's song "Alice Is at It Again," in which the parents took a more practical view of their daughter's wicked ways.

The serial killer is awesomely bright—a member of Mensa, we are told—and he keeps several jumps ahead of the police by bugging just about every telephone in town. In time the investigation centers on a rich old Virginia family called Battle, whose members are variously crazy, diseased, addicted, degenerate, and homicidal. The novel abounds with bizarre scenes that exist to provide cheap thrills. A minor character sells stolen drugs to a mysterious woman who conceals her identity. One night she performs a striptease for him: "As if sensing his thoughts, transparent as they were, she reached behind her, undid the clasp, and the bra fell to the floor and her breasts sprang free. Kyle moaned and almost dropped to his knees. This was, without doubt, the greatest night of his life."

Things grow curiouser and curiouser. The killer is caught but escapes from his cell by means I can only call ludicrous. A bit later, the fiend is about to chop someone's head off, but "before he could bring it down on her neck, the handle of the ax exploded." This is thanks to Maxwell's sharpshooting. In a shootout a moment later, "Beating odds of probably a billion to one, the two bullets had collided." Beating odds of probably a billion to one, I survived this novel with my sanity intact. With this book, Baldacci has entered the James Patterson Really Bad Thriller Sweepstakes.

Trace
By Patricia Cornwell

In decades past, when I first encountered the work of certain writers—Michael Connelly's *The Poet,* Elmore Leonard's *Fifty-two Pickup,* Lawrence Sanders's *The Seduction of Peter S—* I knew I had to go back and read everything they had written because they were that good. *Trace* is the first of Patricia Cornwell's immensely popular Kay Scarpetta novels I've read, and my reaction was the opposite. You couldn't pay me to read another of her novels. The main problem has to do with her characterization—one might say her deification—of her heroine, the forensic pathologist Kay Scarpetta, and we will get to that, but first let's examine her plot.

Scarpetta, five years after she was unjustly fired as Virginia's chief medical examiner, has been called back to Richmond to investigate the unexplained death of a fourteen-year-old girl. She is rudely treated by the misfit who has succeeded her but she concludes, with the help of her loyal sidekick Pete Marino, that the girl was murdered. Meanwhile, down in Florida, a young woman who is living with Scarpetta's niece, Lucy, has been beaten almost to death in Lucy's $9 million mansion. The victim is hustled off to Aspen to be cared for by Benton Wesley, Scarpetta's semi-estranged boyfriend, even as Lucy, who runs a fabulously successful private detective agency, tries to find out who is stalking her. We readers soon learn the secret that takes Scarpetta and Lucy longer to uncover—that the culprit in both cases is a nutcase named Edgar Allan Pogue who once worked for Scarpetta.

Pogue, although homicidal, is no more repulsive than various other characters. Scarpetta's bête noire is her successor, Dr. Joel Marcus, "a small thin man with a small thin face and a small thin stripe of dirty gray hair on the back of his small head, as if nature has been trifling with him." We are endlessly told of this awful fellow's jealous loathing of Scarpetta. We even learn of Dr. Marcus's bizarre phobia—he is afraid to go out of his house on the days that the garbagemen come ("big dark men in their big dark clothes.") We learn, when Scarpetta returns to her old office, that one of her former colleagues has fallen apart: "Fielding has lost most of his hair and his once attractive face is puffy and blotchy, his eyes runny. He sniffs a lot." Two minor participants in a staff meeting are described as "a big, horsey woman with a horsey face" and "an overweight, homely young woman . . . her face glowing like a halogen heater on high." Cornwell brings people onstage only to scorn them. A hotel employee, briefly glimpsed, is a "pimply-faced young man," a neighbor is "rich and pampered and addicted to Botox," a waitress "clicks her way over in her little stilt-high pointed shoes" and "Up close, she is old."

All this ugliness only underscores Scarpetta's magnificence. One admiring female sees her thusly: "She is an attractive woman in a powerful way, not a big woman but strong-looking in a midnight-blue pantsuit and midnight-blue blouse that sharpen her handsome features and set off her short blond hair.

Her hands are strong but graceful and she wears no rings." Her sidekick Marino rhapsodizes, "If only all women cared as little as she does about things that don't matter. If only all women cared as much as she does about things that do matter." When she touches him, "He would know that hand anywhere, that strong, sure hand." We are not surprised when Marino reveals that he has long lusted for Scarpetta.

Scarpetta has a lover, of course. Benton Wesley is a fine specimen, with his "hard, tan, handsome face," and he is "rich, very rich" and becomingly modest ("He has never quite understood why Kay loves him intensely and unconditionally"), but in this novel "Scarpetta and Benton are not in a good place." Oh, Lord, please let Scarpetta and Benton be in a good place again—there's so much bad in the world, surely we deserve that! Cornwell doesn't conceive of Scarpetta as a heroine on the scale, of, say, Sue Grafton's Kinsey Millhone, but more like a figure in Greek mythology, a Minerva, a goddess. I was therefore pleasantly surprised, a bit later, to find Edgar Allan Pogue, the nutcase who wants to kill Scarpetta, comparing her to "the god who sits on top of Mount Olympus, the biggest god of all gods." If Edgar Allan Pogue and I agree on something, it must be true. I don't know if Cornwell's fans enjoy the Scarpetta novels because of or despite her being a superhero who deserves to be worshipped the way girls used to worship Wonder Woman. If you aren't put off by Cornwell's forensic pathologist as a modern Minerva, you might find *Trace,* and perhaps her other books, to be enjoyable reads. But once was enough for me.

When *Trace* came in, I read a couple of chapters and told my editor it was awful and I didn't want to review it. She said Cornwell was a highly successful writer, and if the book was awful we should tell our readers. She was right, of course. The *Post* prints my e-mail address and the Cornwell review prompted a flurry of messages. A handful protested my vicious attack on their heroine, but far more readers thanked me. Many of the latter said that Cornwell's early novels had been good but she had gone astray. Some cited news stories about an FBI agent who shot his wife, allegedly because she had become involved with Cornwell when the writer visited the FBI training center in Virginia. One reader said, "As Patricia Cornwell's personal life spins out of control, her characters' lives more and more reflect her desperate fantasy of perfection victimized." Another said, "Thank you for letting us know that there is no point in hoping for a miraculous reversal of Ms. Cornwell's writing career." But my favorite message was this: "I appreciate your speaking out for a lot of other disgusted readers—or ex-readers—of her stuff. Beat up on Patterson too, while you're at it. He deserves it." Amen, brother!

The Face of the Assassin
By David Lindsey

As I read David Lindsey's *The Face of the Assassin,* literary associations kept springing to mind. I thought of what Monroe K. Spears told our class about T. S. Eliot's "The Waste Land" many years ago: "There is an element of impenetrable mystery about the poem." There are mysteries about this novel too, mostly along the lines of "What the hell is going on here?" I recalled, too, what a celebrated New York editor once said when I complained that I found Robert Ludlum's novels unreadable: "Patrick, those novels are intended to be read by weary businessmen setting out on transcontinental flights; they don't care about writing or logic, but they adore vast conspiracies that will keep their minds occupied." Lindsey's conspiracy-rich tale is clearly in the great Ludlum tradition.

A CIA undercover agent is found out by some cutthroats in Mexico City and suffers a wretched death. Just before he dies, he realizes that his tormentors have torn out his tongue and tossed it to a dog that "wolfed it down." We move to Austin, and meet Paul Bern, widower and forensic artist. He is in his studio with Alice, his seventeen-year-old goddaughter, who is brain-damaged but has an uncanny ability to tell when people are lying. A woman brings Bern a skull that she thinks is her husband's. Although Alice warns that the woman's story is false, Bern agrees to study the skull.

We suspect that the skull is that of the undercover agent who died in Mexico City. The truth is even more complicated—the dead agent was the twin brother that Paul Bern never knew he had. This twin had infiltrated a terrorist cell that is poised to kill thousands of people in the American heartland. Bern is summoned by a CIA operative, an elegant Mexican named Vincente Mondragon, who has "only eyeballs and teeth." It seems that the leader of the terrorist operation had his henchmen slice off Mondragon's face. This sinister fellow urges Bern to go to Mexico City and impersonate his dead twin so the terrorist plot can be thwarted. Bern tries to decline the assignment, but the man with no face stoops to blackmail: if Bern does not comply, the CIA will frame him for raping his beloved brain-damaged goddaughter. Bern submits. Upon arriving in Mexico City, he is consoled to learn that he has a sexy undercover partner, in both senses of the word, named Sabella.

The main action of the novel, involving various kidnappings and shootouts in Mexico City, is dumb beyond belief and is punctuated by amazing bits of writing. My favorite was this: "There was a loud smack, and her head flew apart in a liquidy red spray, drenching him in the living warmth of her last moment." You can read books for a lifetime and not come across a sentence like that.

Even in summary, it will be seen that this story is rich in literary associations. The use of twins of course evokes Shakespeare. The man with no face recalls Mason Verger, "noseless and lipless," in *Hannibal*. Poor Alice, who twice warns Bern that people are lying to him, suggests other crime-solving sidekicks that stretch back to Holmes and Watson. And Mondragon is all but Lear-like as he bewails his fate: "God, God, God, how he wanted a face."

At the end of *Huckleberry Finn*, when Jim is held captive in a shed, Huck and Tom debate how to free him. Sensible Huck notes that they can steal the key and have Jim out in a matter of minutes. But Tom insists they must free the prisoner the way it is done in books by "the best authorities," and that means smuggling a rope ladder to Jim inside a pie, digging a tunnel into his cell (and a moat around it if time permits), and giving Jim some rats to keep him company. All this is Twain's satire of the romantic fiction of his era, but it is relevant to certain overwrought thrillers today.

If the CIA knew that a terrorist was about to kill thousands of Americans, the sensible approach would be to send in a hit squad to zap the guy forthwith. But that's too easy. So we get novels in which the terrorist can only be stopped by a forensic artist with a dead wife and a brain-damaged goddaughter who is blackmailed by a man with no face into going to Mexico City to impersonate the twin brother he never knew who unfortunately was murdered and had his tongue fed to a starving dog. That's the Tom Sawyer approach to fiction, and I can only hope it gives comfort to weary businessmen on their transcontinental flights because it makes my poor head hurt.

The Eleventh Commandment
By Jeffrey Archer

As I write this, Jeffrey Archer's latest is already on the best-seller lists, so my warning may come too late to save you from this piece of nonsense. If not, caveat emptor. Archer's hero, Connor Fitzgerald, is both the CIA's most deadly assassin and a saint. We know he's an assassin because we see him kill someone in the opening chapter. We know he's a saint because he loves his wife and daughter, won a Congressional medal of honor in Vietnam, and is adored by all. The fact that he kills people does not detract from his saintliness because he only kills very bad people whom the president of the United States has told him to kill.

His troubles begin when the president tells him to go kill a very bad man who is about to be elected president of Russia. At least, he thinks the president told him that. Actually, an evil female FBI director has tricked him with snippets of presidential speeches that have been rearranged into a rather stilted presidential phone call that our saintly assassin, who's not real quick, takes to be the real McCoy. One howler follows another in this ill-conceived chain of events. Jeffrey Archer is both a best-selling novelist and a leading figure in Britain's Conservative Party. One assumes he is an intelligent and sophisticated man. Why he is writing claptrap like this is anyone's guess.

Kindly note that this review appeared before Archer was sent to prison for giving false testimony about whether he hired a prostitute. I kicked him when he was up, not down. Perjury about his sex life strikes me as forgivable—better men than he have done it—but his novel is not.

The next book is a romance novel, not a thriller, and I have no idea why the *Post* sent it to me, but it was my duty to sound the alarm.

The Rescue
By Nicholas Sparks

Nicholas Sparks, his publisher says, is one of America's most beloved storytellers. Having once forged a career as one of America's least beloved storytellers, I paid close attention to this man's art. In this case his formula involves putting a beautiful and virtuous damsel in distress in a small North Carolina town, where she meets a good-hearted hunk with a commitment problem. Toss in a kid who needs a dad, stir frequently with big action scenes, confront that darn commitment problem, and—presto!—they live happily ever after.

The damsel is Denise Holton, whose virtue failed her only once, when she inexplicably joined in a one-night stand with a handsome devil named Brett Cosgrove (Sparks has a way with names), which led to the birth of Kyle. A mysterious disability has Kyle, at age four, still talking baby talk that Sparks helpfully translates ("I wuff you, Money" = "I love you, Mommy"). Denise, working night shifts in a restaurant, dreams of her Prince Charming, and one night he appears in the person of Taylor McAden, a volunteer fireman blessed with bulging muscles and eyes the color of the sky. (Her eyes are "the color of jade, exotic and mysterious.") They meet when Denise, driving in a storm one night, bangs into a tree. When she comes to, Taylor is there to rescue her, but Kyle has wandered off in the direction of a nearby swamp. In the novel's first big action scene, the fearless fireman finds the boy, which soon leads to a rather chaste courtship of the boy's mom.

But why is this paragon still a bachelor at thirty-six? What is wrong with Mr. Right? It is, of course, that darn commitment problem, which is what the novel is all about. He wants to go hunting with his pals. She wants to talk about his feelings. She fears there is something "dark and unknowable" inside him. (We're all that way, Denise; get used to it.) "What do you want from me?" the poor guy cries. What she wants is a ring on her finger, but there are many complications before that blessed moment arrives. This is a novel in which men are lovable dopes, and women gab, gossip, giggle, and endlessly roll their eyes, as in: "She rolled her eyes. 'You really are a goob.' "

Upon publication, this novel shot to the top of the best-seller lists, so Sparks is clearly filling some deep national need, but I truly don't know who would suffer this maudlin tale—except perhaps lovesick young women in search of romantic guidance. Alas, the lessons they would learn here would not improve their prospects. *Cosmo* or a good cookbook would do more good.

Isn't this amazing stuff? The weirdo who thinks Kay Scarpetta is a goddess? Bullets that miraculously collide in midair? The U.S. attorney general crawling around in a dog collar? Terms of endearment like "You really are a goob"? Where is the Bad Writing Hall of Fame when we need it?

So what are we to do about all this deplorable fiction? In the long term, our nation must spend fewer billions on foreign wars and more on literacy programs. In the short term, reviewers (heroic fellows, for the most part) must steer people away from this schlock and toward all those good writers out there.

We would also do well to look on the bright side. There is so much wonderful writing. To be a book lover in America today, able to enjoy the wealth of fine writing that we and the rest of the world produce, is to be blessed. Ultimately, the purveyors of crap are only a nuisance.

19.

The Question of the Series

From its earliest days, crime fiction has often been presented in series form. The writer invents an intriguing hero and brings him or her back for book after book. There are advantages for all parties concerned. We grew up with the Hardy Boys and Nancy Drew. Later, Travis McGee and Kinsey Millhone became friends who drop by every year or two. For writers, a series means not having to reinvent the wheel with each new book; your hero and his or her world are established and you can concentrate on plot. For ambitious writers, the series makes possible a depth of characterization impossible in a single novel. Publishers, of course, love a successful series. For them, it's a gold mine.

Still, for many years the series was a literary stepchild. According to literary mythology, great writers should surprise us each time with some new burst of creativity. In fact, many of our best novelists have sometimes used recurring characters—Hemingway's Nick Adams stories, Fitzgerald's Pat Hobby stories, Faulkner's Snopes family, Roth's Zuckerman novels, Updike's Bech books—but the mythology endured and the series was long regarded as bargain-basement writing, fine for Ellery Queen and Agatha Christie, suitable for the masses, tolerated in Trollope, but generally disdained by the literary world.

Things have changed. When I started writing novels in the 1970s, I worked with some very good editors, but none suggested that I consider a series—being young and foolish, I would probably have been insulted if they had. After the success of *The President's Mistress* in 1976, I thought vaguely about bringing its protagonist back for another novel, but I didn't. Today, a young novelist with my journalistic knack for action and dialogue would be drawn to a crime series; if not, his publisher would push him in that direction.

Crime writers who are serious about their craft endlessly agonize over the series, and often alternate between a series and stand-alones. Dennis Lehane once said, "I think Spade and Marlowe remain icons because they didn't wear out their welcome. Would Chandler be Chandler if he'd written eighteen Marlowe books?" He added, "I think any series is going to run down and you don't know where the tipping point is. You never heard a writer say, 'The fifteenth novel in my series, that was the best one.' " Of course, Lehane began his career with a series and then gambled on *Mystic River* and won. Many writers admire what Lehane did but aren't willing to gamble.

Writers can become prisoners of success. Conan Doyle tried to kill off Sherlock Holmes but was forced by popular outrage to bring him back. John D. MacDonald would leave Travis McGee for more ambitious fare—his best-selling *Condominium* was an example—but always returned to his bread and butter. I sometimes think of Hannibal Lecter as Thomas Harris's Frankenstein monster—will he destroy the monster or will the monster destroy him?

Many writers have a love-hate relationship with their series. The publishers—greedy devils—push for a book a year. This year's hardback and the paperback of last year's book can be timed to support each other. Writers finish one book and start the next the same day. Vacations are postponed and families ignored in the struggle to meet deadlines. It's insane—these are successful writers—but once you're riding the tiger it's hard to dismount. Some of the most successful writers become CEOs, contributing their names and not much else to a great many bad books.

Starting a series is like a marriage—there's always the chance that you've guessed wrong. Some writers—MacDonald, Connelly, Rankin—chose well. Others have changed directions. Daniel Silva started one series, wasn't satisfied, and moved to another that suited him better. Pelecanos's first series reflected the wild years of his youth; as he matured it no longer fit and he began one about someone quite unlike himself. Some prolific writers have juggled two or even three series at the same time. Sometimes a series just happens. *Red Dragon* wasn't intended to start one and Hannibal Lecter was only its third most important character; later, Harris realized that the jailed cannibal was the finest flower of his art and contrived to free him.

Pelecanos, a supremely independent man, told me this when he was agonizing over whether to write a stand-alone, continue his Derek Strange series, or start a new one:

> The pro of series fiction is, if the books are successful, the promise of a long career. The con is generally the loss of artistic freedom and the death of the dream. To be locked into a series character is exactly the same as having to go to a job you hate day after day. It's just another kind of handcuff, something I have been running away from my whole life. The exhilarating thing about being a writer is not knowing where you are going next. And also the possibility that you will write that one great novel. Those dreams are dashed when you take the blood money. Because no one ever said that the tenth novel in the series was as good as the second or third. The drop in quality is inherent in the concept.

He added,

> It's simply not plausible for one character to have so many violent adventures and encounters that many times. Most police officers never even have to pull their service weapons once in their entire careers. But fictional private detectives pull them, and use them, in series fiction time and time again. And they seem to be unscarred by committing these acts of murder themselves.

I must disagree. Pelecanos knows what's best for Pelecanos, but I think Michael Connelly has shown that these problems can be overcome. Harry Bosch has killed in the line of duty and been deeply scarred by the experience; his scars and soul-searching are central to his series. I don't think that the survival of either Bosch or McBain's Steve Carella has made their series less believable. Readers gladly suspend disbelief to keep a favorite character coming back.

Connelly has thought a lot about how to sustain interest—his own and his readers'—in the Bosch series. He has shifted to stand-alones, moved between a first- and third-person narrative, and had Harry leave the LAPD and return.

"My stand-alone novels are strategically placed to give my batteries a chance to recharge on Harry," he says.

> I try to change things up, challenge myself, and do whatever I can to keep momentum and my interest high. The upside of a series is the opportunity to show evolution of character and place. The downside is that the longer you write a series the more you are begging reality. Could such a character exist and keep on and always win the day? The way I look at it is that the series is the war and each book is a battle. Harry wins the battles but will he win the war? There has to be a toll for what he does. He goes into the darkness—how much darkness has seeped into him? That's the essential question of the series.

More than anyone else except McBain, Connelly has created a cast of characters who come and go in his books and offer him endless possibilities for plot development. The reporter Jack McEvoy stars in the stand-alone *The Poet*, returns for a lesser role in *The Narrows*, and will probably be seen again. Terry McCaleb had his own stand-alone, returned to co-star with Harry in *A Darkness More Than Night*, and then was killed in a third novel. The killer called the Poet, after escaping in his first novel, was killed by Bosch in a later one. Eleanor Wish was an FBI agent in the first novel, went away, married Harry, vanished again, returned with a child, and was last heard of in Hong Kong.

Perhaps most dramatically, Mickey Haller, the half brother Harry never knew about until they met briefly in an early novel, abruptly became the star of the 2005 stand-alone *The Lincoln Lawyer*. Perhaps Connelly will pair Harry and his half brother in some future novel, as he once paired Harry with Terry McCaleb. Connelly says he wrote *The Lincoln Lawyer* in three months, after many talks with a real-life lawyer who was his model. Mickey Haller is a cynical, semishady criminal lawyer, but his ex-wives love him and readers did too. *The Lincoln Lawyer* was the best seller of Connelly's books, perhaps because legal thrillers have a bigger audience than police procedurals, perhaps because Haller is a more colorful, crowd-pleasing character than Bosch. Maybe Connelly will alternate Bosch and Haller novels, or maybe he will end the Bosch series and concentrate on Haller. But whatever he chooses to do, Connelly's success with the Bosch series—and that of McBain, Burke, and a few others—has led me to rethink my views on the potential of a crime series.

The main reason that even the best series have rarely been considered serious literature has been that they follow a formula. Rule number one is that the hero will survive to fight again. That formula has sold billions of books, but serious writing has long been thought to reject formulas. Hamlet doesn't survive for a sequel; Dick Diver is not heard from again. Death is serious; narrow escapes are not. In one novel discussed earlier, the detective hero is shot dead at the end. It was a stunning moment, an all but unprecedented act that carried a good novel to a higher level, because it reflected the reality that heroes often fail. Of course, humankind longs for happy endings. They may not be art but they offer consolation and hope. That's why for centuries stage managers kept rewriting Shakespeare's tragedies. Ophelia lives! Hamlet rules!

The Bosch novels prove that a crime series can transcend genre. Connelly has been writing the novels in "real time," which means that Harry is well into his fifties now. Connelly says he thinks he has only three or four more Bosch books in him, and whether he chooses to have Harry die in the line of duty or enjoy a deserved retirement, the excellence of the series has already placed it at the highest level of popular fiction.

It doesn't matter if Harry has survived near-fatal scrapes in a dozen books—some cops do survive. It isn't necessary for Harry to die for the Bosch series to be either believable or great. It *is* great, in the way that Anthony Trollope's Palliser novels or the Holmes stories are great. The whole is more than the sum of the parts. As Connelly says, each book is a battle in a longer war. Harry has earned the right to win that war—or die trying. It is splendid to write a great novel, but it is no less admirable to write a great series. A dozen or more novels, uneven individually, can become one heroic achievement.

20.

Parting Shots

Is the thriller triumphant?

At this writing, the most recent evidence is the *Publishers Weekly* list of hardback best sellers for 2005, which includes about 130 novels that sold more than 100,000 copies. By my count, between a third and half of them can be called thrillers: probably about forty percent, depending on how you define the term. Many of these best sellers aren't to my taste, but they are part of the phenomenon along with those I admire. The thrillers among *PW*'s top thirty include:

1. *The Broker.* John Grisham's latest sold more than 1.8 million copies.
2. *The Da Vinci Code.* After three years and 40 million copies sold—and with the paperback edition finally out—Dan Brown's miracle drops to second place.
3. *Mary, Mary.* James Patterson had an amazing—some would say appalling—four books in the top fifteen.
5. *Predator.* By Patricia Cornwell.
8. *The Historian.* Elizabeth Kostova's literary thriller, based on the Dracula myth.
10. *Eleven on Top.* Janet Evanovich, a one-time romance writer, pioneered the chick-lit thriller with her Stephanie Plum series,

which Janet Maslin of *The New York Times* called "the mystery-novel equivalent of comfort food."

14. *S Is for Silence.* Sue Grafton's nineteenth and one of her best.

15. *The Camel Club.* By David Baldacci.

18. *Forever Odd.* Dean Koontz writes about an odd fellow named Odd Thomas who sees Elvis and other dead people.

27. *The Lincoln Lawyer.* Michael Connelly's biggest sales yet, about 440,000 copies.

28. *No Place Like Home.* The prolific Mary Higgins Clark tells of a girl who accidentally shoots her mother and faces more woe when she grows up.

30. *Broken Prey.* Another crowd-pleaser for John Sandford.

That's fifteen thrillers among *PW*'s top thirty, if we count all four Pattersons. After that, *PW* lists about a hundred more novels. Those that sold between 300,000 and 400,000 copies included the veteran Clive Cussler's *Polar Shift;* a special illustrated edition of *The Da Vinci Code* (proving yet again that there's a sucker born every minute); *Consent to Kill* by Vince Flynn, one of Tom Clancy's loyal disciples; *Origin in Death* by J. D. Robb, part of a series about an NYPD detective in 2059, actually written by the best-selling romance novelist Nora Roberts; *The Ambler Warning* by Robert Ludlum, whose books, like the poor, are with us always; *Point Blank,* the latest of Catherine Coulter's "romantic thrillers" about FBI agents confronting love and crime; and Dean Koontz's *Velocity.*

Those with sales between 200,000 and 300,000 included Michael Connelly's *The Closers,* in which Harry Bosch returns to the LAPD; literary thrills in P. D. James's *The Lighthouse; On the Run* by Iris Johansen; *Rage* by Jonathan Kellerman; and *Prince of Fire* by Daniel Silva.

Thrillers with sales between 100,000 and 200,000 included *Cold Service* and *School Days* by the veteran Robert B. Parker; *Two-Dollar Bill* and *Iron Orchid* by Stuart Woods, who writes in the Parker tradition; *The Scorpion's Gate,* a terrorism thriller by former White House aide Richard A. Clarke; *The Innocent* by Harlan Coben; the literary adventure *No Country for Old Men* by Cormac McCarthy; *Without Mercy* by Jack Higgins; *Vanish* by Tess Gerritsen; *Double Tap* by Steve Martini; *Dance of Death* by the talented team of Douglas Preston and

Lincoln Child; *The Twelfth Card: A Lincoln Rhyme Novel* by Jeffrey Deaver; *One Shot* by Lee Child, wherein Jack Reacher does much violence in the heartland; *Company Man* by Joseph Finder; *Tyrannosaur Canyon* by Douglas Preston, which at one point takes us inside the mind of a killer dinosaur some 65 million years ago; *Fire Sale* by the admirable Sara Paretsky; *Blood Memory* and *Turning Angel,* well-written novels of southern violence by Mississippi-based Greg Iles; and *Straight into Darkness* by Faye Kellerman.

By comparison, I counted fewer than ten literary novels on *PW*'s list, excluding the literary thrillers already mentioned. They included John Irving's *Until I Find You* (which led this group with about 266,000 books sold), E. L. Doctorow's *The March,* Ian McEwan's *Saturday, Memories of My Melancholy Whores* by Gabriel García Márquez, *Gilead* by Marilynne Robinson, *Zorro* by Isabel Allende, and *Extremely Loud and Incredibly Close* by Jonathan Safran Foer.

In short, thrillers are now the mainstream of American popular fiction. We need to recognize that the best of them are as impressive as the best literary fiction. Of course, if you care about books, there's never enough space to give credit to all the good ones. I'm speaking on behalf of one sort of fiction that I enjoy, but others will with equal fervor champion feminist fiction or Eastern European novels or magic realism or whatever. Still, when we are allocating praise and prizes, we should pay some attention to what large numbers of literate Americans are reading.

The literary world reached a dubious milestone in October 2004 when a National Book Award panel nominated five little-known women writers who all live in New York City for the annual NBA fiction award. Two were first novelists, and according to the *Times* only one of their books had sold more than two thousand copies. No doubt all parties involved are good people with the best of intentions, but what about all those other good people out there who are looking for interesting accessible fiction and getting precious little help from the alleged experts? The novelist Tom McGuane called the nominations a "meltdown" for the NBA, and that estimable critic John Leonard expressed dismay that *The Plot Against America* wasn't nominated.

Clearly, judges who snub Philip Roth aren't likely to consider Pelecanos, Furst, Littell, Leonard, Lehane, or Connelly, and we are left to wonder if our literary establishment has drifted into the outer realms of irrelevancy. If we are going to have book awards that purport to be national, they should be open to all comers, not just to regulars at the 92nd Street Y. Personally, I'd rather see the National Book Awards decided by the next ten people who walk into my neighborhood public library than by the geniuses who picked the five white chicks from the Big Apple.

Let us be wary of literary elites. They are not that different from political elites or sorority-house elites; they seek to accumulate and keep power, and they favor their friends. They often inhabit a world that most of us would find exceedingly strange. The invaluable Janet Malcolm wrote a *New Yorker* essay about Gertrude Stein's 900-plus-page *The Making of Americans*. She said of the book, "It is believed to be a modernist masterpiece, but it is not felt to be a necessary reading experience. It is more a monument than a text, a heroic achievement of writing, a near-impossible feat of reading."

The Making of Americans is an extreme case, but at a certain level literature tends toward the incomprehensible. James Joyce's *Finnegans Wake* is another example, and some of today's postmodernists are no walk in the park. Too many people, awed by the academy and highbrow critics, fear that if they don't understand a book the fault must be theirs. It ain't necessarily so. There are writers out there who are unreadable simply because they don't think clearly, and others who equate obscurity with profundity.

I recently set out to read a novel by one of the most highly regarded of today's literary novelists. I was doing fine until its third paragraph, when the author introduced an "alarm bell of anxiety" in a suburban home and proceeded to elaborate:

> By now it had been ringing for so many hours that the Lamberts no longer heard the message of "bell ringing" but, as with any sound that continues for so long that you have the leisure to learn its component sounds (as with any word you stare at until it resolves itself into a string of dead letters), instead heard a clapper rapidly striking a metallic resonator, not a pure tone but a granular sequence of percussions with a keening overlay of overtones; ringing for so many days that it simply blended into the background except at certain early-morning hours when one

or the other of them awoke in a sweat and realized that a bell had been ringing in their heads for as long as they could remember; ringing for so many months that the sound had given way to a kind of metasound whose rise and fall was not the beating of compression waves but the much, much slower waxing and waning of their *consciousness* of the sound.

Is this man serious? After repeated readings, I have a vague sense of what he's trying to say, but he could have said it better in ten or twenty words and spared me a headache. Still, I was grateful to him for giving me fair warning of what lay ahead. I murmured my thanks and quit his novel right there, on page two, because life is too short to spend it wrestling with sentences like that. Apparently not everyone agreed, because the novel won the National Book Award, but I do not regret my decision. Perhaps I will return to it in my old age, after I have reread Shakespeare and Ed McBain.

A few years back, Tom Wolfe published an essay called "My Three Stooges" that was as fascinating, audacious, and self-serving as Raymond Chandler's celebrated "The Simple Art of Murder" more than fifty years earlier. Wolfe was inspired by the fact that Norman Mailer, John Updike, and John Irving had all dismissed his 1998 novel *A Man in Full* as journalistic—entertaining, they sniffed, *but not literature.* Wolfe responded by calling his best seller a piece of "Zolaesque realism" and pointing out that all three of his critics had recently published more esoteric novels that had "sunk without a bubble." In truth, he declared, these "old codgers" had been frightened because his novel was "an example—a highly visible one—of a possible, indeed, the likely new direction in late-twentieth and early twenty-first-century literature: the intensely realistic novel, based on reporting, that plunges wholeheartedly into the social realism of America today, right now—a revolution in content rather than form—that was about to sweep the arts in America."

The sort of novel America urgently needs, Wolfe argued, was in the tradition of Balzac, Dickens, Tolstoy, and Zola and, among Americans, Dreiser, Lewis, and Steinbeck. I don't think Wolfe is, as he would have it, the heir to this tradition, but he described quite well the strength of the best thrillers. They are not only providing skillful popular entertainment, at their best they are producing the social realism that Wolfe called for and that today's literary writers rarely attempt.

I mean the realism of books like *Mystic River* and *Done for a Dime*, and virtually everything by Pelecanos, Connelly, and Ian Rankin. Pelecanos's Derek Strange novels, in particular, are remarkable simply as reporting on black Washington, but they go deeper, into the dreams and heartbreaks of their characters, to a degree that defines them as art. The novels of Alan Furst and Robert Littell, too, explore modern history and politics with the artistry of the finest literature.

We need, in all realms of creativity, less emphasis on genres and more on excellence. In music, you can put labels on, say, Hank Williams, Louis Armstrong, Elvis Presley, Billie Holiday, Bob Dylan, and Robert Johnson, but by whatever name they are great artists and should be evaluated as such, not as representatives of this or that genre. The same is true in fiction. Is Harry Bosch a less interesting character than Bellow's Herzog or Roth's Zuckerman? Is Ed McBain's Isola a less compelling world than John Cheever's suburbs? Is *Mystic River* a less impressive novel than *An American Tragedy*? Are Pelecanos's Derek Strange novels less powerful portraits of the dispossessed than *The Grapes of Wrath* or *Thieves Like Us*? We could debate these questions, but the writers should be judged on the insights they provide and the pleasures they give, not on the basis of labels.

George Bernard Shaw had Eliza Doolittle remind us that ladies are not what they are but how they are treated. Writers are like that. They need to be appreciated for what they are. If you want to argue that Jonathan Franzen, Michael Chabon, and Jonathan Safran Foer are three of America's best young writers, fine, but they're not necessarily better or more significant than Connelly, Lehane, and Pelecanos simply because some people put the latter three in a different category. If the first three win National Book Awards and the second three don't, let's not accept that as gospel; let's take a look at who's doing the judging and what cultural blinders they bring to the task.

Ultimately, change will come from readers who know what they like and won't be duped into reading books that bore them. Let me close with the words of an American writer who scorned those who tried to pin tags on him. In his novel *Romance*, Ed McBain has a writer protest when someone calls his books what McBain's own novels were often called—police procedurals.

Not procedurals. *Never* procedurals. And not *mysteries,* either. They were simply *novels* about *cops.* The men and women in blue and in mufti, their wives, girlfriends, lovers, children, their head colds, stomachaches, menstrual cycles. *Novels.*

Novels. How sweet and various they are, what good friends they make, what joy and comfort they provide. Let us savor them and—most urgently—make up our own minds about them. That, in this world, is always a triumph.

Personal Favorites

Yes, we all like lists. Here's mine, not of the "best" thrillers but of ones I have particularly enjoyed. A couple I have reservations about but still consider required reading. Some are widely acclaimed, like those by McBain, MacDonald, Connelly, Turow, and Harris. And several are little-known novels that I admire and want to tell others about. A great crime series should ideally be read in its entirety and in the order the books were written; Connelly's Harry Bosch books are an example. But if you said you didn't have time to read them all and put a gun to my head, I would say to begin with two of the strongest early books, *The Last Coyote* and *A Darkness More Than Night,* then move forward to the more recent novels that begin with *City of Bones.* I confess that I've skipped around a lot in McBain and MacDonald and never thought it mattered much.

Dashiell Hammett: *The Maltese Falcon*
Raymond Chandler: *The Long Goodbye*
John D. MacDonald: The Travis McGee novels
Ed McBain: The 87th Precinct novels
Elmore Leonard: *LaBrava*
Lawrence Sanders: *The First Deadly Sin*
Charles McCarry: *The Tears of Autumn*
Robert Littell: *Legends*

Alan Furst: *Night Soldiers*
Scott Turow: *Presumed Innocent*
Sue Grafton: the Kinsey Millhone novels
Walter Mosley: the Easy Rawlins novels
Thomas Harris: *The Silence of the Lambs*
George Pelecanos: the Derek Strange novels
Michael Connelly: the Harry Bosch novels
Dennis Lehane: *Mystic River*
Ann-Marie MacDonald: *The Way the Crow Flies*
Ian Rankin: the Inspector Rebus novels
James Lee Burke: the Dave Robicheaux novels
John Lescroart: the Hardy-Glitsky novels
John Burdett: *Bangkok 8*
Michael Gruber: *Tropic of Night*
David Corbett: *Done for a Dime*
Charlie Huston: *Caught Stealing*
Peter Abrahams: *End of Story*
John Lawton: *Bluffing Mr. Churchill*
Adrian McKinty: *Dead I Well May Be*
Karin Slaughter: the Grant County novels

About the Author

PATRICK ANDERSON, who for several years has written a weekly book review for *The Washington Post,* is the author of nine novels and three previous books of nonfiction. He served as a speechwriter in the Kennedy and Clinton administrations and in Jimmy Carter's 1976 presidential campaign. He lives in Washington, D.C.

About the Type

This book was set in Sabon, a typeface designed by the well-known German typographer Jan Tschichold (1902–74). Sabon's design is based upon the original letter forms of Claude Garamond and was created specifically to be used for three sources: foundry type for hand composition, Linotype, and Monotype. Tschichold named his typeface for the famous Frankfurt typefounder Jacques Sabon, who died in 1580.